Financial Fitness *for* Life

Financial Fitness for Life

Jerry Mason

This publication is designed to provide accurate and authoritative information in regard to the subject matter covered. It is sold with the understanding that the publisher is not engaged in rendering legal, accounting, or other professional service. If legal advice or other expert assistance is required, the services of a competent professional person should be sought.

Associate Publisher: Cynthia A. Zigmund
Managing Editor: Jack Kiburz
Interior Design: Lucy Jenkins
Cover Design: Scott Rattray, Rattray Design
Typesetting: the dotted i

© 1999 by Dearborn Financial Publishing, Inc.®

Published by Dearborn, a Kaplan Professional Company

All rights reserved. The text of this publication, or any part thereof, may not be reproduced in any manner whatsoever without written permission from the publisher.

Printed in the United States of America

99 00 01   10 9 8 7 6 5 4 3 2 1

Library of Congress Cataloging-in-Publication Data

Mason, Jerald W.
    Financial fitness for life : advice from America's top financial planning program / Jerry Mason.
        p.   cm.
    Includes index.
    ISBN 0-7931-3361-0 (paper)
    1. Finance, Personal.   I. Title.
HG179.M3466   1999
332.024—dc21   99-32271
                                                CIP

Dearborn books are available at special quantity discounts to use as premiums and sales promotions, or for use in corporate training programs. For more information, please call the Special Sales Manager at 800-621-9621, ext. 4514, or write to Dearborn Financial Publishing, Inc., 155 North Wacker Drive, Chicago, IL 60606-1719.

Dedication

I dedicate this book to our children and their spouses:

    Matthew and Bonnie Mason   Andrew and Natasha Mason
    Amy and Kelly Ethington   Laurie Mason
    Belinda and Ryan Frost   Julie Mason

In appreciation for hiring my financial planning students:

    American Express Financial Advisors   Merrill Lynch
    Arthur Andersen   Northern Trust
    Edward Jones   SunAmerica
    Equitable   T. Rowe Price
    Lord Abbett   USAA

Contents

Preface xi

Acknowledgments xiii

1. **Take Control of Your Financial Future** 1
   Identify steps you must complete to gain a greater sense of financial control as you achieve your goals and objectives.

2. **Calculate Your Net Worth** 12
   Figure out how much you are worth in dollars and cents.

3. **Get Organized** 23
   - Identify goals to last a lifetime.
   - Set up a system so that you can file and quickly find any document.
   - Assemble your team of advisers.

4. **Where Does Your Money Go?** 43
   Discover exactly where you spend your money. You will then create a spending plan to help you fund your goals and increase your net worth.

5. **Stop Piling Up Debt** 65
Develop and implement a strategy so that you no longer need to borrow money.

6. **Get Out of Debt** 76
Develop strategies you can use to become debt-free. Check to make sure your credit report is accurate.

7. **Win at Credit Cards** 99
Learn how to get the most from your cards while avoiding their pitfalls.

8. **Examine Your Social Security Account** 113
Check to make sure that the financial data in your file at the Social Security Administration are current.

9. **Maximize Your Employee Benefits** 119
Make sure that you are taking full advantage of all financial benefits offered by your employer.

10. **Update Your Auto and Property Insurance** 129
Evaluate your auto and property insurance, improving coverage and reducing premiums.

11. **How Healthy Are Your Health and Disability Policies?** 144
Learn how to get the best coverage for the least cost.

12. **Update Your Life Insurance** 162
Make sure your life insurance coverage is adequate and cost-effective.

13. **Funding Financial Independence** 178
Determine the amount you need to be investing each month to achieve financial independence.

14. **Investing in Stocks and Bonds** 197
Understand the basics of investing in stocks and bonds.

15. **Buying and Selling Mutual Fund Shares** 210
Understand the basic steps in creating a mutual fund portfolio.

Contents

16. **Annuities** 227
    Understand the pros and cons of owning annuities.

17. **Give Your Money Away** 236
    Give back to a society that has given you so much.

18. **Make Your Taxes Less Taxing** 241
    Understand the steps to take for reducing the time and stress associated with paying taxes.

19. **Pay Uncle Sam Only What You Owe** 249
    Identify tax avoidance strategies you can use to reduce your tax liability.

20. **Love What You Do** 262
    Focus on keeping your career on track and your résumé fresh.

21. **Make Sure You Have a Plan for Your Estate** 279
    Make certain that your estate plan reflects your current thinking with particular attention paid to your dependents.

Epilogue 297

Index 299

Preface

If you went to a money doctor for a financial checkup, would your fiscal condition earn a passing mark? Or are your finances giving you a pain that aspirin won't help? If you want to get into better financial shape, *Financial Fitness for Life* can serve as your personal trainer or counselor. This is the personal finance book that breaks down the money management process into manageable steps you can complete to gain control over your finances. As you work through the financial exercises, you will sense an improvement in your financial well-being. When you finish the book, you should be financially fit and on track to fund important goals while experiencing significantly less financial stress.

For more than 20 years, I have spent my time and energy developing professional financial planners. The financial planning program at Texas Tech University, where I teach, is the best in the country. The financial strategies discussed in this book are the identical strategies that I teach my students and that I include in professional development programs for financial planners. Read *Financial Fitness for Life* and you will learn the techniques professional planners use when working with their clients.

You do not need to become a financial planner to handle most of your financial affairs. *Financial Fitness for Life* will put you in charge of your finances. You decide what is important to you financially and what you want to accomplish with your money. As you work through these financial exercises each week, you will gain greater control over your finances and will discover that it takes you less time to manage your finances than you thought.

Too often financial advisers examine only one aspect of your financial situation and often exclude important aspects of your finances. Work through the exercises in *Financial Fitness for Life,* and as your financial condition improves, so should other aspects of your life. You will experience less financial stress and will free up both time and energy to pursue other aspects of your life.

Financial Fitness for Life is different from other investing and personal finance books in the following ways:

- This book focuses on financial issues that should interest you today, that is, topics that you need to check on to make sure that you are in top financial shape.
- It is so easy to implement the ideas. If you work through all the chapters, you will have completed a financial examination of your finances. Much like a physical exam, each chapter will not only help you identify problems, but also will show you steps to complete to resolve your money issues.
- You can start immediately reading about the topic that is currently of greatest concern to you. While there is a natural flow beginning with the first chapter, you can begin anywhere.

Most readers, like my clients and my students, have one or more destructive beliefs about money. You will be challenged to confront beliefs that may contribute to current financial mismanagement.

Financial Fitness for Life breaks personal money management into simple steps that anyone can complete. Assignments within each chapter can be completed in one to two hours or less. To make real progress toward becoming financially fit, you need to work through each assignment. And whether you are 16 or 106, you will benefit from the exercises in this book. Over the years I have worked with hundreds of clients. I know firsthand that most people can improve their financial performance in most, if not all, financial areas discussed.

Financial Fitness for Life includes numerous links to other excellent resources. Each chapter includes 800 numbers, addresses, and Web sites for resources that make it possible for you to find additional information helpful for answering important questions. In many ways, this is a handbook, guiding you through daily financial decisions, enabling you to make better decisions that become an integral part of your financial life plan.

Readers wishing to ask Dr. Mason questions about their personal finances can contact him at www.askmoneydoc.com.

Acknowledgments

No writer creates a book alone. I wish to recognize individuals who have reviewed part or all of this manuscript and provided helpful feedback. However, I alone am responsible for the ideas and information included in *Financial Fitness for Life*. Shannon Kennedy reviewed the entire manuscript. Vance Grange, James Mason, Karen Thomas, Maxine Sweet, Phil Hamman, and Tammy McNutt each reviewed one or more chapters.

A special thank you to Artie Limmer who shot the photo on the cover.

I especially appreciate the help and support of my wife, Joyce, who carefully reviewed each chapter.

1 Take Control of Your Financial Future

Identify steps you must complete to gain a greater sense of financial control as you achieve your goals and objectives.

When I first met Irene and Jose, I could not recall having met more stressed-out individuals. Neither smiled. Both sat slumped in their chairs. Each talked in a monotone. Each avoided eye contact with me. Everyone I see has at least one financial problem, but Irene and Jose seemed to have them all. Jose was behind in his student loans, his child support, his car payment, his mortgage payment, and his credit card payments. Jose owed the IRS nearly $30,000 in back taxes, and he was two months behind on his payments to the bankruptcy trustee. Irene spent every dime Jose brought home and more. When they finally put together a spending plan, Irene and Jose were spending $1,400 more a month than they were bringing in. Yet they refused to cut any expenses. While I try to refrain from suggesting where people might cut back, I was amazed that Irene spent more than $400 a month on music lessons for their three children and was not willing to reduce the number of lessons. Neither was she interested in having the poodle's hair trimmed less often than once a month. Every person has his or her sacred cows, expenditures that they are not willing to reduce or eliminate. Irene had corralled an entire herd of sacred cows. I finally had met clients who refused to let me help them, I thought. They were equally uninterested in helping themselves.

You may never have walked in Irene and Jose's shoes or may think that Irene and Jose have it much better than you. I hope your finances are in better shape than theirs. No matter how well you manage your finances, you can do better. As you improve, you will gain more control over your present situation as well as your future. As you work through the activities in this book, you will become increasingly fit financially.

Answer the true-false questions on pages 3 and 4 as accurately as you can. These are not trick questions, but your score will provide insight into your present financial management style. Please do not read the answers until you have finished.

This list of questions is not comprehensive, and you may not totally agree with my answers before you read this book. My primary concern is not that you agree with me, but that as you work through the exercises in this book you gain increasing control of your finances.

If you would like to have greater control of your finances, you may need to focus on your financial beliefs and behavior.

Your Financial Beliefs

Many of your money problems can be traced back to your financial behavior. One of the primary factors dictating your behavior is your beliefs. Almost everyone subscribes to more than one dysfunctional belief about money and what it can do. Almost all of us believe that money can do more for us than it actually can.

Which of the following beliefs listed below do you think is true?

- People with more money are happier than those with less.
- People with more money are smarter than those with less.
- The more money you can accumulate, the happier you will be.
- Lottery winners are happier after they have won the lottery.
- You can buy almost anything you really want with money.
- Most people who work hard have more money than those who do not.
- There is nothing negative about having lots of money.
- Money is the single best motivator of children.
- You can actually buy happiness with money.
- You can solve almost any problem with money.

As you have probably figured out, rarely are any of the above statements true for anyone. However, most people think they are. We label these ten ideas destructive beliefs. Your believing one or more of them can help explain why managing your finances is not as satisfying and rewarding as you think it should be. As you read through this book, I discuss these and other distorted beliefs in greater detail.

Financial Fitness Quiz

T / F   1. If I had 10 percent more money to spend, my life would improve.

T / F   2. I feel good about the amount of money that I donate to worthy causes.

T / F   3. I look forward to retiring because I then will have time to do things I cannot do now.

T / F   4. I currently invest 10 percent of my income.

T / F   5. I work at my job more than 50 hours per week.

T / F   6. I know best how to spend my family's money.

T / F   7. People with more money are happier than people with less.

T / F   8. I buy at least ten lottery tickets per year.

T / F   9. People who drive expensive cars are trying to buy status.

T / F   10. At least once during the past 12 months, I have taken a course to help me do my job better.

T / F   11. Offering children money is a great way to get them to do what parents want them to do.

T / F   12. Because the stock market scares me, all my money is in bonds and CDs.

T / F   13. I have money that I can spend each month without having to explain or defend my purchases.

(continued)

Financial Fitness Quiz
(continued)

T / F   14. I never plan how I want to spend my money.

T / F   15. If I had more leisure time, I would be happier.

T / F   16. I have a hobby that I really enjoy.

T / F   17. Several times during the past year a creditor has called me.

T / F   18. Several times during the past year I have made the minimum payment on a credit card.

T / F   19. Complaining is a waste of time when a product or service does not work as it should.

T / F   20. Were I to die today, my loved ones could find all my important papers.

T / F   21. Were I to die today, I would leave behind enough money to pay off all of my financial obligations.

T / F   22. I earn interest every month on the money in my checking account.

T / F   23. I have reviewed my credit report during the past 36 months.

T / F   24. I am not accumulating debt.

T / F   25. I know what my net worth is.

T / F   26. If I become unable to make my own financial decisions, I have appointed someone to make them for me.

Your Financial Behavior

Your behavior also is governed by your knowledge of money management strategies. I have taught a basic personal finance class for 20 years. Most students are not satisfied with their score on the first exam. Why? Because they believe that they know everything about handling money. Actually, most know very little. Your experiences have taught you more than a college student knows. However, to be in control of your finances and on track to fund important goals, you should be implementing each of the strategies discussed in this book.

Answers to the Quiz

It is time to find out how you did on the true-false quiz. Congratulate yourself if 18 or more of your answers agree with those discussed below. Do not be surprised if you don't earn a passing grade; most people don't. Their dysfunctional beliefs about money combined with their lack of knowledge about financial strategies defeat them. The answers that follow are brief; you will encounter each of these ideas again in greater detail throughout the book.

1. False. If I had 10 percent more money to spend, my life would improve. Quality of life rarely correlates with the amount of money you have, but it does correlate with how well you manage your money.

2. True. I feel good about the amount of money that I donate to worthy causes. Americans are a generous people. Some of us give away more in a year than we actually save and invest. Most of us could give even more if we managed our finances better.

3. False. I look forward to retiring because I then will have time to do things that I cannot do now. Many people fantasize about retiring. They see it as a time to do things that they currently do not have time to do. Anything a person plans to do during retirement can be done now in moderation. Only a foolish person saves himself or herself for retirement, thinking that finally they can do the things they could never afford to do while working.

4. True. I currently invest 10 percent of my income. This is the golden rule of financial independence. Only a few people have employers who have set up such generous retirement plans that they do not need to put aside 10 percent for retirement. For most of us 10 percent is the minimum, and the later we start following this rule, the larger the percentage we need to invest.

5. False. I work at my job more than 50 hours per week. My first question is always: Why? If you really love your work and do not have a family, maybe you can break this rule. If not, why are you working so many hours? What do you believe all these hours are buying you? Many people who work long hours use work as an excuse to avoid spending time with their family. Such people are often poor delegators; they do not manage work responsibilities well. They find it difficult to distinguish between what really needs to be done now and what really does not matter. If you are guilty of working more than 50 hours a week, keep a time diary next week. At the end of the week answer these questions:

- How many hours were spent on extremely important tasks that only you could do?
- How many hours could have been delegated?
- How much time did you spend on the phone or answering e-mails that really were a waste of time?
- How much time was wasted in committee meetings? How much time spent visiting with coworkers?
- How much time did you spend working on your personal agenda?
- How much time did you spend on projects that were not really that important?

No one is going to believe that you spent even 80 percent of your time on extremely important tasks that only you could do. People who do spend that kind of time usually don't know how to tackle jobs efficiently.

6. False. I know best how to spend my family's money. The answer may be true if you are single and responsible for no one else. You may think you know how best to manage the family's money, but you need to seek input from family members. Many people who answer true actually use this belief as an excuse to control all the money in the family.

7. False. People with more money are happier than people with less. Unless you are living below the poverty level, researchers cannot find a correlation between money and happiness.

8. False. I buy at least ten lottery tickets per year. You must have answered true to question 7. Research shows that lottery winners are no happier than the general public.

9. True. People who drive expensive cars are trying to buy status. Most wealthy people do not drive expensive cars. Most people who drive an expensive car lease the car because they cannot afford to buy it.

10. True. At least once during the past 12 months, I have taken a course to help me do my job better. You are your most valuable investment. To stay on the cutting edge of your job, career, or profession, you need to invest at least 40 hours a year in educational activities.

11. False. Offering children money is a great way to get them to do what parents want them to do. The younger the child, the less effective money is as a motivator. While a child might prefer money, there are usually more effective motivators. Using money can often do more damage than good.

12. False. Because the stock market scares me, all my money is in bonds and CDs. People who put most of their money in bonds and CDs don't want to lose their principal. However, bonds can be extremely risky if interest rates rise. Several years ago bonds lost 20 percent of their value in one year. Over the long haul, stocks far outperform bonds and CDs.

13. True. I have money that I can spend each month without having to explain or defend my purchases. Anyone who has to explain or defend purchases is controlled by someone else and needs help now.

14. False. I never plan how I want to spend my money. Anyone who plans how to spend money (and follows that plan) achieves more with their money than those who do not.

15. False. If I had more leisure time, I would be happier. The amounts of leisure time people have and their sense of happiness are not related. Life quality does correlate with what one does during his or her leisure time. For many of us, work time is more satisfying than leisure.

16. True. I have a hobby that I really enjoy. People with hobbies rate the quality of their lives higher than those who do not have hobbies.

17. False. Several times during the past year a creditor has called me. You know the answer to this one. Calls from creditors are red flags that something is seriously wrong with your finances.

18. False. Several times during the past year I have made the minimum payment on a credit card. Same answer as question 17.

19. False. Complaining is a waste of time when a product or service does not work as it should. Knowing how to complain effectively is a money-saving skill.

20. True. Were I to die today, my loved ones could find all my important papers. We hope that this is true. If not, you create a real financial problem for the loved ones you leave behind.

21. True. Were I to die today, I would leave behind enough money to pay off all of my financial obligations. Anyone who answers false may have created serious financial problems for his or her loved ones.

22. True. I earn interest every month on the money in my checking account. There is no acceptable excuse for not using an interest-bearing checking account.

23. True. I have reviewed my credit report during the past 36 months. If you have not, it is past time that you did. If you do not know why, read Chapter 6 carefully.

24. True. I am not accumulating debt. If you answered false, you have a serious problem that needs your full attention now. Read Chapter 6 carefully.

25. True. I know what my net worth is. Most people who answer this question false tell me that they really do not like to keep score. What they are really admitting is that they are afraid to find out that their net worth is too little.

26. True. If I become unable to make my own financial decisions, I have appointed someone to make them for me. This response can only be true for you if you have an up-to-date durable power of attorney for financial affairs or living trust.

How many of your answers did not match? No doubt you have raised valid reasons when you disagree with an answer. However, most people who are winning the money game answered these questions as indicated above. The more your answers match these, the more control you have over your finances.

Gain Greater Control by Simplifying Your Financial Life

Everyone wants to control his or her own destiny; none of us likes to feel that someone else exercises control over us. Each of us wants to be free to do whatever we want with our life. However, freedom comes with a price tag. Can you remember how you looked forward to getting your first driver's license? That license was your ticket to having greater control over your life. You knew that when you got that license your parents would have less control over you. You soon realized that you needed your own car. You had to insure the car. The car liked gas. You had to repair it. You also paid a stiff price when you received a ticket.

Driving was desirable; you did have more control over your life, but that new freedom came with a heavy price. You had to get a job to pay for the car. You surrendered some of your freedom when you submitted to the boss who controlled when you worked and what you did while at work. In many ways, the car gave you greater control over your life, but it also controlled you in ways you had not expected.

> **Hot Tip**
>
> I use the word *control* often in this book. I hope you realize that when talking about controlling money, I do not mean that you make all of the financial decisions in your family. Control in this context is similar to manage, and manage implies teamwork.

Who doesn't want to control his or her future? For most of us, finances play a key role in achieving that freedom. Are you free today to always do what you want? There are consequences based on the choices you make that may limit your control in the future.

You can gain greater control over your life by trying to simplify your financial affairs. The following strategies will be discussed in greater detail throughout this book:

- Invest 10 percent of your income.
- Give away 10 percent of your income.
- Develop and use a spending plan to fund important goals.
- Automatically fund savings accounts to store dollars for unexpected expenses.
- Keep a current, accurate balance in your check register.
- Use a money management software program to track your spending.
- Stop using all but one or two of your credit cards.
- Get out of debt.
- Insure potentially large financial risks.
- Keep your will updated.
- Find time each day to share with family and friends.
- Set up and use a filing system to hold all your important documents.

Your Mission Statement Worksheet

If I asked you to describe your life's mission, what would you tell me? If your life lacks focus and meaning, write your own mission statement. Such an exercise forces you to reexamine who you are and what you are trying to accomplish. Mission statements are short—no more than one to three sentences—and the shorter the better. Yours should reflect your life's purpose. You should enthusiastically, even passionately, want to accomplish goals that support your mission statement. Your mission statement needs to be compatible with your training, talents, desires, and interests. Yet it needs to be broad enough to cover a lifetime of activities. My mission statement: Help individuals and families improve the quality of their lives by better managing their economic resources. Now that you have read mine, write yours:

_____

_____

_____

_____

_____

_____

_____

Read it often and revise it as needed. Your mission statement should inspire you. Everything you do should be compatible with your mission statement. It is the template you use to give your life direction and purpose.

The ideas in this book should challenge your beliefs about what money can do. Strategies are designed to help you gain greater control over your finances. Your financial future depends on the decisions you make now. If you really want to gain greater control over your life and your money, decide now to question what you currently believe about money. Be willing to develop new financial habits. Increased control requires that you make changes in the way you think about, and the way you manage, your money. Only you can assess the costs of continuing along your present road or changing to a new one. You can become more financially fit. Start by following the directions in the next chapter to create your net worth statement.

2 Calculate Your Net Worth

Figure out how much you are worth in dollars and cents.

> When Tammy and David Fry first sat down in my office, they seemed to self-destruct in front of me. I listened as they tried to answer my question, "How can I help you?" Apparently their finances were in such a mess that they could not even explain their basic problem. When they started to slow down, I suggested they needed a picture of their current financial situation. The best way to do that would be for them to figure out their net worth. I explained that net worth is the difference between the assets a person owns and the liabilities they owe. Put another way, net worth would be the amount of money they had left if they sold everything they owned and then used the proceeds to pay off all of their debts. David told me that if they did that there would be no money left.

He was right that day. He and Tammy had a negative net worth; they actually owed more money to creditors than the current market value of everything they owned. A negative net worth is pretty typical for people in their early 20s who have only been working full-time for a year or two and have student loans to repay. However, the Frys were in their 40s.

Your net worth is a measure of your personal wealth. It can be

- zero (assets equal liabilities);
- positive (assets are larger than liabilities); or
- negative (liabilities are larger than assets).

If you have a negative net worth, you are currently insolvent. Unless you recently graduated from college, a negative net worth usually means that your finances have been or are currently out of control.

Because your net worth changes every day, a net worth figure only reflects your net worth on the day you filled in the blanks on the statement.

How much is your current net worth? Before you start to fill in the blanks on your net worth statement, check the following.

1. Define assets and liabilities. As you fill in the blanks on the net worth statement, you will be required to come up with numbers for assets (what you own) and liabilities (what you owe). Each asset is listed at its current market value, which is the amount you would receive if you sold the item today. For example, the market value of your car is the amount that you would accept and a buyer would offer were your car for sale. When listing assets, don't reduce them by the amount of a loan used to buy an item. For example, the Frys' Mustang had a market value of $9,000, and they owed $7,000 on the loan they took out to buy the car. Under assets the Frys listed the Mustang as being worth $9,000. Where did they come up with that number? They checked the prices of similar Mustangs listed in the want ads of their local paper. They also could have found the value of their car by checking a copy of the *Kelley Blue Book* or by going to its Web site: www.kbb.com.

Liabilities are debts you owe someone else. A liability is a benefit you have received but have not paid for, such as the Frys' $7,000 Mustang loan. A bill for a service that you have not yet received is not a liability. For example, if you receive a bill this month for next month's auto insurance, next month's auto insurance is not yet a liability, although it will be next month if it remains unpaid.

If the Frys' only asset was the Mustang and they had no other debt, their net worth would look as follows:

The Frys' Net Worth Statement

Assets	
Mustang	$9,000
Liabilities	
Subtract the Mustang loan	($7,000)
Net Worth	$2,000

2. The date on a net worth statement is the date the statement is created.
People often select one of the following times to calculate their net worth:

- Their birthday
- End of a school year
- April 15
- End of the calendar year

If you want to see how your net worth changes from year to year, create your net worth statement on the same date each year. Whatever date you select, all assets and liabilities must be valued as of that date. For example, if you date your net worth statement March 31, the balance in your checking account should also be as of March 31.

3. Net worth statements contain from one to four or more columns of financial data. Some of you will have only one financial column as did the Frys. The sample net worth statement in Figure 2.1 has four columns. If you are single, record this year's figures in column one. Log next year's data in column two. You can then compare the numbers to see where your net worth in growing and where it is declining. A year from now if the Frys' only asset is still their car and their only liability is their auto loan, will their net worth be higher or lower? The answer: That depends. Cars are depreciating assets, so the Frys' car will be worth less a year from now. However, during the next year they will make 12 more car payments, so their loan balance will also be lower.

> **Hot Tip**
>
> **M**any people calculate their net worth at the end of the calendar year because they receive annual statements from creditors as well as financial institutions that handle their investment accounts. Unless you are reading this book in January, you will need to contact many of your creditors and institutions handling your investment accounts to obtain current balances.

Couples often use a format that includes four columns of financial data:

1. The first column holds one person's data.
2. The second holds the other person's data.
3. The third column holds financial data for items they own together.
4. The fourth column combines all the data from columns 1, 2, and 3.

Couples have a choice in calculating their net worth. Either use the four columns as described above to show one year's data, or combine data, using a single column for one year's figures. The remaining three blank columns could be used to hold numbers for future years.

The format of the net worth statement in this chapter has separated assets into three categories:

1. *Cash assets.* Assets that are cash or near cash, such as money in a checking or savings account. Such assets are extremely liquid, meaning that they can be converted to cash in a day or two without losing any of their value.

2 / Calculate Your Net Worth   15

Figure 2.1 Sample Net Worth Statement

1. December 31, 2000

2.	Joe	Julie	Together	Combined
3. Assets				
Cash assets				
Checking	$ 500	$ 1,000		$ 1,500
Investment assets				
Retirement account		4,000		4,000
Personal assets				
Honda Civic	8,000			8,000
Buick Skylark		9,000		9,000
House			90,000	90,000
4. Total assets	$8,500	$14,000	$90,000	$112,500
5. Liabilities				
Honda Civic loan	(4,000)			(4,000)
Buick Skylark loan		(5,000)		(5,000)
House mortgage			(50,000)	(50,000)
6. Total liabilities	(4,000)	(5,000)	(50,000)	(59,000)
7. Net worth (Total assets less Total liabilities)	$4,500	$9,000	$40,000	$ 53,500

2. *Investment assets.* Investments represent ownership in businesses (such as owning stocks) or a creditor relationship with a business or government (such as owning bonds) or retirement accounts. Such assets change in value from day to day depending on what happens to the business and the economy. Over a long period of time, most investment assets should increase in value.

3. *Personal assets.* Most personal assets, such as clothing, furniture, electronic equipment, and cars, depreciate in value. Some personal assets such as a house or collectibles may appreciate.

Liabilities are sometimes divided into two groups:

1. Short-term liabilities: debts that are to be paid off in full during the next 12 months. An example would be a doctor's bill or a credit card balance.
2. Long-term liabilities: liabilities like a home mortgage, car, or student loan that may require many years to repay.

Complete Your Net Worth Statement as follows:

1. Record the date when the financial data were collected.
2. List your name in the space over column one, leaving the three remaining columns for data from future years. If you have a partner, fill out the statement as completed in Figure 2.1.
3. Assets
   - Cash assets are selected from the following list:

     Cash
     Checking account balance
     Savings account balance
     Emergency fund
     Certificates of deposit
     Money market account

   - Select investment assets from the following list. You may have to contact firms that have your investment accounts to obtain current balances.

Hot Tip

If you do not have a money management software system, now may be the time to buy one. The following programs have net worth statements that you can complete with your own data:

Managing Your Money
203-452-2600
www.mymnet.com

Microsoft Money
800-426-9400
www.moneyinsider.msn.com

Quicken
800-446-8848
ww.quicken.com

You can also complete your net worth statement by going to the following Web sites:

www.tdbank.ca/tdbank/tdam/mfplgpnw.html

www.armchairmillionaire.com/schwab/investing/networth.html

www.loanvalue.com/loanvalue/javascript/calnetw.htm

Your Net Worth Statement

1.
                Date: _____

2.   _____ _____ _____ _____

3. **Assets**

4. **Total assets**

5. **Liabilities**

6. **Total liabilities**

7. **Net worth**

Stocks
Bonds
Mutual funds
Individual retirement
  accounts (IRAs)
Real estate
Businesses

401(k) or 403(b) retirement
  plan balances
Profit-sharing plan balances
Keogh plan balance
Trusts
Annuities
Precious metals (gold, silver, etc.)

- Select personal assets from the following list. While you can check local newspaper want ads to estimate the market value of your home or car, you are going to have to make an educated guess about market values for most of the other items. You might be able to research some on the Internet. Most used items, such as your furniture, clothing, or appliances, are probably worth significantly less than their cost.

Home
Automobile
Furniture
Clothing
Jewelry
Antiques

Computer equipment
Camera equipment
Boat
Sports equipment
Electronic equipment (TV, CD player,
  VCR)

4. Add together the market value of all assets.
5. Select liabilities from the following list. Your monthly statements from creditors should provide balances for most of these debts. In some cases you will need to contact creditors to find out some of your current loan balances.

Utilities
Rent
Medical/dental bills
Insurance premiums
Credit card balances
Taxes
Auto
Education/student loans

Mortgage
Family
Medical
Home equity
Margin account
Life insurance
Installment loans (washer-dryer,
  for example)

6. Add together all liabilities.
7. Compute your net worth by subtracting the total for liabilities from the total for assets.

Are you surprised by the size of your net worth? What does this number actually mean to you? Is it larger than you expected? Do you think it is too low? A financial adviser will want to know the amount of your net worth. A counselor also will want to know several things about you. Why? So he or she can determine how well you are doing in funding important goals.

How old are you? If you are a college student, your net worth is likely to be negative. Within two or three years after graduating, your net worth should turn positive. Several years before turning 30, you should start accumulating investment assets. By the time you are in your 40s, total investment assets should be larger than your personal assets. As you age, your investment assets should become an increasingly larger percentage of your total assets.

> **Hot Tip**
>
> Did you have a difficult time finding all the paperwork you needed? Chapter 3 will help you set up a filing system, so that you always will be able to find what you need when you need it.

At what age do you want to achieve financial independence? This information is critical when evaluating if you are adequately funding financial independence right now.

What is your family status? Are you single? Are you a parent? How many people depend upon you financially?

How much income do you need to live on each month? This number, when compared with your current income, will tell your financial counselor how much you can invest each month to adequately fund your retirement.

What are your beliefs about investment risk? Anyone interested in helping you achieve your financial goals and increase your net worth will carefully consider your attitudes about investments. Have you invested your money in ways that are compatible with your feelings about risk? For example, someone who does not want the value of investments to decline is less likely to own investments where the principal could decline in value. Because most investments have the potential to drop in value, some people only keep their money in certificates of deposit or insured savings accounts.

How large is your net worth? If your net worth is in excess of $500,000, you have made significant progress toward becoming financially independent. However, net worths of this size and larger also indicate the possibility of estate planning problems, including paying substantial federal estate taxes at your death. Future chapters will look at estate planning problems and how you can resolve them.

To measure how well you are doing, a financial counselor might divide your net worth by the number of years you have been employed. Such a number measures how much you have been able to accumulate on average for each year you have worked.

How much debt do you have? This is what a loan or mortgage officer considers when looking at your net worth statement. There are two key issues here. More than one year of data is helpful, so you can answer the following question: Is your debt load increasing or decreasing? Unless you are borrowing to finance a college education, or you just purchased a house or car, your debt balances should be declining.

If you owe too much to too many creditors, you are likely to be turned down when you apply for another loan. For example, a lender may evaluate your debt load by dividing the total amount of your liabilities by the total amount of your assets. The resulting number tells you the percentage of your assets that you have purchased using debt.

Lenders also want to see what assets you own that they could sell if you default on the loan. If you have few investment assets, they are likely to charge you a higher interest rate or reject your loan application.

How can you increase your net worth? A financial counselor or loan officer can tell quite a bit about your present financial situation if he or she has your answers to the above questions. To become financially independent, you need to make sure that your net worth is growing. Unless you are either in college or have already celebrated your 85th birthday, your net worth should increase from year to year. Here is what you need to do to make sure this happens:

- *Pay down both short-term and long-term debt.* Debt is suffocating millions of people. Financial bondage, caused by debt, is closely associated with alcohol and drug addiction, crime, marriage disruption, poor job performance, and child and spousal abuse. We discuss how to deal with debt in Chapters 5 and 6.
- *Buy investments.* Financial independence depends on your adopting the Golden Rule of financial independence: Invest 10 percent of your gross income. In Chapter 14, we will discuss strategies you can adopt to practice this objective.
- *Over time your investment assets should appreciate in value.* Most of your investments should also generate income. Use such income to buy more investments (not to support your lifestyle). We discuss this topic also in Chapter 14.

How much should your net worth increase each year? While that depends on your answers to the above questions, your net worth should grow at least 15 percent to 20 percent per year until all nonmortgage debt is repaid. Examine the sample net worth statement in Figure 2.2.

Figure 2.2 Sample Net Worth Statement April 15, 2000

	Current Year	Last Year	Two Years Ago
Assets			
Cash	$ 1,000	$ 1,000	$ 1,000
Investments	9,000	6,400	4,000
Chrysler LeBaron	7,000	8,000	9,000
Total assets	$17,000	$15,400	$14,000
Liabilities			
Credit cards	$ 1,000	$ 3,000	$ 4,000
Car loan	2,600	4,000	5,000
Student loans	8,000	10,000	11,500
Total liabilities	$11,600	$17,000	$20,500
Net worth	$5,400	($1,600)	($6,500)
Changes in net worth	$7,000	$4,900	

We hope you noticed the following:

- Net worth is improving and is now positive.
- Debt has decreased substantially.
- Assets are increasing, but not as fast as debt is declining because the car depreciates.

Examine your net worth statement to identify your strengths and weaknesses. Can the numbers that make up your net worth pass this test? Are all your debt balances declining? Is each investment asset appreciating at an average annual rate of at least 7 percent (10 percent is better)?

Until you can answer "yes" to these questions, you will make little or no progress in achieving financial independence. Anyone who continues to pile up debt is not likely to have the money to purchase investment assets, because money that should be invested is serving debt.

Nothing says more about your progress toward becoming financially fit than positive improvement in your net worth. Calculate your net worth at least once a year. So you will remember to compute your net worth again in 12 months, write "compute NW" on the appropriate date in your calendar. By computing your new worth, you have taken an important first step toward gaining more control over your finances. You also will be ready when a financial institution wants you to provide information about your net worth. Now that you know your current net worth, you can evaluate how well you are doing in achieving such important financial goals as financial independence.

3 Get Organized

- Identify goals to last a lifetime.
- Set up a system so that you can file and quickly find any document.
- Assemble your team of advisers.

> Once upon a time a teenage boy created a list of things he wanted to accomplish during his life. Some goals were not too unusual: become a black belt in karate; type 60 words a minute. Others stood out: climb the Matterhorn; land a plane on an aircraft carrier; publish an article in *Fortune* magazine. His list included over 120 activities. During his life he has accomplished most of them. Recording his dreams gave his life a long-term perspective, yet enriched each day as he planned how he was going to achieve his next goal. His list has provided the source of inspiration that has enabled him to live far more dreams than most people have.

Focus on Your Goals

Without goals, we drift through life unsure of what is important, what is a distraction, or where we are going. Do you want to get acquainted with someone? Ask that person about his or her goals. Any financial adviser or counselor wants to first know what a client's goals are. When advisers ask clients to bring a list of their goals to the next meeting, many clients show up empty-handed. Why? People are so afraid of failing to achieve what they might write down that they shield themselves from defeat by not identifying their goals.

Would your life be richer and more satisfying if you made a list of goals? Would you have more to look forward to? Find out.

During our life, we spend our money and our energy in three ways:

1. Doing
2. Having
3. Becoming

What do you want from your life? Did you first think of career aspirations not yet achieved? Such dreams fit somewhere on your list. Try to think about all aspects of your life.

What do you want to do, to have, and to become? Too often when people write about goals, the examples are limited to having things. A certain amount of pleasure comes from anticipating buying something. My wife and I look forward to the new computer that will enable us to connect with the Internet at home. For many years I dreamed of owning a 1965 Mustang. Once I finally owned it, I enjoyed driving it, but it soon had so many problems that I dreamed about the day when I no longer owned it. You may have heard that the two greatest days in the life of a boat owner are the day it's bought and the day it's sold. I suggest to clients that they put wish lists for each member of the family on the refrigerator. Listing things you want is satisfying.

Wish lists are great places to record things we want to have or to do in the immediate future.

Are we always in the process of becoming? I know that I am becoming older and so are you. But what else do you want to become? Maybe your goal is no more challenging than becoming a better tennis player. Maybe you want to learn to play the mandolin. Do you know someone who wants to become a brain surgeon? Too many adults in their 30s and 40s tell me that it is too late to learn anything new. Here's how I respond: You are likely to live into your 80s or 90s. Even if you only live five more years, you will derive joy and satisfaction during the process of becoming what interests you. In fact, once we stop growing, we start shrinking. Life stands still for no one. When we have no more challenges that stretch us, much of the zest that makes life worth living slips away.

To identify the goals that you want to fund right now, please complete the following three steps:

1. Record as many of your goals as you can on the Personal Goals Worksheet.
2. Select a minimum of two goals that you want to achieve in the near future.
3. Define these goals so that you know exactly what you must start to do now to achieve them.

When you start filling in your wish list, identify dreams in all three areas: doing, having, and becoming. Creating a wish list is really a brainstorming activity.

Write goals down without judging. Do not critique your goals. Refuse to let your current financial condition, your family situation, or your health keep you from recording a goal. I have always heard that medical school will not accept anyone older than 30, yet my cousin, who is in his 40s, is attending medical school. Reading the stories in Canfield and Hansen's *Chicken Soup* books reminds me that people can and do achieve their impossible dreams. Will you achieve every goal you list? I hope not. Adding goals to your list is a lifelong activity. When you die, I hope someone finds your list and thinks, "Wow! No wonder you loved life so much."

Your goals do not have to involve only you. A balanced life involves others. Some of your most satisfying experiences come from helping others. For example, if you are not yet a parent, then you may dream about having children. Perhaps you, like the young man mentioned at the start of this chapter, plan to serve a mission for your church. Maybe you would like to volunteer some of your time working for a community service organization. You are not likely to focus all your goals on helping the disadvantaged, as Mother Teresa did. However, some of your most satisfying goals, when realized, will involve making a difference in others' lives.

When you list goals, many of them are one-time accomplishments like walking on the Great Wall of China or hiking in the Swiss Alps. Some of the more satisfying will be activities that you experience repeatedly, such as growing flowers or tracing your family history. Identify some goals that can involve you for the rest of your life and that you will never complete.

One final suggestion: as you list each goal, list steps that describe appropriate actions for fulfilling your goal. John Goddard defined his goals using terms such as *explore, photograph, study,* and *climb.* Action verbs help you better visualize what you plan to accomplish.

Are you married? Ask your spouse to create his or her list, too. Assign priorities to your most important goals. Ask your spouse to do the same. Then compare. Are you surprised at some of your spouse's choices? You are more likely to fulfill certain activities when you work together.

No matter what your current situation, select at least two goals that you want to experience as soon as possible. List them on the following worksheet. You may want to work on more than two, but two should be the minimum. Many of your goals may not require any money to achieve, but some will require substantial sums. As you gain greater control over your finances, you will be able to start planning and funding more of your goals. Notice that the worksheet for listing your goals requires you to answer some specific questions about each goal.

Let's look at an example. One of Fred and Virginia's goals is to go Volkswalking in Bavaria, Austria, Switzerland, and Italy. Here is how they filled out the worksheet:

	Start Date	Cost
Goal #1 Spend 3 weeks Volkswalking in Bavaria	July 2000	$3950
Step 1: Save $190 a month	Nov. 1998	3800
Step 2: Join European Volkswalking Association	Sept. 1999	25
Step 3: Order two passports	Jan. 2000	150
Step 4: Obtain airline tickets	Jan. 2000	*
Step 5: Obtain current tourist literature, maps	Feb. 2000	75

*No cost because using frequent flyer tickets.

Notice that the goal is specific:

- What: Volkswalking
- When: July 2000 for three weeks
- Where: Bavaria, Austria, Switzerland, Italy
- How much: $3,950

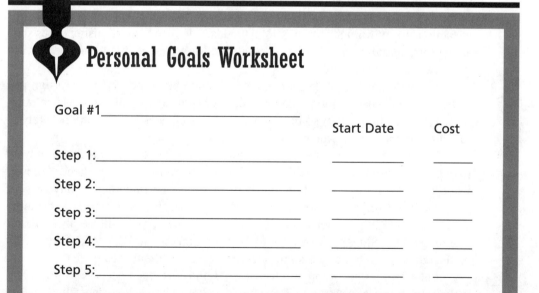

Personal Goals Worksheet

Goal #1 _____

	Start Date	Cost
Step 1: _____	_____	_____
Step 2: _____	_____	_____
Step 3: _____	_____	_____
Step 4: _____	_____	_____
Step 5: _____	_____	_____

Personal Goals Worksheet
(continued)

Goal #2 _____
                                                          Start Date   Cost

Step 1: _____   _____   _____

Step 2: _____   _____   _____

Step 3: _____   _____   _____

Step 4: _____   _____   _____

Step 5: _____   _____   _____

Goal #3 _____
                                                          Start Date   Cost

Step 1: _____   _____   _____

Step 2: _____   _____   _____

Step 3: _____   _____   _____

Step 4: _____   _____   _____

Step 5: _____   _____   _____

Goal #4 _____
                                                          Start Date   Cost

Step 1: _____   _____   _____

Step 2: _____   _____   _____

Step 3: _____   _____   _____

Step 4: _____   _____   _____

Step 5: _____   _____   _____

Creating this goal required that Virginia and Fred create a budget. They figured their costs as follows:

Airline tickets	No charge
Passports	$ 150
New walking shoes	200
Lodging (hostels)	1000
Food	1000
Rental car + gas	900
Volkswalking fees	120
Gifts, souvenirs	400
Miscellaneous	480

Fred and Virginia now have a clearer idea of the steps they must take to prepare for their European vacation. While they have no control over weather, sickness, or accidents, they have created a plan that enables them to make the trip. I hope they take their cameras.

Until you write down your dreams, they remain just that: dreams. Writing them down greatly increases the likelihood that you will accomplish them. Why? Because many of us like to cross things off lists. We are more likely to focus on achieving goals that we have written down. Writing them down adds a certain concreteness and direction to our life. On blustery winter days, refer to your list of goals and you will find yourself escaping for a few seconds or minutes as you see yourself fulfilling one or more. Wintertime is also a great time to take those concrete steps you must complete to fulfill your goals.

You should be able to fund most of your goals in less than three years. However, some goals, such as retirement or college, often require decades of saving and investing. I discuss more involved funding strategies in later chapters; ten or more years are required to fund the primary goals discussed in those chapters.

Hot Tip

You will probably need airline tickets to participate in many of the activities on your goal list. Consider using a credit card and a telephone company that allow you to accumulate frequent flyer miles. Recently, CitiBank offered one free round-trip to Europe to new cardholders who purchased a European airline ticket with their CitiBank Visa card. Diner's Club offered 10,000 frequent flyer miles for applying for its card. MCI offered 5,000 miles for switching to its long-distance service plus five frequent flyer miles for every dollar spent on MCI calls.

Financial Checkup Checklist

- List a minimum of five "doing" goals.
- List a minimum of five "having" goals.
- List a minimum of three "becoming" goals.
- Fill in all the steps for at least two goals.

After you create your spending plan in Chapter 4, come back to this chapter so you can include the amount of money you need to save regularly to achieve your two goals. When you want to add another goal, please do. Remember to record the date when you achieve each goal.

File and Find It Again

At times, does it seem you are buried under a flood of papers? In case of an illness, accident, or emergency, could you find important documents? How quickly could you locate your car title, birth certificate, or Social Security card? Do you maintain organized tax files, or is April's arrival the signal to start the annual income tax paper chase? Have you ever misplaced important documents needed to respond to an IRS audit or to file an insurance claim? If you died today, could your family find all your important documents, including your will, passbooks, stock certificates, and key to your safe deposit box?

Tommy and Lilly Chan had a hard time finding any document. Because they did not bring most of the needed paperwork to the first two visits in my office, we decided to hold the third meeting in their home. When I arrived I was surprised to find a neat, orderly house. However, that third meeting took an hour longer than it should have as they played "hide and seek" looking for needed papers. Before I left that day, we discussed setting up a filing system much like the one you will read about next. They followed these instructions to the letter. On the fourth meeting I tested their system, and they could retrieve every document I requested in less than seven seconds. More than anything else that I may have done for the Chans, in a small way I helped them simplify their life because they spent so much less time finding and refiling papers.

Your personal computer will not eliminate your need to store important documents. The word *document* refers to any piece of paper that goes into one of your folders. Legal papers, repair bills, receipts, and insurance policies are considered documents. Each year you will continue to receive dozens of documents that need to be stored where you can find them quickly. Some original documents that cannot be replaced, like a marriage license, need to be copied and the originals stored in a fireproof safe or in a bank's safe deposit box.

Keeping track of your paper flow need not be complicated or time consuming. A good filing system will help you accomplish the following:

- Protect important, original documents in a safe place.
- Discard papers that you no longer need.
- File all important papers.
- Retrieve all important papers quickly.
- Enable other family members to find important papers.

You will complete four steps in setting up and operating your system.

1. Acquire file folders, hanging folders, large envelopes, and a file box or filing cabinet.
2. Set up your filing system.
3. Collect and file your documents and papers.
4. Once a year go through all the files and discard as appropriate.

Step 1: Get the Needed Supplies

Buy colored file folders; it is easier to find and refile papers when all file folders do not look alike. You also need large envelopes (10"×13") in which to place papers that you will eventually discard. You will need a file drawer in which to place your hanging folders. Insert several file folders in each hanging folder. Do you have an empty drawer or can you empty a drawer in a filing cabinet or desk? If no drawer is available, go to your nearby office supply outlet and purchase a metal or cardboard file box. You may need to install a metal rack in the drawer on which you can place the hanging folders. You will need a second file box, a file drawer, or a filing cabinet to hold papers placed in storage. Most items in storage can be discarded eventually.

Step 2: Set Up Your Filing System

You need a file for every type of document. Any important original document that cannot be replaced should be kept in a fireproof safe or safe deposit box. Only photocopies of such originals should be kept in folders at home. Create a folder titled "Safe Deposit Inventory," where you keep a list of all items stored in the safe deposit box.

Figure 3.1 is a fairly long list of potential labels or titles for file folders. You will not need folders for most of these topics, but you are likely to need one or two for topics not on this list. I have grouped folders by major filing categories and suggest that you file folders alphabetically within these categories. Experience has shown that when folders are not grouped by topic, they are harder to locate.

> **Hot Tip**
>
> Place original documents identified by this star (*) in your safe deposit box or safe.

Figure 3.1 Labels for Your File Folders

BANKING

    Bills due this month
    Bills due after this month
    Checking account transactions/statements
    Credit card transactions/statements
    Credit report
    Get out of debt
    Savings account transactions/statements/passbooks

CHILDREN

ESTATE PLANNING

    Durable powers of attorney
    Letters of last instructions
    Living will(s)
    Umbrella liability policy
    Will(s)*

(continued)

Figure 3.1 Labels for Your File Folders
(continued)

FINANCIAL PLANNING

    Annuity policies
    Financial statements
    Life insurance policies
    Retirement needs analysis

HOUSEHOLD

    Buy/sell home
    Complaint letters
    Homeowners/renters policy
    Household inventory
    Pictures of valuables
    Property tax assessment/appeal
    Repairs: home/appliances
    Subscriptions
    Warranties/guarantees

JOB

    Benefit statement (from employer)
    Résumé

INVESTMENTS

    Brokerage account transactions/statements
    IRA transactions/statements
    Mutual fund transactions/statements
    Retirement account transactions/statements

MEDICAL

    Dental and medical bills paid (this year)
    Dental and medical insurance policies

Figure 3.1 Labels for Your File Folders
(continued)

MEDICAL (continued)

    Disability policies
    Immunization records
    Long-term care insurance policies
    Medical reimbursement account transactions
    Optical records
    Prescriptions

PERSONAL

    Advisers
    Certificates/licenses
    Divorce/separation papers
    Frequent flyer mile statements
    Goals
    Legal papers
    Pictures

TAXES

    Receipts for this year's transactions
    Forms, schedules, and publications

VEHICLES

    Accident records
    Buy/sell vehicles
    Insurance policies for vehicles
    Leasing
    Oil change/maintenance
    Registration/titles*
    Repair records

Step 3: Find and File All Your Documents

Unless you are already well organized, documents and papers will be found all over your house. Finding all your documents and placing them in appropriate folders takes time. Don't forget to check your garage, your car, and your desk at work. Be sure to go through boxes in which you already store important keepsakes. You also need a copy of every document in your safe or safe deposit box. Start a list of all documents that you cannot locate. Many of these will eventually materialize, but you will have to replace those that you cannot find.

> **Hot Tip**
>
> Someone in your family or household should be responsible for filing each new paper or document. However, all family members need to be aware of the need to save papers. Have a box near your file where members can place papers as they receive them. The person doing the filing should find a convenient time each week to file or discard all papers placed in the box.

Step 4: Discard Annually

Discard papers that are no longer needed. Unless you discard annually, your files will become clogged and bloated. When you file any paper, use a pencil to record on the item when it should be discarded.

Place papers you want to keep longer than a year into permanent storage with the discard date visible. Once a year spring clean your files. An ideal time is when you prepare your income tax return. Toss papers you no longer need; place others in permanent storage. Select a dry place that is free from temperature extremes. I suggest that you avoid attics and basements.

A few documents can never be thrown away. The originals should be kept in your safe deposit box. Documents to be retained forever include the following:

- Adoption papers
- Marriage licenses
- Baptismal certificates
- Birth certificates
- Divorce decrees
- Deeds/Titles to property you own
- Loan documents (if you still owe—or are owed—money)
- Naturalization papers
- Military discharge papers
- Stock certificates

- Trusts
- Wills (Destroy old wills when a new will is drafted.)

Organize Yourself

You will manage your papers more effectively if you select the same time each week to handle your "paper shuffle." You need a place to work that is as free as possible from distractions. Your home office should be close to your file drawer or filing cabinet. It's hoped a computer or typewriter is handy. If you do not have space in a drawer, you can place stamps, tape, scissors, pens and pencils, envelopes, and your checkbook in a box labeled "Stamps and Office Supplies."

Control your paper chase as follows:

- When you receive a bill that should be paid in a few days, file it in the folder "Bills due now." Bills not due until next month go in the folder "Bills due later."
- When you receive a letter that requires an answer, file it in "Correspondence to answer."

How many of these important papers do you carry in your wallet or purse?

- Auto insurance card
- 800 number if you lose your credit card
- Driver's license
- Health insurance card
- Medical card

Have you recorded the following?

- Your blood type
- Your donor instructions
- Allergies (are you diabetic, epileptic?)
- Whom to notify in case of accident?
- Minisized living will

You also need to record important personal information on the Personal Data Worksheet. Make a photocopy of this form for each family member; fill it out, and keep it in your personal data folder. Use a pencil to fill in the blanks.

Setting up a filing system takes time, but the rewards are many. In the long run you will save time when trying to find documents. You also are less likely to lose or misplace important papers. Filing certain documents related to income taxes, insurance policies, and estate planning papers is discussed more thoroughly later.

Personal Data Worksheet

PERSONAL DATA FOR _____

Birth date _____

Social Security number _____

Driver's license number _____

Passport number _____

Marriage date _____

Name of spouse _____

Naturalization date _____

Military discharge date _____

Name of former spouse: _____

Divorce/Death date: _____

Name of father _____

Maiden name of mother: _____

Location of will _____

Name of close relative _____

Relative's address _____

Financial Checkup Checklist

- Locate a filing cabinet, box, or drawer.//
- Label the file folders.
- File all documents in their proper folders.
- Check to make sure you have key documents such as your driver's license, health insurance card, and auto insurance card in your purse or wallet.

Create Your Own Professional Dream Team

The lifeblood of any financial counselor is new clients. At the start of my first meeting with a client, I always ask: "How may I help you?" Every answer is different. When I put that question to Mr. Martin, he exploded. We had both watched the 6 PM local news a week before when the lead story focused on a local financial adviser who had just been arrested. While the story provided an example to be discussed by my classes, Mr. Martin realized that most of his investment dollars had been stolen by a childhood friend whom he trusted. I just listened for a considerable period of time while Mr. Martin let off steam. Once again a trusted professional had cheated someone.

We all want to work with competent, honest professionals who will complete their work for us promptly and charge a reasonable fee. The vast majority of the professionals I know pretty much fit this definition. Some professionals charge substantial fees or take forever to finish their work, but few are dishonest and most are reasonably competent.

Make a list of the names of professionals with whom you wish to continue working. The discussion that follows this list is designed to help you find competent professionals:

- Accountant
- Attorney
- Clergy
- Financial counselor/planner
- Insurance agent(s)

- Stockbroker
- Banker
- Physicians
- Dentist

Common Mistakes When Working with Professionals

Billing. Always get the estimate in writing for doing the work you want. Most people who complain about being overcharged never received a written quote. Most professionals are paid in one of three ways:

1. By the hour. Some professionals, like plumbers, may start the meter when they leave their office or their last job. Others will bill you for work done at their office, including time spent with you on the phone.
2. By the project. These professionals give you an estimate for completing the entire job. If the job includes parts, make sure that each part is clearly identified and that the prices are itemized.
3. By commission. Most of the financial products that you buy include a commission paid to the salesperson or financial adviser. You have every right to ask what that sales fee will be. Increasing numbers of professionals disclose commissions without your having to ask.

Shoddy or unfinished work. Never pay for work until it is completed to your satisfaction. In a few cases you may be required to make a deposit to start a job. When a job is expected to take several weeks to complete, partial payment is often required when certain milestones have been reached. A sure sign of a con is a request for most or all of the money up front.

Here are the four steps you must complete when you have a complaint about shoddy or unfinished work:

1. Keep all original documents.
2. Contact the professional and request that the work be finished or redone.
3. If the professional refuses, contact your credit card company and ask to have the professional's charge reversed. You can expect a credit in three to five weeks. A client of

> **Hot Tip**
>
> Get in the habit of paying for professional work with your credit card. Any time you order work done in the state where you live and the bill is $50 or more, pay with a credit card. Why? You can have the amount you were charged refunded if the work is unacceptable.

mine gave a travel agent a check for $20,000 for a summer vacation. The travel agent used the client's money to take a trip himself. Had the client paid with a credit card, she could have gotten the $20,000 returned.
4. When work is not completed according to the agreement, withhold payment. If delays continue, terminate the project and go elsewhere. You may want to visit with an attorney if you are bound by a written contract or if substantial work has been completed.

Finding a Professional

Better professionals obtain their clients by referral. You are likely to be happier with professionals who have been referred to you by a friend or another professional. Want to find a doctor? Ask a nurse. Want to find a divorce attorney? Contact a trial lawyer. Want to find a financial planner? Get referrals from your banker or certified public accountant. Want to find an electrician, ask a plumber. This system is not foolproof because sometimes a professional receives a kickback from the person to whom he or she refers clients.

Before selecting any professional, try to come up with three referrals. You want someone who is competent, honest, reasonable, and meets deadlines. Seek out someone with whom you feel comfortable. This means that you actually need to visit with each professional before you select one. Ask the following questions:

- How long have you been doing the type of work I need to have done?
- What kinds of clients do you usually work with?
- What percentage of your practice is represented by this type of work?
- How do you determine what to bill your clients?
- What types of products do you usually sell?
- Why should I work with you?
- Can you give me the names of three clients whom you have worked with during the past six months?
- To what professional organizations do you belong?
- What professional designations, certifications, or licenses do you hold?
- Will you actually be doing the work, or will a colleague do it?

Also consider the following:

- How pleasant and professional is the rest of the staff?
- How convenient are the professional's office hours?
- How convenient is parking?
- If you need round-the-clock assistance, is it available?
- If this professional (such as a stockbroker or financial planner) will be sending you monthly or annual reports, how readable are they?

Rely as much on your intuition as you do on the facts and figures shared with you. Did you immediately feel comfortable with the professional? Did you have the impression that you could trust this person completely? Did you sense that this person was concerned about helping you?

Checking Out a Financial Adviser

Because this book focuses on helping you better manage and control your money, please review the following before committing to work with a financial planner or adviser. Few universities offer degree programs in financial planning, so a professional you work with should have earned at least one of the following certifications:

- **CFP**—Certified Financial Planner. He or she has passed a rigorous examination covering investments, retirement and estate planning, insurance, and income taxation.
- **CLU**—Chartered Life Underwriter. He or she has passed a series of examinations primarily about life insurance planning, but some estate and income planning is included.
- **CPA**—Certified Public Accountant. He or she has passed a rigorous examination about accounting to include corporate and personal income taxation.
- **CFA**—Certified Financial Analyst. He or she has passed a series of challenging examinations primarily about investing.

While having one of these certifications is no guarantee of competency, you have every right to be suspicious of anyone who has not earned any of these certifications if that individual is providing financial planning advice.

Discuss in detail how you will be charged for services. Expect to encounter one of the following approaches. At the start of the conversation, ask for a copy of the form ADV-Part II that the planner files

> **Hot Tip**
>
> Be suspicious of anyone who may have only RIA or Registered Investment Advisor on their business card or stationery. Almost anyone can become an RIA by contacting the Securities and Exchange Commission (SEC), completing the ADV (or adviser) form, paying a fee, and passing the National Association of Securities Dealers (NASD) Series 65 examination. All RIA really means is that someone is registered with the SEC.

with the SEC; this form details how the planner is compensated. Most planners are paid in one of the following four ways.

1. *Fee only.* A client pays a flat fee for services or charges an hourly rate. A competent planner should be able to save you, or make you, significantly more money than he or she charges for services provided.
2. *Fee-based payments.* Fee-based advisers charge 1 to 3 percent of the assets they manage for their clients.
3. *Fee-offset payments.* Fee-offset planners charge either an hourly rate or a flat fee for service. They also sell products and deduct the commission earned, when a client buys a product, from their basic fees.
4. *Commission.* A commission-based planner's total compensation is earned from the products you buy. Some consumers feel strongly that financial advisers cannot be objective when commissions are involved. This is no doubt true in some cases, just as there are a few doctors who order operations not really needed by their patients. Some attorneys hate to close cases, knowing that as long as they can keep the case going, the money train continues to roll. The potential for conflicts of interest is always present in most professions.

Referrals

You can obtain referrals on planners in your area by contacting the following organizations:

American Institute of Certified Public Accountants	888-999-9256	www.aicpa.org
Institute of Certified Financial Planners	800-322-4237	www.icfp.org
International Association for Financial Planning	800-945-4237	www.iafp.org
National Association of Personal Financial Advisors	888-333-6659	www.napfa.org
Society of Financial Service Professionals	800-392-6900	www.agents-online.com

While each of these groups should do their own due diligence on the referrals sent to you, I suggest that you also contact the following two groups before calling a referral.

Securities and Exchange Commission	800-732-0330	www.sec.gov
National Association of Securities Dealers	800-289-9999	www.nasdr.com

These two watchdog agencies can provide information about a planner's background, including complaints filed against him or her, fines paid, and disciplinary action taken. You can also find out if the planner is the subject of a current investigation. The absence of negative information about a planner is not the same as a clean bill of health. You may also want to check with your state's security commission. You can contact the North American Securities Administrators Association at 888-846-2722 (www.nasaa.org) to obtain the phone number of your state commissioner or to hear many informative alerts about investment fraud.

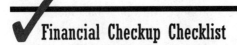

Financial Checkup Checklist

- Put together your own financial dream team—don't wait until disaster strikes!

- Be sure each member of your team has the appropriate credentials and is someone you feel comfortable with.

4 Where Does Your Money Go?

Discover exactly where you spend your money. You will then create a spending plan to help you fund your goals and increase your net worth.

> The first time the Thompsons phoned, I learned that they owed $100,000 on their credit cards. Although they were not past due, they were $50,000 behind on payments to the IRS. I asked them to prepare a list showing where their money came from and where they thought it went during the previous 12 months. Soon after they arrived for their first visit, I asked to see the list. Their total inflow was $300,000. However, total outflow was $235,000, leaving $65,000 unexplained. The Thompsons had experienced Parkinson's Second Law in action: spending rises to meet (or exceed) income.

You're Earning More . . . But

Have you ever thought: "When I graduate from college and get a real job, I will finally have enough money"? "When my spouse starts working, our financial problems will go away"? "Now that I have received a sizable raise, I can easily balance my budget and put money away for retirement"?

The Thompsons' income put them in the top 1 percent of American families, but they experienced a spending problem common to a majority of families from all income levels. The Thompsons didn't know where their money went. They also answered far more of the following questions with a yes than they wanted to admit. How do you answer these questions:

- Do you have a difficult time making your money stretch between paydays?
- When you have an unexpected car repair or medical bill, are you forced to pay the bill with your credit card?
- Do you and your spouse fight about money?
- Are you unable to invest 10 percent of your income each month?
- Too often, do you make the minimum payment on a credit card bill?
- Are you currently behind to one or more creditors?
- Do you believe that you can't afford enough life insurance?
- Do you never take the vacations you dream about?
- When you are depressed, do you go shopping?
- Do you buy your children things you cannot afford?
- Are your debt balances growing?
- Are you unable to adequately fund at least one goal?

If you answered yes to even one of these questions, then you may have a serious money problem. In Chapter 1, I discussed how your money beliefs strongly influence your financial behavior. If you continue managing your money today in the same way that you always have done, you will reap the same financial results. A major key to better managing your money is changing certain aspects of your financial behavior. In this chapter, you will be asked to perform several financial tasks that you probably have not attempted before.

The behavior we recommend is commonly practiced by individuals who can easily answer no to all of the previous questions. If you want to become more physically fit, then you know some of the behavioral changes that you would be required to make. The same is true if you want to improve your financial fitness. Change is never easy, especially at the start when you must develop some new skills and develop several new habits. Much of the success you can experience in managing your money depends on completing all the exercises in this chapter. Remember, if you don't change several aspects of your financial behavior, then your financial results will remain the same.

Have you ever visited your favorite ATM after work on Friday but have only a vague idea on Monday morning where all those dollars went? Does your inability to account for those dollars annoy or upset you?

Are you in the same boat as the Thompsons? One simple exercise will help you find your answer. Fill in the following Cash Flow for the Past 12 Months Worksheet. First, try to remember all sources and amounts of income that you received for the past 12 months. Next, describe where you spent your money. This might be the only time when the total for your inflow will be larger than the total for your outflow.

Cash Flow for the Past 12 Months Worksheet

Inflows:

Source: Amount:

_____ _____

_____ _____

_____ _____

_____ _____

    Total inflow: _____

Outflows:

Descriptions: Amount:

_____ _____

_____ _____

_____ _____

_____ _____

_____ _____

_____ _____

_____ _____

_____ _____

_____ _____

_____ _____

_____ _____

_____ _____

    Total outflow: _____

Unless you have been using Quicken or some other software program that tracks spending, your numbers probably don't provide a complete picture of where you spent your money. You are unusual if you have identified all the places your money went during the past 12 months. You are typical if you have forgotten several spending categories. Do answers to the following questions concern you?

- What was the dollar amount of miscellaneous items? Ideally, less than 3 percent of spending should be identified this way. Miscellaneous items often serve as a catchall category when you really don't know where you spend your money.
- What percentage of your outflow went to credit card and installment debt (like a car loan)? The higher the percentage, the less control you have over spending.
- What percentage of your outflow did you save to fund short-term goals? As a minimum, you need to be putting money away for at least two short-term goals, as discussed in Chapter 3.
- What percentage of your outflow did you save to fund financial independence? The accepted minimum is 10 percent of your gross income. Although I discuss financial independence in detail in a later chapter, investing less than 10 percent earns you a red flag.

Track Your Spending

Later in this chapter you will create your own spending plan. However, unless you track your spending for the next 30 days, when it is time to create your spending plan your numbers will be no better than the ones you recorded on the cash flow worksheet. When you track spending, you need to record every transaction you make (to the penny) whether you pay with a check, credit card, or cash. This task may sound tedious. You may be afraid to find out where your money goes. You may feel that this assignment is confining. Dietitians often have their patients track their eating habits to learn how to manage—and improve—their diets. Accurately tracking your spending is essential to managing—and improving—your money diet.

The Thompsons were not especially pleased when I asked them to track their spending. However, 30 days later, what the numbers showed amazed them. Like most of my clients, they spent more than they expected. The Thompsons told me what I usually hear after a client has tracked his or her spending for the first time: "I spent more than I planned because I had several expenses this month that don't occur most months. This month was not typical." After the second month of tracking their spending, people start to realize that every month they pay for certain expenses "that don't occur most months." No month is ever typical! Every month you will spend 10 to 20 percent of your income, or more, on expenses that occur only once or twice a year.

Spending Diary Evaluation Worksheet

Your next assignment is to complete the Spending Diary Evaluation Worksheet. Before you start tracking your spending, estimate where your money will go. After completing the following steps, you will have a better idea of where you spend your money.

Step 1. In the Spending Diary Evaluation Worksheet, fill in column one by describing each of your spending categories. Actual numbers go in column two. Check your cash flow statement (that you completed at the start of this chapter) to make sure you have identified all expenditures you plan to make this month. From now on, when you list expenditures, list them in the following order:

1. List *needs* as a group first. List needs in order of priority with the highest-priority need listed first.
2. List *wants* as a group second. Start with your most important want and list the remaining ones in order of their priority. If you have a significant other, then complete this list together.

The following suggestions can help you better define expenditures:

- Identify personal purchases you make with your own money.
- Separate food consumed at home from food eaten in restaurants.
- Include an emergency category.
- You may need a miscellaneous category.
- Consider a separate category for alcohol, tobacco, and lottery tickets.
- Don't forget expenses that may occur during the next 30 days but don't occur most months.

Step 2. Record the dollar amount you expect to spend in column two for each expenditure listed in column one. You may need input from other family members when creating these spending targets.

Step 3. Track your spending for at least 30 days (90 days is better) to discover where your money goes. Record your spending in a small spiral notebook. For the next 30 days, record every purchase you make. This exercise works best when you record a purchase to the penny at the same time you make it. If you wait until the end of the day, you will forget certain purchases or fail to remember exact

Spending Diary Evaluation Worksheet

Spending Categories	This Month Target	This Month Track	Next Month Adjust	Next Month Target
_____	_____	_____	_____	_____
_____	_____	_____	_____	_____
_____	_____	_____	_____	_____
_____	_____	_____	_____	_____
_____	_____	_____	_____	_____
_____	_____	_____	_____	_____
_____	_____	_____	_____	_____
_____	_____	_____	_____	_____
_____	_____	_____	_____	_____
_____	_____	_____	_____	_____
_____	_____	_____	_____	_____
_____	_____	_____	_____	_____
Total:	_____	_____	_____	_____

Figure 4.1 Typical Page from a Sample Spending Diary

DATE	TO	AMOUNT
4/16	County tax office	$56.86
4/16	Kmart: meat, tea	15.24
4/18	McDonald's	4.08
4/18	Pete's	9.72
4/19	Guadalupe Church	25.00
4/19	Burger King	2.03
4/19	Jalapeno	14.56
4/19	Texaco: gas	9.42
4/19	Wal-mart: clothes	51.09
4/19	Builder's Square	10.24
4/19	Kmart: cleaning supplies	14.01
4/19	McDonald's	5.26
4/20	Whataburger	6.60
4/20	United: medication	10.00
4/20	United: salads	5.62
4/21	Sonic	6.99
4/21	Lowe's: cash	5.00
4/22	United: eat	3.86
4/22	Francis: loan	15.00

amounts. For this exercise to be truly effective, you need the support of other family members who also spend the family or household income. Invite others, such as a spouse, to track their spending too.

Observation: Initially, most people tell me that tracking their spending is a total bore. But they also respond that the exercise soon starts to bear fruit. This one behavior change, perhaps more than any other, will put you in touch with how you manage or mismanage your dollars. Many people who initially think they do a great job managing their finances come to the opposite conclusion after tracking their spending for a month.

STOP! No need to read any further in this chapter until you have tracked your spending for 30 days.

Step 4. Refer again to the Spending Diary Evaluation Worksheet. After you spend 30 days tracking your spending, fill in the blanks in column three, entitled "Track." Before you do, you'll need to create your own worksheet like the following one, Where My Money Went. You will need a wider piece of paper because you are likely to have more than six spending categories.

Step 5. Record totals of your actual expenses for each category under Track in column three of the Spending Diary Evaluation Worksheet. Were you surprised

Where My Money Went Worksheet*

Food (home)	Food (out)	Gas	Clothing	Recreation	Personal
_____	_____	_____	_____	_____	_____
_____	_____	_____	_____	_____	_____
_____	_____	_____	_____	_____	_____
_____	_____	_____	_____	_____	_____
_____	_____	_____	_____	_____	_____
_____	_____	_____	_____	_____	_____
_____	_____	_____	_____	_____	_____
_____	_____	_____	_____	_____	_____

*On the top line of your sheet, record all the spending categories that you included in column one of your Spending Diary Evaluation Worksheet. Next, go through your spending diary and jot down each expenditure under the appropriate category heading. When you have recorded all the expenditures from the 30-day period, total each column.

by how much you spent in some areas? Many of my clients are amazed at how much goes for eating out, clothing, recreation, cigarettes, or lottery tickets. Did you end up with more spending categories than you started with?

Step 6. Next month you may want to spend more in some areas and less in others. For each expenditure compare this month's targeted amount with the actual amount spent. How much do you want to change each target for next month? Record that amount in column four entitled "Adjust." For example, Celecia targeted that she would spend $120 on food at home this month. She actually spent $140. She thinks she can get by spending less than $140 next month but it may take more than $120. So she decides to try and reduce last month's actual spending by $10. Her spending diary would appear as follows:

	This Month		Next Month	
Spending Categories	Target	Track	Adjust	Target
Food at home	$120	$140	$10	$130

When your actual expenditure was less than expected in an area (and that month's spending seemed typical), you now have more money to allocate elsewhere. If you exceeded a spending target, then you must either increase next month's target (as Celecia did) or leave that target the same but make a conscious effort to spend less on that expense. Celecia's target for eating out was $60. However, her actual total was $95. She did not realize that she ate out so much but has decided she does not want to change that target.

	This Month		Next Month	
Spending Categories	Target	Track	Adjust	Target
Food at home	$120	$140	$10	$130
Food out	60	$ 95	$35	$ 60

You can spend less if you really want to. For example, many people who smoke (whether they plan to quit or not) want to spend less on tobacco. Once they realize how much they are spending, they set next month's target below this month's actual expenses. Many do spend significantly less. With the new lower target in mind, they do not buy tobacco products as often. They know they are trying to cut back and feel guilty when they record the purchase in their spending diary.

Tracking spending brings most people face-to-face with what they actually spend. When they see where their money is going, many people realize that the effort they made earning the money was far greater than the satisfaction they derived from many of their purchases. One or more of the following experiences are common:

- Most people are able to spend less in areas where they want to cut back. For example, many start taking their lunch to work two, three, or more

days a week if they are trying to cut back on the cost of eating out. By spending less in several areas, they now have the needed dollars to increase spending in other areas, such as leisure activities or retirement.
- You are likely to change the way you spend some of your money. Many people start to question purchases they have always made. One client got in the habit of buying a coffee latte and pastry on the way to the office each day. He was astounded when he realized that this daily purchase cost him over $70 a month, so he eliminated his daily ritual. As you evaluate your spending, you are likely to realize that for many purchases the pleasure received just doesn't last long enough to justify the time you spent earning the money.
- By keeping a spending diary, many people shift dollars from lower priority areas to more pressing areas such as sending more money to their credit card company or increasing savings for short-term and longer-term goals.

You should now have accurate numbers to use in creating your spending plan for next week.

Money brings out so many emotions in each of us. We want to manage our money well. We want to feel that we are in control of our spending. Yet most of us do not earn high marks as money managers. We seem to act as if money can manage itself. You will receive little benefit in trying to set up and follow a spending plan before you know where you spend your money. A record of where you spend your money will be most helpful when you sit down to create a plan to help you better fund important goals.

Cheryl and Bob seemed pleased that I was willing to visit with them at home so they didn't need to hire a baby-sitter. After I declined a cup of coffee, the three of us sat around their kitchen table. The longer we talked, the more apparent it became that Cheryl was not a happy camper. Bob worked two jobs. He was rarely home. When he was, he seemed so stressed that Cheryl worried about his health. Cheryl wanted the income from Bob's primary job to support the family, and she wanted the income from his second job to fund several goals, including the chil-

Financial Checkup Checklist

- Estimate where you spent your money for the past 12 months.
- Track your spending for 30 days.
- Complete the Spending Diary Evaluation Worksheet.

dren's education, replacing both of their cars, and retirement. They had not yet started putting funds away for college or cars. Bob thought they needed a lot of the money from his second job to meet day-to-day expenses. I wasn't surprised when Cheryl mentioned that during their nine years of marriage, she and Bob had never tried budgeting.

Financial counselors often ask new clients to put together a budget or spending plan before their first meeting. Financial advisers evaluate the financial issues raised in the following questions the first time they sit down with a new client:

- Is the client funding important goals?
- Is the client investing 10 percent of his or her income?
- Are debt balances increasing or decreasing?
- What percentage of a person's take-home pay is going to service nonmortgage debt?

Counselors add together credit card payments, installment loan, car loan, and student loan. The percentage of the person's take-home pay servicing nonmortgage debt sends the following signal:

- Less than 10 percent—probably OK
- Between 10 and 15 percent—tight budget, borrowing must stop
- More than 15 percent—a financial crisis is brewing or has settled in

If the adviser is satisfied with the answers to the above questions, he or she often does not continue to examine the spending plan. However, if the person does not answer the questions to the adviser's satisfaction, the adviser checks to see if spending is out of control in certain areas. I refer to these areas as *sacred cows*. Everyone has at least one. Most people have several sacred cows; some people have a herd. A sacred cow is a spending category in which the client spends far more than the average person. To get their spending plans to balance, I advise clients to give their sacred cows less feed. This they do by cutting back on sacred cow expenditures. What are your sacred cows? Some of the more common ones are discussed below.

Food. What is the total amount you spend on food each month? Americans now eat nearly 50 percent of their meals away from home. Eating has become a recreational sport. We want convenience, taste, and ambiance. Sometimes we opt for fast food because it is quick and inexpensive. At other times we are willing to spend considerably more when our taste buds want a treat. Most of us could significantly reduce what we spend on food if we had to. Compare your food budget with four budgets created by the U.S. Department of Agriculture (USDA) presented in the table below. Which U.S. Department of Agricultural food budget comes closest to your own? Can you switch to a less expensive food budget?

Monthly Cost of Food at Home

	Thrifty	Low-Cost	Moderate	Liberal
Single adult male (20–50)	$117	$150	$187	$226
Single adult female (20–50)	105	131	159	204
Child 1–2	64	79	93	113
Child 3–5	70	87	107	128
Child 6–8	85	114	143	166
Child 9–11	101	130	166	193

Source: U.S. Department of Agriculture, *Family Economics and Nutrition Review,* vol. 10, no. 1, 1997.

Restaurants. How much of your food budget was spent on eating out? This number is often larger than most people realize. Reductions here can produce significant savings. Look at what you spend for lunch. Do you go out for lunch five days a week? What does your average lunch cost? How much could you save if you brown-bagged it two or three times a week?

I had a client who purchased a latte every morning on the way to work. At $2.15 (including sales tax) each, the amount did not seem like much each day. However when we multiplied the $2.15 times 250 workdays a year, the amount of $537.50 shocked him. He was 40 at the time. I told him that if he had invested that $2.15 every day since he graduated from college, he would now have at least $25,000. He almost started to cry.

Wardrobe. What was the total amount you spent on clothing? Put every clothing item you bought during the past 12 months on your bed. Would you spend your clothing dollars differently if you could redo all those purchases? People become defensive when you suggest that they spend too much on clothing. Unlike food, where the USDA has created food budgets, no spending guidelines exist for clothing. However, most people spend between 5 and 10 percent of their income on clothing, but such statistics don't serve as guidelines for you. If you don't know how much of your income is spent on clothing, maybe you need to find out.

Home. How much of your income goes for housing? Unless you live at home and your parents pick up the tab, you may be spending more dollars on housing than any other item. Which of the following housing expenses do you pay: rent or mortgage, utilities, telephone, cable, insurance, property taxes, repairs, maintenance, and/or furnishings? When all the expenses are added together, the number can be depressingly large.

How can you cut your cost of housing? If you lease, you can move to a less expensive place. If you own, moving down in housing may not be easy, but it may make a lot of sense.

Transportation. What is the total amount you spend on transportation in a year? People rarely understand just how much of their income is spent on cars. Cars are the first or second largest expenditure in most budgets. We are not always aware of how much it costs to own and operate a car because there are so many separate expenses. Add together car payments, insurance, gas, repairs, licenses, parking/traffic tickets, maintenance, upkeep, and parking fees. Even if you are not making loan payments, most cars cost more than $2000 a year to operate. Twelve monthly payments more than double this amount. Too many people spend too much of their income on vehicles. Most families would have plenty of room in their budget if they sold one of their vehicles. Park one vehicle for a month and see what it is like to get by without it. You may value the money you save more than the inconveniences.

Identify your sacred cows. They cost a lot to feed and maintain. What can you do to cut back the expenses required to take care of them? By now you have tracked your spending for several days. As you keep careful records, you will find several places you can cut back. You need to identify such areas before you seriously try to create a spending plan.

Almost everyone will get more out of their money if they develop a plan for spending it. The discussion that follows lays out a basic approach for creating such a plan that seems to work for most people. If you don't think this approach will work for you, pay attention to another strategy found near the end of the chapter.

Creating a Spending Plan

You may have tried creating and following a budget. Chances are your budgeting efforts failed, and you felt frustrated and discouraged. You probably got caught in one or more of the following traps.

Trap 1. When you sat down to create your budget, you did not have good financial data. By tracking your spending, you end up with better data than when you guesstimate the numbers.

Trap 2. Unless you live alone, seek input from all members of your household; make creating a spending plan a group effort. Without input from everyone, the numbers are not as realistic as they need to be and the budget is likely to fail. Household members are not likely to help you stick to the budget if you didn't ask for their input.

Trap 3. In creating a budget most people fail to distinguish between expenses that occur each month from expenses that only occur a few times a year.

These nonmonthly expenses are real budget wreckers. For example, were you able to pay cash (or write a check) the last time you had to repair a car or pay a medical bill? If you paid with plastic, you only added to your debt problem. Have you finally paid for last summer's vacation? How about last year's Christmas or Hanukkah gifts? When you tracked your spending, you focused on expenses that you pay every month. If you don't plan for nonmonthly expenses, those expenses knock a hole in your spending plan when they show up.

To complete this worksheet, refer to check registers and credit card statements. There are several ways to budget nonmonthly expenses. Each way relies on the following three concepts.

1. Calculate what you spent on each nonmonthly expense for the past 12 months. These numbers can vary from year to year, but your recent spending is the best data you have. Fill out the form on the following page.
2. Set up one or more savings accounts to hold funds until needed. How many accounts do you need? Depending on your circumstances, you may want one dedicated to car and home repairs, one for medical expenses, one for gifts and vacations, one for insurance premiums, one for education fees, and so on. It may be less expensive to set up these accounts at a credit union. Banks usually want too large an initial deposit to open such accounts. Credit unions will usually allow you to maintain lower account balances and make more free transfers than banks. A savings account that holds funds for nonmonthly expenses serves as your emergency account. When you pay a nonmonthly expense such as a car repair with a check, transfer the amount of the repair from the savings account back to your checking account.
3. Set up automatic monthly transfers that sweep dollars budgeted for nonmonthly expenses into one or more savings accounts. No one has the discipline to make such transfers each and every month. Let your bank or credit union do the transfer automatically.

It is now time to fill out your spending plan. Copy the form on page 58 using paper with more lines for outflows. You will need to refer to your goal statement, your spending diary, and your nonmonthly expenses.

Record descriptions of your income and expenditures in column one. On the lines under the column headed "Inflows," record all sources of cash such as your take-home pay, child support, Social Security, and the like. Under "Outflows" list all expenditure categories. List needs first, such as food and rent or mortgage payment. Next list your wants in order of their priority. List your most important wants first.

Too many couples fight about money. Too often neither partner has his or her own money to spend. When creating expenditure categories in column one, make sure that a personal category is included. Once you agree on the amount that each

Annual Nonmonthly Expenses Worksheet

	Past 12 Months
Home repairs	$ _____
Car repairs	_____
Medical/Dental	_____
Auto insurance	_____
Vacation	_____
Gifts	_____
Donations	_____
Appliances	_____
Birthdays	_____
Christmas/Hanukkah	_____
Education	_____
Property taxes	_____
Payroll taxes	_____
Total	_____

Your Spending Plan

Inflows	Monthly Targets	First Payday His Targets	First Payday Her Targets	Second Payday His Targets	Second Payday Her Targets	Third Payday His Targets	Third Payday Her Targets	Fourth Payday His Targets	Fourth Payday Her Targets
Pay:									
Pay:									
Total									
Outflows									
Automatic Transfers									
Total Outgo									
Difference									

gets to spend, remember not to criticize how the other spends his or her personal funds. For example, if your partner wants to spend 100 percent of personal money on lottery tickets, that's his or her business.

Select *inflows* from the following list:

- Gross income (before any deductions) or take-home pay
- Interest
- Dividends
- Rents
- Bonuses/commissions
- Child support
- Alimony
- Public assistance (such as AFDC, WIC)
- Social Security
- Pension
- Tax refund
- Gifts/inheritances
- Scholarships and grants
- Loans

Select *outflows* from the following list:

- Income taxes (federal, state, local)
- Social Security
- Life insurance
- Disability insurance
- Health insurance premiums
- Saving
- IRA contribution
- 401(k)/403(b) contribution
- Keogh contribution
- Emergency fund
- Donations
- Rent/Mortgage payment
- Property taxes (may be included in mortgage payment)
- Homeowners insurance (may be included in mortgage payment)
- Car loan
- Credit card interest paid
- Installment loan
- Family loan
- Education loans
- Union dues
- Telephone

- Natural gas/heating oil
- Electricity
- Cable
- Water/Garbage/Sewer
- Food (home)
- Food (away)
- Gas (auto)
- Clothing
- Car repairs
- Medical/Dental/Optical
- Personal care
- Recreation
- Vacations
- Education
- Child care
- Allowances
- Tobacco/Alcohol
- Dues/Membership fees
- Domestic help
- Subscriptions
- Licenses
- Tuition and fees
- Books

Insert numbers into column two. Look at income figures first. When entering your salary, use take-home pay. Your employer withholds part of your income to pay federal, state and, in some places, city income taxes. Dollars were also withheld for Social Security taxes, medical insurance premiums, contributions to a company retirement account such as a 401(k), and possibly a medical or dependent care reimbursement account. Your paycheck probably shrinks 15 to 40 percent before you get your hands on your money. When you don't know exactly how much cash you may receive from a particular source, make the estimate low.

Now fill in the number for expenditures. Refer to your schedule of non-monthly expenses, your list of goals, and the summary of your spending diary. A review of check registers, canceled checks, and credit card statements can help supply useful information about expenditures. Unless you have kept accurate records, many numbers are only guesses.

Once all the numbers are recorded in column two, compute totals for inflows and outflows for the month. Compare the totals. Inflows must be equal to or greater than outflows. Before you go any further, recheck your work and then answer the following questions:

- Did you forget one or more expenses?
- Were your estimates of some expenditures too low?
- Did you make a math mistake?
- Were all payroll deductions included (such as medical premiums)?
- Did you report all income?

If inflows are greater than outflows, did you

- overestimate income sources?
- underestimate expenditures?
- include all expenditure categories?

Try to reduce expenses (since it can take months to implement a strategy to increase income). Examine each expense and ask, "Can I eliminate, postpone, or reduce this expense?" How much do you have to reduce expenditures? Start with the lowest priority "want," which should be at the bottom of the column. You can often balance inflows and outflows if you can reduce each of your lower priority wants by as much as $5 to as much as perhaps $50.

What expenses can you eliminate?

- Subscriptions to newspapers and magazines (read them at the library or on the Internet)
- Service contracts on appliances
- Cigarettes, lottery tickets
- Cable TV
- Dues for organizations in which you no longer participate
- A car or pickup (Take a train, bus, or taxi; walk; or car pool.)

How can you reduce expenses?

- Phone less; phone when rates are lowest; use e-mail
- Brown-bag lunch instead of eating out
- See first-run movies at the dollar theater (or wait until they come out on video)
- Use two-for-one coupons when you eat out
- Buy it used or rent it instead of buying it new

What expenses can you postpone?

- An expensive vacation
- Braces
- A new car
- A new outfit

Need more ideas? Check Jonathan Pond's *1001 Ways to Cut Your Expenses* (Dell).

Continue to reduce expenses until your total for outflows is no larger than your total for inflows. Once your monthly spending plan balances, you have achieved a significant milestone. If you are single and have only one payday a month, you can skip the next section. Singles with more than one payday a month and couples still have work to do.

> **Hot Tip**
>
> **A**utomate your budget as much as you can. Is your paycheck automatically deposited to your checking account? If not and your employer offers direct deposit of your paycheck, sign up for it.

Advice for Couples

Kim and Kelly have just balanced their budget. They feel good that they are funding two important goals, are making more than minimum payments on their credit cards, are setting aside funds in savings accounts to pay nonmonthly expenses, and have included a personal spending category in their budget. However, they still have an important issue to discuss. Who is going to manage the money, making sure that spending does not exceed budget targets? Like most couples, they share this responsibility. Since they are both paid only once a month, their remaining task is pretty simple. They go down the spending categories and decide who will be responsible for each one. They agree that Kim will pay for food, utilities, credit card payments, and child care; Kelly will make the mortgage payment and fund the vacation and the repair account. They will split the personal, gas, and clothing accounts evenly. The appropriate numbers are recorded in columns three and four on Your Spending Plan worksheet under their names. When they total the expenditures for columns three and four, Kim's comes to $2,100 and Kelly's to $2,800. These two amounts match each of their take-home pay amounts. Had take-home pay not matched their planned expenditures, the partner with the surplus would need to transfer funds to the partner with the deficit. Each now knows how his or her income should be spent.

More Than One Payday a Month?

A monthly budget is not much help if you are paid twice a month or even more often. When you receive your first paycheck, your monthly budget is not too helpful since it doesn't indicate which bills to pay from that first check. If you are single and are paid weekly, you need to create a budget for each payday. If you are married but have more than one payday during the month, you will need to create spending plans for each partner for each payday.

All of this may seem like a lot of work. It is at first, but the benefits are huge if the budget balances initially, categories are included for funding goals, and reserve accounts are set up to store money for nonmonthly expenses. Spending plans for each payday are essential when you're trying to manage your money well. It is equally important for partners to decide together who is to be responsible for making sure that spending doesn't exceed each budgeting target.

How many of the following expenditures can be paid (or saved) automatically without your having to write a check?

- Mortgage
- Utilities
- Mutual fund purchases
- Car payment
- Any other loan
- Nonmonthly expenses such as repairs, gifts, vacation
- Funding for a goal

Automatic transactions save you time and money and help you become a better money manager. Create a budget to increase the likelihood that important goals will be funded and that debt will be paid down. Automatic transfers increase the likelihood that you will satisfy these objectives. You may be able to get by without creating and following a spending plan if you are willing to automate your financial system:

Set up automatic transfers to pay as many expenses as possible, especially the funding of important goals like retirement and nonmonthly expenses such as repairs, gifts, and a vacation. Make sure that your employer deposits your paycheck directly to your checking account.

Review Periodically

No matter what your financial situation, you and your partner (if you have one) need to review how well all of this money managing is working. Remember, a spending plan is made up of spending targets. Your main concern is that you

- fund high priority goals;
- are on track for getting out of debt;
- fund nonmonthly expenses;
- have personal money to spend; and
- do not run out of money before payday.

> **Hot Tip**
>
> For this system to work, you must remember to subtract transfers from the balance in your check register. If you want to use this system, every time you write a check or withdraw money from an ATM, record that transaction in your check register and calculate the current balance. While you do need to keep an up-to-date balance in your check register, you may not need to follow a budget.

Expect to make adjustments in two areas. (1) Some targets are too low; however, to raise one, another has to be lowered. (2) One partner may no longer want to be responsible for managing a certain account; for example, this year my spouse asked me to take responsibility for buying gifts.

Recommendation: My favorite book about budgeting, written by Joe Dominguez and Vicki Robin, is *Your Money or Your Life* (Viking). This is a great book for couples to read out loud to each other.

Few people enjoy setting up a budget. However, without a spending plan that you can follow, you are not likely to fund important goals. Most people who don't budget spend more than they earn each month. Almost no one who budgets effectively piles up credit card debt; most people who do not use a budget have significant credit card debt. Four keys make budgeting work:

1. Decide where you want your money to go.
2. Set up automatic transfers to handle goals and nonmonthly expenses.
3. Create a spending plan for each payday.
4. Couples need to make sure that spending does not exceed targets for which they are individually responsible.

It takes far more time to set up a budget than it does to follow one. During the first year that you're trying to use a spending plan as a guide, you, like most people, need to make several adjustments to your spending targets. But positive results show up as soon as you attempt to ensure that your spending matches your targets. If you really want to become financially fit, set up and follow a budget.

Financial Checkup Checklist

- Get your monthly budget to balance.

- If you have a partner, decide who will be responsible for what expenditures each month. Better yet, do this task together.

- If you have more than one payday a month, create a spending plan for each payday.

5 Stop Piling Up Debt

Develop and implement a strategy so that you no longer need to borrow money.

> When Lilly came into my office, she was nearly in tears. Less than two hours earlier, she and her daughter Shannon had been standing at a cash register in the mall. The clerk had been polite as she explained to Lilly that none of her five credit cards would accept the purchase Shannon wanted to make. Both Lilly and Shannon just stood there and cried. When Lilly had called me two weeks before to set up an appointment, she told me she was having credit card problems. As she sat in my office and retold the store experience, she cried again.

Over the years I have met many people with problems similar to Lilly's. Whenever people like Lilly are depressed or upset, they stuff plastic cards into their pockets, purses, or wallets and head to the nearest mall. Spending money to try to solve problems is as much an addiction as is gambling, alcohol, drugs, and tobacco. A credit card addict experiences the same pains and feelings of depression and withdrawal common to any addict who is trying to escape.

Not everyone who is buried under a pile of debt is a credit card addict. In Lilly's case, her addiction explained why she had maxed out her cards (and didn't realize that she had). If you don't have any debt, you can skip this chapter (unless you want to read it to see how helpful it could be for someone you love). If your only debt payment is a mortgage or student loan, you may not have a debt problem. If you have only two or three debts, you may be managing your debt load OK. I don't have to tell you that as you accrue more debts, the greater the stress you will feel trying to make payments each month. If you have no debt load at all, you should be able to fund all of your important financial goals. Most people who cannot adequately fund their retirement could if they were debt-free. Chapter 6 focuses on strategies you can use to become debt-free, while this chapter sets the stage by discussing what you must do to stop borrowing.

You first need to determine if you have a serious debt problem. Although you probably know if you do, these questions may help you focus on your debt problems. They provide clues in helping you develop a strategy to stop borrowing.

Shopping Till You Drop

If you are carrying more debt than is comfortable, perhaps you are one of those who shop till they drop. This situation covers the largest number of people who have created seemingly impossible debt loads that they are struggling to pay off. However, within this group there are three very different types of shoppers. If you have shopped until you did drop and your debt load reflects it, do you belong to one or more of the following three groups?

1. If you head to the mall when you feel depressed or bored and use your plastic to make purchases that you cannot pay off in full when your statement arrives, you may have a serious problem. Most people who realize that they are addicted to shopping believe that money does indeed buy happiness (or at a minimum, an escape from pain). When the need to shop takes control, such people lack the strength to resist. It is almost as if their brain says: "Go shopping, and you will feel better." Like robots, they grab purse or wallet and the car keys. Their next conscious moment occurs when they "wake up" in the mall's parking lot. At that time such shoppers actually receive a rush of adrenaline much like a gambler outside a casino or an alcoholic entering a bar.

   Most people confuse pleasure with happiness. Addicts are not happy people, but they do derive initial pleasure just before starting to satisfy their cravings. For the addicted shopper, that pleasure may last until he or she returns to the parking lot. On returning home, addicted shoppers come face-to-face with the obvious fact that their recent purchases have only made things worse. The depression that follows once they enter the house is worse than the depression that drove them to the mall.

   My concern is for individuals whose shopping sprees have driven them to the point where they cannot service their debt loan. There is noth-

Assessing the Seriousness of Your Debt Problem Worksheet

Check off those statements that describe your situation. Use a pencil so that you can erase your answers if you want someone else to complete this assessment tool.

Answer each of the following questions yes or no. If you answer yes to more than two questions, you have a problem.

Are you

____ using a credit card to buy groceries because you don't have cash?

____ using a credit card to eat out when there's no money to buy groceries?

____ refusing to open mail from creditors?

____ requesting higher limits on credit cards?

____ thinking about applying for a debt consolidation loan?

____ borrowing money from family and friends?

____ making minimum payments on credit cards each month?

____ applying for new cards so you can get a cash advance to make payments on maxed-out credit cards?

____ assessed late fees on credit card statements?

____ receive phone calls from creditors?

The more statements that you checked off, the more serious your problem. However, it is possible to be carrying a heavy debt load and not have checked off any of the above statements. If you didn't check off any of the above statements, yet feel strangled by debt, increasing any of your current debt balances or taking on more debt could be the straw that breaks you.

ing wrong with experiencing the pleasure that results from shopping when the shopper can handle his or her debt. But the pleasure that you experience because you buy an item you need is vastly different from the temporary high a shopper receives who has gone shopping to temporarily escape feelings of depression or anxiety.

If you realize that you cannot implement the strategies discussed in this chapter and in chapter 6, you should seek professional counseling. Treating factors that cause shopping addictions is beyond the scope of this book.

2. Fortunately, most shoppers who pile up credit card debt do not have a serious addiction problem. However, such shoppers do need to examine their beliefs about money. This is not a pop book about the psychology of money, but I want to discuss a concept known as the "locus of control." Everyone has a locus of control. Where we have positioned it in our lives has a great deal to do with our overall sense of happiness and well-being.

Therapists talk about the locus of control as either internal or external. People whose locus of control is external feel they have little or no control over their life. A person with an external locus of control sees himself or herself as a victim. Such people are easy to recognize. They are rarely happy; they always talk about themselves, especially their problems. Their glass is always half empty. They see themselves as constantly being manipulated by others, such as a spouse, child, or boss. They want to escape but lack the courage. Such people seem to derive their happiness by complaining. Many people with an external locus of control engage in shopping, seeking short-term pleasures as a way to escape their problems.

People who have positioned their locus of control internally are people you and I like to be around. When you meet them, they are more concerned about you than they are about themselves. They know that they control their own lives, that they are the masters of their own soul. They take responsibility for their own situations. When they have a problem, they focus on how they are going to solve the problem. They see their glass as half full. Most of them are not phony Pollyannas who are always sickeningly positive about everything. People who learn to internalize their locus of control live happier, more fulfilling lives than their counterparts. They are a lot less likely to head for the mall when they are down mainly because they are rarely down. When they are down, they don't see shopping as a way to raise their spirits.

3. A third group of people belong in the "shop-till-you-drop" category. These people hate budgeting; they hate keeping track of how much they owe;

and they love to shop. Shopping for them is truly a recreational sport. Before they head for the mall, they put on their uniform of sneakers and jogging suit like any trendy amateur athlete. The game ball is their plastic credit card. Like many amateur athletes, they make their own rules for playing the shopping game. For example, a sale (any kind of sale) works like a time-out. A sale time-out means that shoppers can spend all the money they want during the sale because the amount charged doesn't have to be repaid for months, or even years, later. They actually believe one retailer's slogan: "The more you spend, the more you save." Another common game rule is that the person who accumulates the most stuff in a one-day shopping spree wins. What such shoppers especially like about their sport is that there are no referees. Such type B individuals can be helped only if they stop using their credit cards and make all their purchases with cash.

If you consider yourself a shop-till-you-drop spender and are only making minimum payments (or close to minimum payments) on your credit cards, you need to cut up the cards.

The Card-Cutting Ceremony

Do not cut up cards by yourself even if you are single and live alone. Card cutting is a group affair. Assemble your family and/or friends. Explain to one and all that from this moment on, you will never charge another purchase. Plead with them not to put you in a situation where you need to borrow. Explain that if they do, they will be out of luck because you are going to cut up each card. Ask them to support you in this effort. Then cut up each card. Place the pieces of each card in a separate envelope and label the envelope with the name of the card. When the balance on that card has been paid in full, send the pieces back to the lender and ask to have your account closed "at the request of the cardholder."

Before you hold this solemn meeting, draft a document similar to the one below.

I, _____ have decided to never again use a credit card. I need your support by never putting me in a position that tempts me to use a credit card. I also ask you to serve as a member of my support group, willing to spend time with me when my desire to use a credit card seems overwhelming.

Leave a space for each person to sign; you sign first. Attach this document to your refrigerator with magnets that you bought with cash.

Failing to Keep Financial Records

If you are carrying an uncomfortable amount of debt, you may not be a shop-till-you drop type, but you may not keep financial records. You are not a compulsive spender, but you have no idea where your money goes. You may have tried budgeting before, but it failed to work for you. You may feel as though you don't have the time to set up and follow a budget. You are often in too much of a hurry to balance your check register. You spend money as needed or perhaps you belong to one or more of the groups discussed below.

Keeping Up with the Joneses

You don't believe that you can buy happiness with money, but you do believe you would be happier if you could keep up with the Joneses next door, down the street, at work, or at church. Your self-esteem is somewhat tied to your ability to demonstrate that you have arrived or are at least on the right road. I like Thomas J. Stanley's book *The Millionaire Next Door*. He points out that most millionaires do not live in expensive houses, nor do they drive expensive cars. In fact, many of them would not have become millionaires had they. Most millionaires, and many on their way to becoming millionaires, are not interested in trying to impress others. Most people need a car to function in our society, but they do not need to drive a Lexus. Did you know that most Lexus drivers cannot afford to own one, so a high percentage of new Lexus drivers actually lease a new Lexus?

I once had a client who was making $250,000 a year but was spending $300,000. He and his wife lived in a million-dollar house, but because their debt level was rising, they definitely were not happy. I calculated that if they sold their present home and moved into a $300,000 house, they would have enough money from the sale to pay off their debts and balance their budget. They sold the house and were glad to be rid of it.

Many people actually need to consider such drastic action. People who have serious debt problems often live in a home they cannot afford, and they usually own too many cars. If I seem to be describing you, you may be surprised to discover that you can actually be happier after a move down in your housing. Mounting debt occurs because you cannot balance your budget without additional borrowing. If you don't keep effective records, you may not even realize why your debt level continues to rise.

Rationalizing Overspending: Blame It on the Children

Perhaps you spend more than you should because you feel you owe it to your children. Children are expensive, but sometimes the amount parents spend on children is not rational. Could you be spending too much on your children? Are you committed to making sure they have it better than you did? Were you really that deprived as a child? If your parents had spent dramatically more money on you, would that have dramatically improved your childhood? For every child who lacks adequate financial support, there is another one whose parents rarely spend any time with him or her. I know of a university president who, on the day before his son left for college, took him out to both breakfast and lunch. This parent suddenly realized that he had never spent any time with his boy, who was now leaving home. The president could not make up the lost time in just one day. While the son was growing up, guilt had driven this father to give his son lots of material things, like a new car when he turned 16. Sadly, the father never found the time to give his son what the boy wanted most, time with his father.

Too often parents want to buy love. Love, like happiness, is not for sale. Such parents need to ask themselves some tough questions, such as: "Why am I spending so much money on my children that I am in financial bondage?" "What are my children learning about managing money from my example?" "What message am I teaching them about what money can do for them?" Most children who grow up thinking that money buys happiness were introduced to this idea at home.

Sometimes parents actually use their children when playing the money game. Such parents' own self-esteem is enhanced because the child drives a new auto, or because the child can afford to escape for skiing weekends, or because the child is enrolled in lessons five days a week. When a child really enjoys musical, artistic, or athletic activities and the parents can afford to support these dreams, fine. But when the child couldn't care less, yet the parent goes in debt to support such activities, both parent and child develop problems.

Resorting to Credit Cards

You may belong to the group of those who have used credit when faced with making a repair to your car or house or when paying a medical or dental bill. You may have also resorted to using credit to pay for vacations or Christmas or Hanukah gifts. Perhaps you have borrowed significant sums to pay college tuition costs for yourself or a family member. Such credit charges stem from three separate sources:

1. You do not save money regularly to fund unexpected expenses such as car repairs. Nor do you save to fund a vacation or gift account. You know each year that such expenses will happen, but you don't know when they'll occur. Most people who have failed at budgeting ignore setting aside funds for expenditures that do not occur each month.
2. You lack adequate insurance coverage to pay for unexpected repairs and medical bills. People often have no insurance or the wrong kind of insurance. Insurance is expensive, so it is not surprising that all of us dislike paying premiums. You are not likely to achieve financial independence if you have an inadequate insurance program. In my practice I have been able to improve each client's insurance coverage yet at the same time save him or her money (often hundreds and sometimes thousands of dollars a year). In a later chapter you will learn how to put a cost-effective insurance program in place.
3. You have not yet established a savings habit. Long-term goals, such as earning a college degree, require you to start putting money away many years before college starts. I cannot understand anyone going into debt to finance a child's wedding. Young couples need to think seriously about the financial impact a child will have on their world. Plan your financial future, and you will be in control when major financial events occur.

> **Hot Tip**
>
> Use credit to buy only items that should last longer than it takes you to pay off the debt. This tip does not give you license to use credit to buy anything that satisfies this criterion. The main point is: Never use credit to pay for vacations, food, clothing, or anything else that will be gone and forgotten long before the credit card bill has been paid.

Unexpected Events

Divorce

A life-changing event has affected you. Once a month for more than eight years I have taught a two-hour workshop attended by individuals and couples who have filed for bankruptcy. While a variety of factors motivated each person to file, several of them have recently experienced a major life-changing event such as the death, disability, or divorce of a spouse.

Divorce is usually a financial disaster for both partners. At the root of many divorces is the inability of the couple to communicate effectively; and statistics show that money problems are a basic cause of many divorces. Actually, it is not money that is the problem but rather the inability of one or both spouses to discuss their money problem or what they consider their money problem to be. For far too long one spouse may have controlled the purse strings. The other spouse always has to ask for money and then account for how he or she spent it; and the one who controls the purse strings may or may not be the one who earns any or most of the income. The person controlling the purse strings may also control other aspects of the couple's life. A major premise of this book is that you must be in control of your life; but I am not advocating that you control anyone else's. If you are divorced, I sincerely hope you can benefit from the strategies discussed in *Financial Fitness for Life*. If you are contemplating divorce, take the following five steps:

1. If you sign on your spouse's credit card, write to the credit card company to tell it that you will no longer be responsible for any charges as of the date of the letter. If your spouse signs on your card, send a similar letter stating that you will no longer be responsible for any charges made by your spouse's using your card.
2. Make sure you have one credit card in your name only.
3. Create a special savings account in your name only and stash as much money there as you can.
4. Try to create two budgets; one for you and one for your spouse. Can either one of you live on these budgets?
5. If at all possible, attend counseling sessions together, especially if you have minor children. Before you file for divorce, ask to read the divorce decree of a friend whose situation is similar to yours. You may be surprised to learn that much of the decree is about children's visitation rights. I hope you will be motivated to try counseling.

Problems in the Family Business

After many years of working with families, I am still amazed by the number of people who cannot manage their own money yet actually try to run a business. Most of them put in long days. They do a lot of things right, but the business finances are often in a mess. Too often they never distinguish between business and family finances. Too often their accountant has failed to insist that they set up two sets of books, one for the family and one for the business.

When I discuss how to stop creating debt, my concern is not business debt. However, when business and family finances are mixed up together, it is difficult to tell which is business debt and which is family debt.

If you find yourself wrestling with this dilemma, see an accountant right away and separate your business and family finances. You will also want to ask your banker for help. Open up a separate checking account for the business. Apply for a credit card for the business. Stop paying business expenses with family finances, and vice versa. If the IRS ever audits you, and they probably will, you will find yourself in serious trouble without separate accounts. Business owners who are buried in debt have a terrible habit of never sending Uncle Sam the Social Security and Medicare taxes that they have withheld from their employees' paychecks. Nor do they send in their business's share of the same taxes. Often their personal income taxes have not been filed either.

Distinguishing Needs from Wants

If you have not yet found yourself in the above scenarios, maybe this one fits you because it usually fits most of us. We live in a land of plenty. Compare yourself with the richest king or queen one hundred years ago and you win hands down. That monarch did not live in an air-conditioned home, didn't have central heating, and didn't have a car, TV, or VCR. We live the good life. Most of us have never gone without, which may be at the heart of our money problems. We do not, or cannot, distinguish between wants and needs. Anything we want, we actually think we need. If needs are not met, a person lacks adequate clothing, a safe place to live, competent medical services, and nutritious food. Often when we are faced with satisfying a need, we end up wanting more than just basic need fulfillment. This is OK unless we have to rely on credit. Jack is hungry. He faces many options, including going home and fixing a meal, stopping at a fast-food outlet, or consuming a gourmet meal. If Jack has the cash to pay for any of the above, no problem. However, if Jack plans to charge this meal and then cannot pay for it completely when his credit card statement arrives, Jack has a problem.

Try this experiment for seven days. Do not make any charge purchases. *Spend money only on items or services that you actually need.* Buy a little spiral notebook that will fit in your pocket or purse. Every time you want to spend money on a want, describe that want in the notebook. Include the time of day you wanted to make the purchase and your reason for wanting the item. Also record how much it would cost to buy the product or service. At the end of the seven days, review your list. Which items do you still want? Assign each item a priority and buy as many items as you want as long as you have the cash to make each purchase. How many items do you no longer want? How much money did you save by not making those purchases? Does there seem to be a certain time each day when you want to satisfy your wants? What else can you do at those times besides spend money?

I learned a long time ago how to handle wants that I do not have the cash to satisfy. I record them on my wish list and then find a book I am reading and read until the desire goes away. This strategy is probably not one that would work for you, so come up with your own.

Many people would never pile up debt if they could resist trying to pay for wants with credit. Surprisingly, the urge to buy most wants goes away in a day or two if you can find a way to delay the urge.

We have discussed strategies that you can use to stop piling up debt. Only you really know why you borrow. Actually, you may not know. Most people cannot identify most of the products and services they received for the money they borrowed. I am not saying that everyone should shun credit and become a cash buyer only. However, if you are buried in debt, you need to stop using credit today. You also may need to read other chapters in this book before you can put all the pieces of your plan in place. If you have a debt problem, you can at least give all your credit cards to a friend and ask your friend not to give them back unless the friend really believes that you have an emergency. If you do not trust your cards with a friend, mail them to a relative or lock them up in your safe-deposit box. If you do not have the strength to cut them up, at least make it difficult to get hold of them.

Financial Checkup Checklist

- Clearly identify reasons why you use a credit card.

- Cut up and return extra credit cards.

- Go an entire week and only purchase what you need.

6 Get Out of Debt

Develop strategies you can use to become debt-free. Check to make sure your credit report is accurate.

When I opened my office door and saw the large box that Paul was holding, my first thought was that he and Mary were moving in with me. I soon learned that the box contained unopened letters from creditors that they had let pile up for the last three months. We first sorted the letters into separate piles, one for each creditor. By the time we finished, 26 piles covered my desk, the tops of my filing cabinets, and the coffee table. Actually only one letter in five contained new information. Most of the letters duplicated payment requests made by previous letters. We even found three envelopes that contained checks. Paul and Mary seemed to feel better after the letters were opened. Fortunately, we did not find any serious threats that, if carried out, could have resulted in serious consequences. Paul and Mary, like millions of other people, thought that by not opening the letters, they could ignore the problems. As the letters piled up around the house, they increasingly felt buried under a blanket of debt.

Nothing limits a person's ability to fund goals more than making debt payments. Most people who are underfunding their retirement accounts site debt payments as the primary reason. Paying down debt can be the quickest way to increase your net worth. If you do not have any debt, you only need to read the section about checking out your credit report later in this chapter. If you are like most readers, though, you will find this entire chapter extremely helpful.

Debt is suffocating millions of Americans. Many of these credit card addicts make only the minimum payment each month on their accounts. If these individuals never charged another purchase but continued to make the minimum monthly payment each month, it would take a decade or two to repay the debt. Look at the numbers in the chart below. JoAnn can make only the minimum payments on her credit card account and does not plan to add to her loan balance. Her outstanding balance is $1,000 and her card's APR is 21 percent. If she consistently sends in $20 a month, it will take her over nine years to pay off this balance.

Making Minimum Monthly Payments Only

$1,000 balance and $20 monthly payments

APR	Total Interest	Number of Payments
10%	$ 280	64
15	540	77
21	1,240	112

Are you making only minimum monthly payments on your credit cards? If you pay just $10 more a month, look how the numbers change. JoAnn decides she can increase her monthly payment by $10. If nothing else changes, she can now pay off the balance in four years and one month (and her APR is still 21 percent); she also saves $770 in interest. Why is this example so dramatic? When JoAnn was making $20 monthly payments, most of the $20 each month went to interest. When she added the $10 to the payment, all of the $10 reduced the loan balance.

Adding $10 to the Minimum Monthly Payment

$1,000 loan balance and $30 monthly payments

APR	Total Interest	Number of Payments
10%	$164	39
15	281	43
21	470	49

Create a Plan to Eliminate Debt

In a previous chapter I discussed what you need to do to stop piling up debt. There is no point in talking about paying down debt if you are still creating it. If you have stopped stockpiling debt, create a plan to pay off the debt you have already accumulated. You can begin by completing the Loan Ledger Worksheet.

Loan Ledger Worksheet

If you are interested in reducing or eliminating your debt load, you should complete this worksheet. If you have more than six loans, you will need to create your own form.

1. Lender/ Loan #	2. Monthly Payments	3. Current Loan Balance	4. APR	5. Secured?	6. # of Payments Behind
_____	_____	_____	_____	_____	_____
_____	_____	_____	_____	_____	_____
_____	_____	_____	_____	_____	_____
_____	_____	_____	_____	_____	_____
_____	_____	_____	_____	_____	_____
_____	_____	_____	_____	_____	_____

1. List the loan number and name of lender in this column.

2. Record your monthly payment.

3. Log your current loan balance here. You may need to call the lender if you cannot find the balance on your most recent statement.

4. APR stands for annual percentage rate. The range for most rates is from 9 to 29.9 percent.

5. Secured creditors almost always require a full payment each month or they will repossess property used as security for the loan. Unsecured creditors will often accept partial payments. Unsecured creditors cannot take anything from you until they win a judgment

Loan Ledger Worksheet
(continued)

against you in court. Credit cards and medical bills are examples of unsecured credit. Unsecured creditors can turn your loan into a secured one if they take you to court and win. No matter how poorly you have repaid the loan and no matter how weak your excuses for making late payments, show up at court. You can usually get the court to postpone its decision—buying you time to respond to the charges. You need this time to negotiate a settlement or file bankruptcy.

6. It's hoped you are currently making all loan payments on time. If not, find out the number of payments you are behind.

Almost every debtor belongs to one of two groups:

1. Those who make payments in full and on time each month
2. Those who do not make all loan payments in full and on time each month

To which group do you belong? I'll first discuss strategies that members of group one can use to get out of debt.

Group One: Those Able to Make Payments in Full and on Time Each Month

Create a debt elimination calendar.

Once you have completed your debt elimination calendar, you may have developed a plan to get out of debt sooner than expected. In column one, fill in the months, starting with next month. Before you fill in the rest of the columns on your debt elimination calendar, prioritize your debts. In column two on the first line, record the

Hot Tip

Recheck your spending plan carefully to try to find extra money to send to creditors. As you saw in the previous example, adding only $10 a month to a payment often dramatically shortens the life of the loan. The larger the payment made on the first loan, the sooner you will be out of debt.

name of the loan you want to pay off first. Most people select the loan with the highest APR, the smallest loan balance, or a loan owed to a friend or family member. In column two record all loan payments required to pay off the first loan you identified. If that loan is a credit card, call the card issuer and ask: "If I do not make any more charge card purchases and decide to make monthly payments of $_____, how many payments must I make to pay off my credit card balance in full?" You can also use a pocket calculator to find the number of payments required to retire this loan or go to one of the Web sites in the Hot Tip on page 82.

The month after you have completely paid off one loan, add the amount of that payment to the next loan you want to repay. For example, suppose you make the final payment on a loan in June. In July, instead of having more money to spend, you add the payment from the first loan to the payment on loan two. Linda, for example, owed only two bills; she was paying the dentist $50 a month and had four payments left. She was paying Visa $100 a month and owed $1,000. The month after the dentist is paid off, Linda adds the $50 to the $100 she sends Visa.

The following example illustrates how a debt elimination calendar works. The total of Jim Bob's monthly payments to all creditors is $500, as shown in the following table:

> **Hot Tip**
>
> Once the first loan is paid off, contact the second lender and make sure it understands and agrees that you want the amount you plan to add to the regular payment to be used to reduce the loan's principal balance. In Linda's case, a credit card such as Visa can easily handle the larger payment. When increasing payments on a car loan, the lender needs to know where to apply the additional amount that you will be sending.

Lender	Monthly Payments	Current Balance	APR	Secured Yes? No?
Visa I	$100	$ 400	22%	No
MasterCard	50	500	20	No
Visa II	25	500	18	No
Car	300	4,300	13	Yes
Dentist	25	800	0	No
TOTAL	$500			

Debt Elimination Calendar Worksheet

	Loan 1	Loan 2	Loan 3	Loan 4	Loan 5	Total
Month	_____	_____	_____	_____	_____	_____
_____	_____	_____	_____	_____	_____	_____
_____	_____	_____	_____	_____	_____	_____
_____	_____	_____	_____	_____	_____	_____
_____	_____	_____	_____	_____	_____	_____
_____	_____	_____	_____	_____	_____	_____
_____	_____	_____	_____	_____	_____	_____
_____	_____	_____	_____	_____	_____	_____
_____	_____	_____	_____	_____	_____	_____
_____	_____	_____	_____	_____	_____	_____
_____	_____	_____	_____	_____	_____	_____
_____	_____	_____	_____	_____	_____	_____
_____	_____	_____	_____	_____	_____	_____
_____	_____	_____	_____	_____	_____	_____
_____	_____	_____	_____	_____	_____	_____
_____	_____	_____	_____	_____	_____	_____
_____	_____	_____	_____	_____	_____	_____
_____	_____	_____	_____	_____	_____	_____

Debt Elimination Calendar
(ignore interest calculations)

Month	Visa	MasterCard	Visa II	Car	Dentist	Total
March	$ 100	$ 50	$ 25	$ 300	$ 25	$ 500
April	100	50	25	300	25	500
May	100	50	25	300	25	500
June	100	50	25	300	25	500
July		150	25	300	25	500
August		150	25	300	25	500
September			175	300	25	500
October			175	300	25	500
November				475	25	500
December				475	25	500
January				475	25	500
February				475	25	500
March					500	500
Total	$400	$500	$500	$4,300	$800	$6,500

Why was the dentist paid off last? Because she did not charge interest. When each loan is repaid, remember to add that payment to the next payment until all loans are repaid. Once Jim Bob is out of debt, what should he do with the $500 he previously sent to creditors? He has several options:

1. Deposit $500 into an emergency fund
2. Invest the $500
3. Spend it
4. Some combination of 1, 2, and 3.

Group Two: Borrowers Who Cannot Pay All Creditors 100 Percent Each Month

Those who have worked and re-worked their spending plan but don't have the dollars to make each promised monthly payment on time should consider the strategies discussed below. When funds are limited, pay financial liabilities listed below in the order of their priority. As used here, priority refers to the swiftness of a creditor to take punitive action.

Hot Tip

Need a Financial Calculator—Try the Web

www.familymoney.com/calc.htm

www.kiplinger.com/ (find the calculators in the Toolbox on the home page)

www.moneyadvisor.com/calc/

Priority Payments:

(1) Mortgage
(2) Car loan
(3) Utilities

These first three are essential because if you fall behind here, you lose your home and your ability to get to and from work.

(4) IRS
(5) Child support
(6) Student loans

Fail to pay items (4), (5), and (6) on time and the state or federal government gets involved. While your wages can be garnisheed to make these payments, that is not as bad as losing your house or car.

(7) Credit cards
(8) Medical bills

Items (7) and (8) represent unsecured loans. The lenders' only recourse is to turn late accounts over to a collection agency or sue the borrower in court. Such initial action is not nearly as drastic as having the government garnish your wages. Your wages can be garnished if a credit card or medical provider takes you to court, but such action is not as swift or as sure as when you're behind to higher priority lenders.

Those who cannot pay all their liabilities in full each month have three options:

1. Contact creditors
2. Seek professional help
3. Bankruptcy

You can contact creditors and try to work out a plan to reduce your payments until you can make all payments as initially agreed. You can contact creditors yourself as long as you haven't previously made payment promises and then not kept them. Start with secured lenders.

Secured Lenders

Secured creditors have a great deal of power over a borrower because they can take back the property that secured the loan. For example, miss a car payment and the repo man will pick it up (probably at 2 AM). Not only does the borrower lose the car but will probably be hit with a deficiency judgment. Here is how a deficiency judgment works. Mike owes $8,000 on his Mustang. Because he failed to make the last payment on time, the repo man picked up the Mustang early Monday morning. The lender took Mike to court and obtained a judgment against him for $3,750, as shown below:

Loan balance	$8,000
Plus repo fee	300
Storage	200
Legal fees	250
Less sales proceeds	(5,000)
Net amount Mike owes	$3,750

The deficiency judgment gives the creditor the right to place a lien on Mike's property, such as his house, or garnish his wages to collect the $3,750. Lenders in some states—Texas, for example—cannot file wage garnishments.

What should you do after missing one payment? Here are some suggestions:

- If you promise the lender that all future payments will be made on time, the lender may be willing to add the missed payment onto the back of the loan.
- If you cannot make full payments in the future, try to negotiate a new loan with a lower monthly payment. There will be more payments to make, and you'll pay more in interest.
- Try to sell the car. Get it detailed—have a professional clean up the car. Remove all personal possessions. Once you receive a firm offer to buy the car—even if it is not as much as you owe—contact the creditor. Some creditors will accept the offer and forgive the difference between the amount that you offer and the amount you still owe. If the lender refuses, tell the lender you are going to visit your bankruptcy attorney.
- Return the car. Before you do, ask the lender if it will forgive the loan balance when you return the car. Get its promise in writing *before* you surrender the car. If the lender refuses, threaten to file Chapter 13 bankruptcy, although the lender may not care.

> **Hot Tip**
>
> Most lenders will tell you that they never take cars back and cancel the loan. However, it is often cheaper for the lender to take the car back and cancel the loan than to go through a Chapter 13 bankruptcy. When someone files a Chapter 13, the odds are good that the loan balance will never be paid in full (and the person going through bankruptcy will keep the car).

Unsecured Lenders

With the exception of student loans, legal judgments, payments to the IRS, and child support payment, if you are late making payments on unsecured loans, such as credit cards and medical bills, you can expect the creditor to do three things:

1. Send negative information about your payment record to the credit bureau.
2. Hassle you with phone calls and personal visits.
3. Take you to court.

Until the creditor obtains a judgment against you, there is little else an unsecured creditor can do beyond steps one and two above. If you receive a summons to appear in court, you should always go no matter what the reasons for not having made payments on time. If you don't show up, the creditor wins by default. The creditor can now place liens on your property, such as your car, home, or bank account, or can garnish your wages. Borrowers should always defend themselves and tell the judge their side of the story. Before the court date, you should do the following:

- Develop a spending plan
- Create a debt elimination calendar
- Contact each of the creditors

Develop a spending plan. Let's use the Quinns as an example. Mr. Quinn's take-home pay is $2,400 a month. After carefully adjusting their spending targets, the family needs $1,750 a month to cover living expenses. This leaves $650 a month for debt payments. The Quinns are supposed to make the following monthly debt payments:

Loan	Monthly Payment
Car	$400
Student loan	100
Visa	50
Discover	60
MasterCard	40
Dentist	50
Hospital	100
Total	$800

Here are the payments I recommend that the Quinns make:

Car	$400 (secured)
Student loan*	$100
Visa	$ 25
Discover	$ 30
Mastercard	$ 20
Dentist	$ 25
Hospital	$ 50
Total	$650

*While not secured, lenders who make student loans can easily obtain wage garnishments. The IRS can also tap tax refunds to repay student loans.

Creating a debt elimination calendar. Next, the Quinns should create a debt elimination calendar using the numbers in the tables. If any of the reduced payments are less than the monthly interest charges for one or more loans, contact the closest Consumer Credit Counseling Service office at 800-374-2227.

Contacting the creditors. Before appearing in court, the Quinns should write to each of the five creditors who are to receive reduced payments, using a letter something like the following:

> Due to (explain why you have fallen behind in your payments and/or cannot now make full payments each month). As you can see from my enclosed spending plan, I cannot make full payments on my debts right now. My monthly take-home pay is $_____; I have $_____ left over after subtracting basic living expenses. I have enclosed a reduced payment of $_____. I will continue to make these payments until I am able to increase them to $_____ as indicated on my enclosed debt elimination calendar. I will not incur more debt until all loan balances are current and I am making full payments to all my creditors.
>
> Sincerely,

If unsecured creditors refuse to accept a reduced monthly payment, send it anyway. If a creditor takes you to court, show the judge your budget, your debt elimination calendar, and your letter to the creditor. Point out that you have regularly made the reduced payments as promised in your letter. The judge will almost always decide with you and throw the creditor's case out of court.

Hot Tip

Make sure you can keep every promise you make to a creditor before sending such a letter.

When Your Account Has Been Turned Over to a Collection Agency

Work with the staff at the collection agency the way you do with a creditor. Unlike the creditor, you can stop collection agencies from contacting you. How? Send them a certified letter telling them never to contact you again. They will not contact you again—except to tell you that they will not contact you. A collection agency can take you to court. If you are making "good faith" efforts, the judge is likely to understand. If the judge sides with the creditor or collection agency, bankruptcy may be your only option.

Seek professional help. Check with your local United Way and government agencies for a referral to someone who can help. Call the Consumer Credit Counseling Service (CCCS) at 800-388-2227 (www.nfcc.org). It charges a modest fee—between $10 and $20 a month.

A CCCS counselor can

- set up a plan to repay creditors;
- get creditors to reduce or eliminate interest on your charge cards;
- help you create an effective budget;
- refer you to appropriate community agencies that can help you with rent, utility, and medical and food expenses as well as other services.

At times, a CCCS counselor will recommend bankruptcy when clients lack the funds to repay their debts according to the CCCS Debt Management Program.

If you have Internet access, check this Web site: www.dca.org. Debt Counselors of America offers a variety of useful booklets for a modest charge and can also help you deal with a wide range of financial issues, including debt problems. Debt Counselors of America does not have a fee schedule; their clients make voluntary contributions for the services they have received.

Call Debtors Anonymous at 781-453-2743 to see if this is an active group in your area. You can also find Debtors Anonymous on the Web at www.debtorsanonymous.org.

When bankruptcy is the only option. If secured creditors won't reduce your secured loan payments so your spending plan can handle payments, you probably are facing bankruptcy—not a pleasant experience. Did you know that it costs money to file for bankruptcy? You should expect to pay from $700 to $2,000 (or more) to file a personal bankruptcy. And bankruptcy does not forgive all obligations. No one can legally get out of repaying legal judgments, student loans, child support, and the IRS! Bankruptcy stays on a credit report seven to ten years.

You get to choose whether to file under Chapter 7 or under Chapter 13 of the Bankruptcy Code. Chapter 7 is popular with borrowers who owe money primarily to unsecured creditors. If you file a so-called Chapter 7, you may have to sell some belongings to repay creditors. But certain property is exempt from sale. You get to decide if you wish to use the exemptions included in the federal bankruptcy law or your state exemptions. A bankruptcy attorney knows if it is better for you to select state or federal exemptions.

You would file a Chapter 13 bankruptcy if you want to keep your house or car, can feel the IRS breathing down your neck, or are behind on student loan and/or child support payments. To file, you must have a regular source of income like a job or Social Security payments. A bankruptcy filing initially stops any and all creditors from contacting you. Anyone filing a Chapter 13 works with a bankruptcy attorney to develop a three-year or five-year spending plan. For the court to approve the plan, the plan must enable you to make up all past due payments to secured creditors, the IRS, student loans, and child support. Such a plan needs to show that you are paying as much as possible to unsecured creditors. In some cases, unsecured creditors are eventually paid in full, but they may not receive any payments during the first year or two of the bankruptcy while past due payments to secured creditors are being brought current. A Chapter 13 bankruptcy filing stops all interest and penalties from all creditors except secured ones (in most bankruptcies, the IRS is not a secured creditor).

Some states like Florida and Texas have enabled millionaires to file for bankruptcy yet not lose their millionaire status. How is this possible? Assume the millionaire lives in a million-dollar house with a mortgage. The millionaire does all she can to pay off the mortgage and then files for bankruptcy. In Florida and Texas, those who file for bankruptcy are allowed to keep their home.

Your Credit Rights

Whether you are in debt or not, you need to be familiar with your credit rights. Many lenders violate those rights from their own ignorance or their belief that they can get away with it because of consumer ignorance. When you believe that your rights have been violated, send a letter to the Federal Trade Commission (FTC), Consumer Response Center, 600 Pennsylvania Avenue, NW, Washington, DC 20580 with a copy to both the lender and your state's attorney general. You may also reach the FTC's Consumer Response Center by calling 202-326-2222; also check the FTC's Web site: www.ftc.gov. Chances are slim to none that the FTC will handle your problem separately. They do want to hear from you, however, because numerous complaints about the same creditor are likely to stimulate action on the FTC's part.

Fair Credit Billing Act

A cardholder who discovers a billing error has 60 days to notify the lender in writing of the error under this federal statute. The lender must respond (but not necessarily resolve the problem) within 30 days after hearing from you. The lender has 90 days to resolve the problem and correct the billing or explain why it believes that no error exists. During the dispute period, the lender cannot bill or take any collection actions against you.

Credit card holders may withhold payment for any defective purchase made with a credit card, but they must satisfy three conditions:

1. The purchase must be for $50 or more.
2. The purchase must have been made within the cardholder's home state or within 100 miles of the cardholder's address.
3. The cardholder must contact the merchant and try to resolve the problem.

If you are the credit card holder and the merchant does not resolve the problem to your satisfaction, the credit card company will remove the charge from your account.

Fair Credit Reporting Act

Under this legislation, a credit bureau must remove negative information from a credit report as follows:

- Erase bankruptcy information after ten years.
- Remove all other negative information after seven years.

You must also be informed when you have been denied credit or turned down for life insurance or employment because of information in your credit report. Following rejection, you have 60 days to request a free copy of the report. And you have the right to insert a 100-word explanation of any disputed information in your credit file.

Fair Debt Collection Practices Act

Under this law, collection agencies may not do any of the following:

- Call a debtor between 9 PM and 8 AM
- Impersonate a law enforcement agency
- Tell other people about the debt
- Call the debtor at work if it is against the employer's wishes
- Threaten the debtor or use obscene language
- Contact a debtor represented by an attorney

- Contact the debtor again if the debtor writes to request no contact. (The collection agency's only option is to pursue the issue in court.)

Truth-in-Lending Act

This law requires lenders to convert all costs of borrowing into an annual percentage rate (APR). It also gives you three business days to cancel any credit purchase when your home is used as collateral. You have the same three-day cooling-off period any time you make a purchase in your home (or not at the merchant's place of business). For example, a door-to-door salesman sells Cheryl a $500 vacuum purchase on Friday at 11 AM. Cheryl has till Wednesday at 11 AM to rescind the purchase and get her money back.

Too many of us owe too much money to too many creditors. The money we send to creditors each month would go a long way toward funding several important goals, including financial independence. If you are in debt, I hope that you have created a debt elimination calendar and are committed to following it faithfully. Such a strategy should work well *if* you implemented the strategies in Chapter 6 so that you no longer need or want to borrow money. Nothing you ever do financially is likely to be as satisfying as getting out of debt. You become increasingly financially fit as each debtor is repaid.

Financial Checkup Checklist

- Complete the Loan Ledger Worksheet.

- Create a debt elimination calendar.

- If you must reduce payments to unsecured creditors, send each creditor a letter explaining how you plan to repay them.

- If you need professional help, contact one of the organizations mentioned in this chapter.

Your Credit Report

When I asked John and Beth how I could help them, Beth said they had recently been denied credit when they applied for a car loan. She went on to say that both she and John never made late payments, so they didn't know why their application had been rejected. When I asked them if they had requested a copy of their credit report, John said that they didn't know how to get one. Once I explained the process, they promised to order their report as soon as they returned home. I offered them the use of my phone to request a copy, but I was told that the rejection letter that had information they needed was on the counter at home.

When they came for their next visit, their problem, actually John's problem, was easy to spot. Placed after John's last name was the Roman numeral III. John was named after his father, who had been named after *his* father. With similar names, creditors may not distinguish between a II and a III, especially since neither father nor son used the numbers regularly. John's problem was complicated by the fact that his father had a history of not paying creditors and several of his creditors appeared on John's credit report. They eventually got John's credit report cleaned up, but it took several months. I told them that John would continue to have this problem for the rest of his life.

Whether you manage credit wisely or are buried in debt, did you know that big computers are watching you? They know how you handle your money. Late with a mortgage payment? Skip a credit card payment? Behind on your student loan? Forget to make a child support payment? Declare bankruptcy? Lose a lawsuit and have to pay financial damages? You expect your credit file to contain information about your history of repaying loans, but did you know items from public records also show up on your report, such as tax liens, judgments, and bankruptcies? Your file identifies firms that want to extend credit to you as well as identifying employers, landlords, and insurance companies to whom you have given permission to check your file.

Information about you is collected by three large companies (Transunion, Equifax, and Experian) and stored on their computers. Any business that subscribes to one of these companies' services has the right to see a copy of your credit report if you fit one of the following circumstances:

- A legitimate borrowing need is initiated by you.
- A judge has requested a copy of your report.
- A lender from whom you have borrowed money wants to review your account.
- You want to become an investor in a business transaction.

There is another way a lender may learn about you. A company may come up with a set of criteria that defines people they want as customers. Such a creditor would like to offer credit to anyone satisfying its criteria. The company sends a list of specific criteria to the credit bureau and asks for the names of individuals that match the creditor's criteria. This process is called "prescreening" or "preselecting." If your data match, the lender sends you an invitation to accept their credit offer.

Check Your Credit Report

You should want to know what your lenders are saying about you. Reviewing your credit report is an especially smart action to take just before borrowing money to buy a home or car, applying for a job, renting an apartment, or obtaining a business loan. Federal law gives you the right to make sure your credit report is accurate.

Your credit report contains a great deal of information about you. Expect to find the following information:

- Birth date and Social Security number
- Your last three addresses
- Your current employer and your most recent previous employer
- Your payment record for most credit obligations
- If divorced, the name of your previous spouse
- Any financial judgments against you
- Negative information about your payment record for utilities, medical bills, and gasoline companies (who rarely report your positive payment history)

Who can legally see a copy of your report? The most likely firms to check on your credit are these:

Someone from whom you have asked for credit. Never give any firm permission to check your credit file unless you plan to use the credit if you are approved. Why? Each firm that requests a copy of your file is listed on your credit report (and stays there for two years). Each lender wants to know if you have recently applied for credit elsewhere. The lender assumes that you might have opened up a new account that has not yet found its way to your credit report. If you did take out a new loan, that loan may make you a poorer credit risk. When a firm checks your credit, that inquiry may be seen as a negative mark by other firms checking your credit for another reason. They may think that if you did not borrow from that firm, you were denied credit. For example: You are shopping for a new car. The salesperson suggests that the dealership check your credit while you are outside kicking tires. The salesperson wants you to know that his or her agency is saving you time in case you decide to buy since your credit information will be ready when you return from checking out the car. Never give anyone permission to check your credit unless (1) you plan to buy something from this company, and (2) you plan to use its financing.

An apartment manager. A growing number of landlords check prospective tenants' credit before they offer a lease. You would too if you were considering renting your apartment or house to a stranger.

An insurance company when you apply for auto or homeowners insurance or $50,000 or more in life insurance. Insurance companies consider that the information in your credit report reflects your character. They do not want to sell life insurance to anyone who may try to defraud them.

A prospective employer. Employers are checking to see if you handle your own finances responsibly. They believe that if you do not, you are not likely to manage their finances any better. Firms usually wait until they have narrowed the search to the top four or five candidates before getting permission to check their credit

A firm when you match its prescreening criteria as explained previously. Some credit bureaus will tell you that even though they collect information about you, they do not rate your creditworthiness. Actually they do. Many lenders ask the credit bureau to condense the information in your credit file into some type of credit risk score. The lender may give a credit bureau a credit-scoring model to use in evaluating credit files. So credit bureaus evaluate the data in your file and calculate what is known as a "risk score." While each lender interprets this score differently, many use it to try and anticipate the likelihood that you will be late with payments or default on a loan. Actually, there are several different credit-scoring models; so your risk score depends on the credit-scoring system used. Even if you could see one of your risk scores, which you cannot, you would not know what it means.

You have a right to see (and should want to examine) a report that describes the information in your credit file for the following reasons:

- Some of the data in your file may be inaccurate.
- Someone else's information may be in your file.
- There may be negative data in your file, but in your opinion the numbers do not provide an accurate picture of what really happened.

If you have not seen your file during the last 18 to 24 months, you probably should. You may obtain a copy of your credit report in several ways. If your credit or job application is turned down because of information in your credit report, the lender or employer is required by law to tell you why it rejected you. The lender must also give you the name and address of the credit reporting agency from which they obtained your credit file. After being

> **Hot Tip**
>
> Anyone who becomes a top candidate when applying for a job that pays more than $30,000 a year is likely to be asked for permission to allow the employer to pull his or her credit report.

denied credit, you have 60 days to request a free copy of your credit report. Contact that credit bureau; tell it that the lender rejected your credit application. Request a free copy of your credit report. Below are the 800 numbers of the three major credit bureaus:

Trans Union	Equifax	Experian
800-888-4213	800-685-1111	888-397-3742
www.tuc.com	www.equifax.com	www.experian.com

Many of my students laugh when I suggest that once engaged to be married, partners should share credit information. They tell me that wanting to see the other person's credit file shows a lack of trust on their part. I tell them that their engagement is the time to thoroughly investigate the other person's attitude and beliefs on a wide range of topics. This is also the time to create a budget together. Each needs to know what obligations the other person has and how well he or she has handled them. My motto, probably borrowed from someone like Twain or Rogers, is: "Before marriage, keep both eyes open; after marriage, keep them half-closed."

Make Sure Your Credit Report Is Accurate

When your credit report arrives, carefully review it. If you have questions about the information contained in the report, call the credit bureau and ask for an explanation.

Focus on these questions and strategies when you review your credit report:

Is someone else's information on your report? Call or write to both the lender and the credit bureau pointing out that this account is not yours. The credit bureau must check out your complaint and make adjustments when it has verified that the information is incorrect. It used to be your responsibility to prove that the information did not belong to you. Now credit bureaus must remove challenged information unless the lender can prove it is correct.

Has a creditor reported incorrect information? Contact both the creditor and the credit reporting agency; explain the

> **Hot Tip**
>
> If you are engaged, I suggest that each of you obtain a copy of your credit report. You should want to know the credit history of your intended, and your significant other has a right to see yours. You would be unwise to cosign a credit application or income tax return with your partner until you have seen his or her credit report. Many spouses have been pulled through bankruptcy when they had perfect credit up to the moment they applied for credit with a partner whose credit history was terrible.

problem and ask that the mistake be corrected. When contacted by a credit bureau, creditors must certify that the negative information they have placed in your credit file is correct.

Do you need to tell your side of the story? Sometimes circumstances beyond your control make it impossible for you to pay on time. Other times, you and a creditor disagree about the amount outstanding. You have the right to write a 100-word explanation telling why such negative data are on your file. Your explanation will be placed in your file for other creditors to read. For example, Jack France disagreed with his credit card issuer about how interest charges were computed. He eventually decided to stop using the card but refused to pay the remaining $5.71 in interest. His credit card assessed a $10.00 monthly fee on the unpaid balance. After six months, the credit card company said that Jack owed $65.71. At that time the credit card company turned Jack's account over for collection. Jack refused to pay the collection agency; he did send in a 100-word statement to the credit bureau explaining why the credit card company said he owed $65.71 and why he felt he had paid it in full.

> **Hot Tip**
>
> Your 100-word statement will stay in your file for seven years. Do not send in such a report unless it satisfies the following criteria:
>
> - You are sending in your statement soon after the negative data are entered into your file. You do not want such a statement in your file after the negative information has been removed.
> - Read your statement carefully. How will this statement sound to creditors three or more years from now?

Close accounts you no longer use. Ever open an account when offered a 10 percent discount on purchases you plan to make that day if you applied for the store's card but now you no longer use the account? Send the creditor a certified letter asking that the account be closed "at the customer's request." Enclose the cut-up pieces of its card too. Three or four open charge accounts are to your advantage *if* payments are made on time. But too many open charge accounts hurts you, especially if they have zero balances; a potential creditor may reject your application if you have available significant amounts of unused credit. How many cards are too many? Everyone's situation is different. More than six or seven is considered too many by most creditors. The more open accounts you have, the more bookkeeping for you when you pay bills and the bigger the hassle (and potential financial loss) if your cards are lost or stolen. Why not limit yourself to two cards? One should be a Visa or MasterCard because they are accepted more places than any other credit card.

Review the list of companies who have seen your file. Your credit record shows all inquiries over the last six months (your file will show potential employers who reviewed it as far back as two years). Inquiries should only come from two sources: (1) those who pay the credit bureau to prescreen everyone in its files and (2) companies you have given permission to see your file. *No one else has the right to see your file and can be fined if they do.* According to federal law, anyone obtaining a copy of your credit report under false pretenses may be fined up to $5,000. You have the right to find out why any firm had access to your file.

> # Warning!!!
> **S**tay Away from Anyone Who Charges a Fee to Clean Up Your Credit Report!

When you do find mistakes in your file, contact the credit bureau immediately. After investigating your request, the credit bureau will notify you if the negative data will be removed or stay on your record. *Negative data will stay on your file between seven and ten years.*

Problem: Since three different credit bureaus are likely to keep a file on you, cleaning up your file at one credit bureau does not mean that you have cleaned it up at the other two. You never know which of the three bureaus a lender, employer, or landlord will check. I recommend that you clean up your file with one agency, and it's hoped that will take care of your major problems and be sufficient unless you are denied credit when a lender received information from another of the big three bureaus.

Avoid any firm or clinic that claims it can repair anyone's bad credit history. No one can legally remove accurate (but negative) information from a credit report (except a creditor), but a credit repair clinic will charge a substantial sum for "dialoging" with a credit bureau. Anything a clinic does accomplish, you can do yourself at no cost, as explained above. All that credit repair clinics usually do is send the credit bureau dozens of letters challenging statements in a person's credit file. These letters rarely are effective in pressuring the creditor or credit bureau to make any changes to a file.

Build or Improve Your Credit

Your good name is worth a lot. If you have been down on your luck, and it is reflected in your credit report, try the following strategies.

- Make all payments on time. If you see a problem ahead, call the creditor before the due date and work out a payment schedule.

- Do not bounce checks. Set up overdraft protection or, better yet, deposit enough money in your checking account so that you earn interest each month.
- If you have not yet ordered a copy of your credit report, do so now. Follow the strategies discussed in this chapter to ensure that your credit history is reported correctly.
- If all of your requests for credit have been turned down, find someone who will cosign a loan for you.
- Apply for a secured credit card. This strategy is discussed in Chapter 7 on credit cards.
- Get out of debt.
- Put money into an emergency account. You need such funds as a backup when you lack the income in a particular month to pay all creditors on time. How much should you save? At a minimum, stash at least one month's income; two is even better. Financial experts often suggest three to six months, but such numbers are not realistic for most of us.

> **Hot Tip**
>
> The best strategy is to make all payments on time. Many creditors will overlook a history of late payments if you make all payments on time for two years.

Periodically, you need to see a copy of your credit report. This is an especially good idea if you are just starting a campaign to get out of debt as discussed earlier in the chapter. If you have not seen a copy of your report lately and are planning on applying for a mortgage or car loan, a new job or apartment, pay the fee and review your credit report. While creditors and credit bureaus claim that they are making a more determined effort to be more careful when entering data

Financial Checkup Checklist

- Obtain a copy of your credit report.
- Close accounts you no longer use.
- If you find errors, call the credit bureau to report the correct information.
- Commit to make all future loan payments on time.

into your files, mistakes do occur. Some people's files have become so messed up that some individuals have had to apply for a new identity (including the difficult task of getting a new name and Social Security number). Such cases usually occur when someone has stolen an unfortunate person's identity. Do all you can to protect your credit and your good name.

> **Hot Tip**
>
> Once you have paid off all your debt (except your mortgage), order a copy of your credit report to make sure all lenders have accurately reported the status of each of your accounts. At this time you would be wise to close any accounts still open that you no longer plan to use.

7 Win at Credit Cards

Learn how to get the most from your cards while avoiding their pitfalls.

Few vices are as controlling as debt or cause us to be more financially unfit. Marge knew. She owed so much on her cards that she could make only minimum payments. She alternated paying one group of six on even months and the other group on odd. Strangely enough, she owned her home free and clear. Yet she lacked the strength to stop using her cards. When I told her that she needed to cut them up, she broke into a sweat. She actually started to exhibit symptoms of withdrawal. Her hands shook as she took over a dozen cards from her purse and put them on the desk. Frankly, I was a little worried as I handed her the scissors. Men and women often cry during a visit, but I had never witnessed a nervous breakdown. I almost did that afternoon.

When Carmenia and Josie came to see me, they didn't have any debt. No mortgage, no auto loans, no student loans; and they paid off their credit card balances in full every month. I did learn that three months before their marriage, they had given a repair contractor a check for $9,000 to cover the costs of remodeling their kitchen. They never saw him again.

These two vignettes provide a picture of one client who abused her cards compared with another client who lost a significant sum of money because of failing to make a purchase with credit cards. Every adult needs to have one card in his or her name, but for every adult who does not have a card, there are dozens who have too many. Think of using cards as a game. What follows is a discussion of the rules that will show you how to win using credit cards. What changes do you need to make to become a better player?

Companies that issue credit cards want you to have something to come home to—their credit card offers. Even people filing bankruptcy receive *preapproved* credit card applications. You probably have something seriously wrong with your credit record if you are not receiving at least one credit card offer a month. No one wants you to believe more strongly that money buys happiness than do the folks who issue credit cards. Some offers are appealing. One bank offers a free round-trip airfare to Europe for a companion when you buy a ticket to Europe. Several companies offer frequent flyer miles for every dollar charged. Another offers $100 in credit if you apply and are approved to use its card. Most offer tempting introductory rates such as 3.9 percent for six months; some rates are even lower and/or last for longer than six months.

> **Hot Tip**
>
> **B**ecause credit card companies are finding it increasingly difficult to sign up new cardholders, they are more likely to respond favorably when you ask them to lower their rate, extend a low introductory rate, or forgive a late or over-the-limit fee. In some cases, they will even forgo the annual membership fee. What do you have to lose by asking?

Before applying for a card, see how well it measures up.

Does the card company charge an annual membership fee?

If you currently use a card that has an annual fee, call and ask the company to drop the fee; many will if they want to keep you as a card user. Travel and entertainment cards (American Express, Diners Club) always require a hefty annual fee; you must pay off the balance in full every month. There is no reason to pay an annual fee!

Does the card offer you a grace period?

A grace period is the number of days between the statement date and the payment date, when no interest is assessed on the charges listed on the statement as long as you pay off the statement balance in full each month and your payment arrives by the payment due date. For example, Bonnie pays off the entire balance on her March statement. The April statement's closing date is April 5; the payment due date is April 25. Her grace period is 20 days. She will not incur any interest charges for the purchases listed on her April statement so long as her check reaches the card issuer by April 25. If Bonnie misses that date, she will be assessed a late payment fee (even if the payment gets there before the next billing or closing date). She will also be assessed interest charges from the date she made each purchase.

You need to know four things about grace periods:

1. Some credit card companies do not offer them.
2. On some cards, like Discover, you must pay off the balance in full for a minimum of two consecutive months to avoid paying interest.
3. The grace period is 25 days for some cards; on others it is 15 or fewer days. A shorter grace period means that payments must be returned more quickly after the statement arrives.
4. Grace periods are an endangered species; more cards are dropping them. If you always pay off your balance in full each month and use a card that does not charge an annual fee, expect to see your grace period disappear if you charge less than $2000 a year.

What annual percentage rate (APR) does the card offer? Unless you have terrible credit, you should be able to get a card with an annual percentage rate below 14 percent. If you now have a card with a higher rate, call the company today and ask that your rate be lowered. Say that you are considering canceling the card because you can get a lower rate from another company. If it doesn't lower your rate, cancel the card *after* you receive your card from the other company.

> **Hot Tip**
>
> Develop the habit of using a credit card company's money for up to 50 days without having to pay interest. Here's how: Matthew's statement closes on the 8th of each month. His card offers a 20-day grace period. Matthew charges a purchase on June 9; the charge doesn't show up until his July 8th statement. His grace period ends July 28. As long as he pays the balance in full each month, he will not be charged interest on the June 9th purchase if his payment reaches the card company on or before July 28. However, if he doesn't pay off balances in full each month, each purchase is charged interest on the date of the charge. In the above example, if Matthew had not paid off the May statement balance in full, interest would be assessed on the June 9th purchase starting on June 9th.

How does your card compute monthly interest? Most cards use one of two systems:

1. *Average daily balance.* Here is how it works: During April William charged $1,000. When his May statement arrived, he sent in a payment of $950, leaving an unpaid balance of $50. On his June statement, however, he will be

charged interest on the average daily balance in May. For 26 days in May he owed $1,000, so he will pay interest on $1,000 for 26 days and interest on $50 for five days. Since Bill did not pay off his balance in full, any charges made in June will be charged interest starting on the day the purchase was made.

2. *Two-cycle average daily balance.* Nancy's May statement arrived. She had paid off the balance in full for April but not in March. On her May statement she will be charged interest for the average daily balance for both March and April. If Nancy pays off the May balance in full, she will not be charged interest on her June statement.

What fees must you pay when you get a cash advance from the card company? This is a game you cannot win, but at least learn the rules. For example, you find yourself in a bind. You need $100 in cash right now because the merchant won't take your check or your credit card. You have two options: (1) get a cash advance from your credit card company or (2) use your debit card to withdraw cash from your checking account.

The choice would be easy if you had the cash in your checking account. On a $100 withdrawal using a debit card, the ATM could charge from 50¢ to $2. For the cash advance from your credit card, the charge could range from 1.5 to 2.5 percent of the amount you withdraw, and the card starts to charge you interest on the $100 the day you get your money. The interest rate charged on cash advances is probably higher than the card's regular annual percentage rate calculated on charged purchases. For example, Shirley takes a $500 cash advance; her card charges her 2 percent, or $10, plus interest of 21.9 percent. Avoid cash advances like the plague.

What perks does the card offer? Some of the better ones include the following:

- *Collision coverage.* People who have a Gold Visa card or MasterCard can decline the collision damage insurance waiver when they rent a car. Collision coverage can cost as much as $12 to $15 a day, so this is a useful benefit if you rent cars.

  Not all cards provide collision coverage; in fact, collision cover-

> **Hot Tip**
>
> Your credit card may cover damage to a rental car anywhere in the world, but it *does not* include liability coverage if you are responsible for injuries or damage to others' property while driving the rental car. You have such liability coverage on your auto policy when driving a rental car in the United States and in Canada. You do not have such coverage when renting a car anywhere else on the planet unless you buy it when you rent the car.

age is not included under most credit cards that employers require their employees to use. Employers sometimes have a separate policy providing collision coverage. Before you rent a car with a company credit card, find out if the card includes collision coverage!

- *Frequent flyer miles.* For every dollar charged, a cardholder earns one mile. For example, Philip charges a new $200 suit using a credit card that awards frequent flyer miles. His next statement from his frequent flyer account should show that he earned 200 miles for the purchase. During the first 30 to 90 days from the date of purchase, the card will replace a lost, stolen or, damaged item. Cards are dropping this coverage, so it must have value.
- *Discounts on the purchase of a new car.* However, these benefits have been cut back or eliminated.

On the other hand, some *benefits you should decline:*

- *Lost or stolen credit card insurance.* If your credit cards are stolen, your maximum liability is $50 for each card. You will not be liable if you report a stolen card before it is used. Card companies often charge $25 to $30 annually for this service. Why pay $30 to save $50 in the unlikely event that your card is stolen *and* the thief uses it before you report it stolen? The possibility of having your cards stolen is another reason for only carrying one card. Someone who had six cards stolen has a potential liability of $300. Even with six cards, the insurance is still a bad buy.
- *Flight insurance:* Every time you fly and charge the ticket on your credit card, the credit card will bill you for flight insurance. There are three reasons for declining this insurance.

> **Hot Tip**
>
> The Gold Visa card or MasterCard will also cover renting cars in many countries. Those planning to rent a car overseas should call their credit card company and ask three questions:
>
> 1. "Will my credit card provide collision coverage if I wreck a rental car in (name the country)?"
> 2. If the answer is yes, then ask, "For how many weeks is the coverage good for?" Some cards only cover you for two weeks (in the United States and overseas).
> 3. "If I have an accident, what is the phone number in (name of the country) that I should call to report my accident?" Obviously, renters need this phone number for each country in which they plan to travel while driving the rented car.

1. If the plane does crash with you aboard, your family can expect a nice settlement from the airline.
2. If someone will suffer financially because of your death, you should already have enough life insurance in place before you fasten the plane's seat belt.
3. If you die in a plane crash, you will not receive the money (I hope your family will). Such insurance is like using your money to buy a lottery ticket for someone else.

- *Disability or life insurance sold by the credit card company to make your credit card payments if you cannot.* Anyone should have enough life and disability insurance to make the payments, so buying it from a credit card company is duplicative as well as expensive coverage.

> **Hot Tip**
>
> To get the best deals on a credit card, you need to satisfy the following criteria:
>
> - Full-time employment with the same employer for at least two years
> - A debt-to-income ratio below 0.25. (Divide your gross monthly income into total monthly debt payments—student loans, auto loan, minimum credit card payments, mortgage or rent payment)
> - No late payments to creditors during the last 24 months

Compare your credit card with others. How well does your card measure up to offers that come in the mail? Compare your cards with those listed each month in *Money* and *Kiplinger's Personal Finance Magazine* or check out the cards at:

    www.ramresearch.com
    www.consumer-action.org
    www.bankrate.com   800-327-7717   ($10 for a report)
    www.cardtrack.com   800-344-7714   ($5 for a report)

Today's top credit card marketing gimmick is the low introductory rate. Card issuers print the rate on the front of the envelope to tempt you to read the propaganda inside.

To sort out the good credit card deals from the bad, make sure you find answers to the following questions.

For how long is the introductory rate good? The offer may state that the rate is good for six months. A closer examination may reveal that if the bank sent the card to you today, only three or four months remain in this six-month period. And the time it takes for the bank to issue the card will use up several more weeks out of the remaining three or four months. Look for offers that lock in the low rate for nine months or longer.

What rate replaces the introductory rate? The permanent rate is almost always above 18 percent, and many times it is higher than 20 percent. Today many card companies tie their APR to the prime rate offered by banks (the prime rate is the rate banks charge their best customers). Card companies' permanent APR is often prime plus 8 to 12 percent. Stay away from prime plus deals. These rates are also a variable APR since the prime rate changes several times during the year.

Is the card company asking you to transfer balances to the new card from current cards for which you are paying a higher rate? This may be an attractive feature, especially if you're given a 1 percent credit for the amount you are transferring. For example, Lolita is tempted to apply for a new card whose introductory rate is 4.9 percent, because her current card's APR is 21.9 percent. She owes $2,000, and the new card is offering to credit 1 percent of the balance transferred (or $20).

The following example illustrates possible savings that may be realized by switching balances from a high-interest-rate card to a lower, teaser rate card that will last for only five or six months after Lou receives the card. Lou's balance to be transferred is $2,000; he plans to make monthly payments of $100. Numbers are rounded to the closest dollar.

> **Hot Tip**
> Always check the box, which should be included in every credit card offer you receive, that defines the card's interest rate, grace period, fees, and the interest calculation used.

> **Hot Tip**
> When the introductory rate period is close to expiring, call the card company and ask it for an extension; many times it will extend the period.

> **Hot Tip**
> A lower introductory rate may apply only to balances you transfer to a new card. Check to make sure that new purchases will also be covered under this introductory teaser fee.

	4.9% APR	21.9% APR
Month		
1st month:		
Payment	$ 100	$ 100
Interest	8	37
Principal	92	63
New balance	1,908	1,933
2nd month:		
Payment	100	100
Interest	8	35
Principal	92	65
New balance	1,819	1,868
3rd month:		
Payment	$100	$100
Interest	7	34
Principal	93	66
New balance	1,726	1,802
4th month:		
Payment	100	100
Interest	7	33
Principal	93	67
New balance	1,633	1,735
5th month:		
Payment	100	100
Interest	7	32
Principal	93	68
New balance	1,540	1,667
6th month:		
Payment	100	100
Interest	6	30
Principal	94	70
New balance	1,446	1,597

By switching to the much lower rate, Lou has saved $151 in interest charges in just six months. Even if he has to pay a 2 percent balance transfer fee of $40, he is much better off by switching. Maybe he can find an offer for a card that will credit his account 1 percent of the amount transferred and not charge the transfer fee.

Some people who are serious about getting out of debt take out a new card every six months when an offer includes both a low introductory rate and an offer to transfer old balances to the new card. People using this strategy should close the old account once the balance has been repaid. So far this strategy does not seem to hurt a person's credit rating.

Billing Errors

Billing errors occur more often than you might think. Keep the receipt from each charge purchase. Compare the charges on each monthly statement with charge slips. Watch out for double and even triple billings. (Duplicate charges are not likely to be next to each other on the statement; sometimes duplicate charges show up on statements from different months.) Look for wrong amounts or charges that are not even yours. If you discover a billing error on a statement, you have 60 days from the statement's closing date to write to the financial institution that sent you the statement. You might call first to see if the institution wants you to write. Describe the error clearly and include the amount and date of the purchase, and provide your name, address, and account number. Send the letter certified. (Pay all amounts on the bill that are correct.) The financial institution has 90 days to correct the error or tell you why it thinks no mistake has been made. Before responding to your letter, the institution cannot

- charge you interest on the disputed amount;
- try to collect the amount; or
- indicate to a credit bureau that the amount is past due.

If the credit card company decides that its original information was correct, it will charge you back interest.

> **Hot Tip**
>
> When cards offer a tempting low rate for a few months, always read the fine print. Many cards will charge a balance transfer fee equal to 2 to 2.5 percent of the amount you are transferring to their card. For example, BankABC sends you checks in the mail offering you a 4.9 percent rate for six months on amounts transferred; however, it charges 2.5 percent on all amounts transferred to its card. Although transferring balances to this card may reduce your interest charges more than leaving your money in your current account, hold out until you are offered a card that does not charge balance transfer fees.

Have you recently been turned down when you applied for a Visa card or MasterCard? The card company must tell you why it denied your application. You also have a right to see a copy of your credit report. If you have been rejected, try consolidating all of your banking services (checking, savings, and car and student loans) at the same financial institution and apply for the credit card offered by your bank. You may be more successful applying for a department store or gasoline company card.

If all else fails, apply for a secured credit card. The limit on your secured Visa or MasterCard will equal the amount that you deposited into a savings account with the institution that will issue the secured card. By using the secured card, you can improve your credit rating *if* you make *every* payment on time. Some company out there badly wants you to have its card. It should not be hard to find.

> **Hot Tip**
>
> **N**ever call 900 numbers to apply for a credit card. These consumer rip-offs make money every minute you talk. When they do have an honest deal for you, they are only offering you something you could have found for free without paying their fees.

Protecting Your Cards from Fraud

To protect your credit cards, *do* take these precautions:
- Sign cards the day they arrive.
- Keep receipts.
- Compare entries on the monthly statement with receipts.
- Shred receipts you don't need for income tax records or warranty protection.
- Never write your card number on anything.
- Before you sign a receipt, check the amount.
- Carry the card issuer's 800 number on a separate piece of paper so you can call when a card is lost or stolen.
- Check your credit report at least once every 24 months to make sure no one else is using any of your cards.
- If you find a mistake on your statement, call the card issuer immediately.
- Consider adding your photo to your card.
- Call the card issuer immediately if your card is stolen or if you receive notice that the card was sent, but you have not received it.
- Memorize your PIN number and never write it anywhere.
- When you move, immediately submit a change of address to the card issuer.

Points to Consider

- You should have one card in your name only; do not give anyone else permission to use this card.
- When cashing a check, *never* use a credit card as identification. Someone who sees a copy of your check with your credit card number written on it can then use your credit card number because your check will have your name, address, and phone number. Someone who has all this information can charge on your card even though they do not have the card itself.
- When making a purchase with a credit card, never give your phone number as identification. Someone with your phone number can use your credit card because they can then obtain your address.
- Each time you are late with a payment, your credit card company is likely to raise the interest rate it charges you. The company may also raise your rate (or cancel your card) if you carry significant balances on competitor's cards *even if you pay on time every month.*
- If you make a purchase in your home state for more than $50 and you have problems with the product or service, you can have that charge removed from your account. Here's how it works: If a product or service doesn't work as you think it should, follow these three steps:
    1. Contact the merchant who sold you the product or service. Ask to have the item replaced or repaired or your money refunded. If the merchant refuses, take the next step.
    2. Send a certified letter to the company that issued your card and ask to have the charge removed from your account. Describe the problem and point out that you returned to the merchant and asked to have your complaint resolved. For example, Amy, who lives in Utah, received a call from a telemarketer in California selling a product for $300. When the product arrived, it was

> **Hot Tip**
>
> Because of the $50 rule, you should always make certain types of purchases with a credit card. Purchases of items that generate lots of consumer complaints, such as electronic equipment, auto and home repairs, travel agent services, and medical services, should always be paid with a credit card. Remember Carmenia and Josie, who gave the contractor a $9,000 check to remodel their kitchen? Had they paid with a credit card, the $9,000 would have been refunded.

not like the product described by the salesman. Amy sent it back to the company and asked it to credit her charge card. When it failed to do so, she wrote her credit card company and asked to have the charge removed. It was.
3. The charge should be removed from your account within two to eight weeks (to give the merchant time to issue a credit). The merchant can take you to court to collect, but that's not likely, because the product was defective or the service was not performed as agreed.

- When traveling abroad, obtain the currency of the country you are visiting by using your debit card at an automatic teller machine (ATM) in that country. (This method assumes that you have the needed funds in your bank account back home). This method is much less expensive than either buying traveler's checks (which often are not as widely accepted as their ads imply) or converting your money (or traveler's checks) into foreign currency. Exchange rates offered by credit card companies are usually the most competitive, and their service charges are lower than fees you will pay at foreign banks. *The most expensive place to convert currency is at an airport or train station.*
- If you are assessed a late payment fee or over-the-limit fee, call and ask to have it removed. If the card company refuses, tell them you plan to cancel this card unless they credit you for this charge.

Debit Cards

Debit cards look like credit cards and can be used in ATMs if you have a personal identification number (PIN). With debit cards, the purchase is immediately subtracted from your checking account balance.

If you report a lost debit card within 48 hours, your liability is capped at $50. After the second day, your liability increases to $500 and remains at that amount for the next 58 days. After 60 days your liability is unlimited. What does this mean? If you fail to report your lost debit card for more than two months, you could lose all the money in your checking account plus all the money in a savings account when you connect the savings account to your checking account to provide overdraft protection. And if you have a home equity loan that deposits money in your checking

Hot Tip

Try to restrict trips to the ATM to once a week; try not to use another bank's ATM.

account when your balance goes below a certain minimum, a thief with your ATM card could withdraw the entire balance of your home equity loan. You would have to repay the loan or lose your house.

Before a financial institution gives you an ATM or debit card, it will ask you to select a PIN number. Avoid using typical numbers like your birth date, address, or part of your Social Security number. When the bank hands you a debit card, it often comes enclosed in a paper sheath. You should know not to write your PIN number on the sheath, but many people do. Thieves love them for it.

Fees associated with using your debit card may be higher than charges for writing checks. Using an ATM is certainly convenient, but for many people an ATM is the hole in their financial system through which money just disappears. Have you ever had no real sense of where the cash you recently received from the ATM went? Are your monthly ATM fees usually in double digits?

Your Credit Card Registry

Make a record of all your credit cards so if a card is lost or stolen, you have the needed information.

Account number: _____ Issuer (Visa, etc.) _____

If lost or stolen, call: 800-_____ Credit limit: _____

Who signs on the account? _____

Too often we only look for ways to save large sums of money. Well, small amounts saved fairly often can grow into large sums. Banks and credit unions that have fewer fees than their competition can translate into a significant amount of money over time. One of the keys of becoming financially fit is finding ways to save a little each month. How you use your credit card accounts can make a definite financial difference.

Hot Tip

Web site www.NCFE.org has a great deal of helpful consumer information about credit and credit card use. If you still have questions not answered in this chapter, check this Web site.

Financial Checkup Checklist

- Cut up all but two credit cards.

- If you do not pay off your balance in full each month, find a card with an APR lower than 14 percent.

- Make sure your card offers a grace period.

- Make all purchases with a credit card if there's a chance you may have problems with the product or service after the purchase.

8 Examine Your Social Security Account

Check to make sure that the financial data in your file at the Social Security Administration are current.

> Selina arrived late at my office. She seemed tired, even exhausted. I had never met her but knew that she had spent 30 years working at night as a janitor. Her health was not good and she wanted to retire. As we visited, she expressed concern that her retirement income from her pension was not going to be enough to live on once she stopped working. She had heard so much negative talk about Social Security that she figured it would not provide her much income. I handed her the Request for Earnings and Benefit Estimate Statement (Form SSA-7004 SM) and asked her to mail it in immediately. A few weeks later, after she received her estimate statement, she called to tell me that Social Security would pay her more each month than her pension.

Currently, Social Security's problems receive a great deal of attention in the press. News articles often imply that Social Security will go broke. The article writers are naive. Social Security is a tax on income just like the federal income tax. Congress will continue to do in the future what it has done for 40 years: raise the Social Security tax rate. Congress uses two strategies to raise revenues from Social Security taxes; it periodically increases the tax rate and raises the amount of income that is taxed.

When people first started paying Social Security taxes in 1937, the tax rate was .005 on the first $3,000 of earned income. So the most anyone paid in Social

Security taxes was $15 ($3,000 × .005). In the 1960s Congress separated Medicare from Social Security; since then each employed person pays both Social Security and Medicare taxes. Although there's a cap on the amount of earned income subject to Social Security, all your earned income is subject to the Medicare tax.

For 1999 you will pay 6.2 percent of your wages in Social Security taxes (wages above $72,600 will not be assessed Social Security taxes) and 1.45 percent of your wages are contributed to Medicare. As you can tell, Social Security taxes have increased dramatically over the past 60 years.

Congress will not allow Social Security to go broke, but it has and will again change benefits. In the 1980s Congress raised the retirement age for every employee born after 1937. Figure 8.1 indicates the age at which you will be eligible for full retirement benefits. Every qualified worker is eligible for reduced benefits once he or she turns 62.

What changes can you expect in the future? Congress will again roll back the retirement age. Expect it to continue to do so every 10 to 15 years. In my opinion,

Figure 8.1 The Age at Which You Will Be Eligible for Full Social Security Retirement Benefits

Year of Your Birth	Age When Eligible Year	Month
Before 1938	65	
1938	65	2
1939	65	4
1940	65	6
1941	65	8
1942	65	10
1943–54	66	0
1955	66	2
1956	66	4
1957	66	6
1958	66	8
1959	66	10
1960 and after	67	0

those born after 1980 are unlikely to be eligible for full retirement benefits unless they live well into their 70s.

At some future date, I expect Congress to base all Social Security retirement benefits on the criterion of need. In other words, if your income during retirement is above a certain limit, you will receive reduced Social Security benefits or no benefits at all.

Obtaining a Record of Your Benefits

Thanks to Dorcas Hardy, who served as the commissioner of the Social Security Administration during the 1980s, you can obtain a record of the Social Security taxes you have paid as well as an estimate of the Social Security benefits you are expected to be eligible to receive. To check on your Social Security account, obtain a Request for Earnings and Benefit Estimate Statement (Form SSA-7004-SM). You can phone 800-772-1213 to receive a copy of the form or go to the Social Security Web site (www.ssa.gov) to process the form.

After you complete the form, you will receive your Personal Earnings and Benefit Estimate Statement. You will need your benefit statement before you can complete your disability analysis (discussed in Chapter 11), your life insurance analysis (discussed in Chapter 12), and your retirement needs analysis (discussed in Chapter 13).

Your benefit statement has two parts.

Your Social Security Earnings Record

You should receive a chart that shows your earnings from the first year that you were employed. Your statement will not show any earnings from the current year and may not yet show your earnings from the year before. If your earnings records do not agree with what is printed on your statement, contact the Social Security Administration at 800-537-7005. However, you can only make corrections on your earnings records for the last three years.

Your Estimated Social Security Benefits

The Social Security Administration has estimated three types of benefits for you: future retirement benefits, disability, and survivor. Estimated benefits are a function of the amount of taxes you pay each year, the number of years you have paid taxes, and the number of dependents you have. In calculating estimated retirement benefits, Social Security personnel assume that your future earnings record will be similar to your income history. These estimates are in today's dollars. For example, Luise is 40 years old, and the Social Security Administration estimates that when Luise turns 62 and is eligible for reduced retirement benefits, he should receive

$650 a month were he to retire then. However, because of inflation, by Luise's 62nd birthday, his actual monthly payments are likely to be more than twice as much as today's $650 estimate.

Retirement benefits. Benefits are defined for three retirement options:

1. Retiring at age 62 (lowest benefit)
2. Retiring at the earliest age you can to receive maximum benefits (somewhere between your 65th and 67th birthday)
3. Retiring at an age you select

> **Hot Tip**
>
> **D**ivorced? If you were married a minimum of ten years before your divorce, you should be eligible to receive retirement benefits that are 50 percent of your divorced spouse's benefits or 100 percent of your own, whichever is larger.

If you're married when you retire, your spouse has a choice of benefits: 50 percent of your benefits or 100 percent of his or her own benefits. (He or she selects the larger of the two.)

Notice that your retirement benefits increase as you grow older. Someone with a Social Security earnings record similar to yours will receive monthly Social Security payments nearly twice as large if he or she defers retirement until age 70 compared with retiring at age 62. At what age should you retire? I explore that issue in Chapter 13.

Disability benefits. To qualify for disability benefits, your disability must be expected to last at least one year or result in your death. A disabled person must wait six months before benefits start. However, most disabled individuals apply two or three times before Social Security agrees to pay disability benefits. Many disabled persons have found it necessary to hire attorneys to appeal Social Security's rejection of their claim in order to receive benefits.

Disability benefits provided by your employer are probably merged with Social Security. For example, Loraine's employer's disability insurance policy promises to pay her $1,600 a month. If Social Security were to pay $1,200 a month, her employer's policy would only pay Loraine $400 (the difference between the $1,200 paid by Social Security and the $1,600 promised by the insurance policy).

Survivor benefits. These benefits are a function of the number of dependents you leave at your death. Children receive benefits until they graduate from high school or have their 19th birthday, whichever occurs first. A surviving spouse will receive benefits if his or her wages are less than $10,000 and one dependent child is younger than 16. For every $2 that the spouse earns above $10,000 ($9,600 in 1999), his or her Social Security benefits will be reduced by $1. When the youngest child turns 16, spousal benefits stop until the spouse turns 60.

Unlike most insurance programs, Social Security benefits are indexed to inflation. The annual increase in payments that occurs each January is tied to price increases experienced during the previous year. This cost-of-living adjustment (COLA) is an important benefit paid for by your tax dollars.

Hot Tip

Medicare provides extremely limited coverage for anyone staying in a nursing home.

Medicare

As your Social Security benefit statement points out, Medicare hospital and medical insurance is a two-part program that helps pay your medical bills. Part A helps pay for hospital costs, and Part B pays part of the expenses occurred when you visit a doctor. Several months before your 65th birthday, visit the nearest Social Security office and complete the forms necessary to apply for Medicare. *You must apply for Medicare at 65 no matter when you plan to retire.* Medicare will cover you once you have applied even if you continue employment after 65. You must pay monthly premiums to receive Medicare benefits.

Reduced Social Security Benefits for Employed Retirees

If you elect to start receiving Social Security benefits once you retire but before you celebrate your 70th birthday, your Social Security benefits will be reduced as follows if you continue to work and your income exceeds the following limits:

- For those under 65: $1 for every $2 you earn above $9,600 for 1999. (This earnings limit is indexed to inflation and adjusted on January 1 of each year.)
- For those from 65 through 69: $1 for every $3 you earn above $15,500 for 1999. For example, Jackie applied for Social Security benefits when he turned 65; however, Jackie continued to work. Jackie is eligible to receive $8,000 from Social Security in 1999 were he not employed.

Hot Tip

This earnings limitation or cap rises dramatically over the next three years as follows:

2000	$17,000
2001	$25,000
2002	$30,000

However, since he expects to earn $18,200 from his job, his Social Security benefits will be reduced by $900 in 1999.

Here is how Jackie's Social Security reduction is calculated:

Jackie earned	$18,200
Less: 1999 earnings limit	(15,500)
Excess earnings	2,700

Jackie's Social Security income is reduced by one-third of his excess earnings or $900 ($2,700 × .333), so Jackie's Social Security check will be $7,100 (8,000 − 900). After Jackie turns 70, his Social Security benefits will not be reduced if he is still employed.

Taxation of Social Security Benefits

Social Security benefits are not included in gross income unless adjusted gross income exceeds certain limits. If you're *single,* 50 percent of your Social Security benefits will be taxed if your adjusted gross income is above $25,000; and 85 percent of your Social Security income will be taxed if your adjusted gross income is above $34,000. If you're *married,* 50 percent of your Social Security benefits will be taxed if your adjusted gross income is above $32,500; and 85 percent of your Social Security income will be taxed if your adjusted gross income is above $44,000.

Social Security will always be controversial. No one can predict changes in the Social Security system, but it will never disappear. To make sure that you get the benefits you deserve, request your estimated earnings statement from Social Security every three years.

> **Hot Tip**
>
> If you are retired and your non–Social Security income is close to the specified limits, ask an income tax professional, such as a certified public accountant or an enrolled agent, to prepare your tax return. In some cases, married couples would pay less in income taxes if they divorced.

✓ Financial Checkup Checklist

- Order your Social Security Earnings and Benefit Estimate Statement.

9 Maximize Your Employee Benefits

Make sure that you are taking full advantage of all financial benefits offered by your employer.

> Zoe and Ralph, both in their middle 40s, were concerned about financing their retirement. They had a right to worry. Neither had put away any money for retirement. Neither expected an inheritance. Yet when I asked how much they wanted when they retired, both seemed to agree on $50,000 annually (in today's dollars). Each was hoping to retire after celebrating their 62nd birthday. I asked what type of retirement plans their employers offered. They said that both employers had set up 401(k) plans. Each employer would match employee's contributions 50 cents on the dollar. Had Zoe and Ralph each contributed $3,000 a year to a 401(k) plan, their employers would have donated $1,500 to each 401(k) account in their name. Why, I wanted to know, were they not contributing?

Too many employees do not appreciate or take advantage of the benefits available from their employers. Employers share some of the blame. Too many employers do a poor job of explaining what benefits they offer. Benefits are rarely explained from a financial planning perspective. Benefit personnel seem to be well versed on how benefits work but often are not trained to help employees understand how each benefit could help. Are you taking full advantage of all the benefits offered by your employer?

Let's examine some of these benefits in greater detail.

120 FINANCIAL FITNESS FOR LIFE

Employee Benefits Worksheet

Which of the following benefits does your employer offer?

1. _____ A defined benefit retirement plan. Benefits at retirement are a function of your average annual salary for the three or five highest-salary years weighted by total years of service.

2. _____ A defined contribution retirement plan. Benefits available at retirement are usually a function of the dollars you and your employer contribute to the plan each year. Popular defined contribution plans include 401(k)s, 403(b)s, and profit-sharing plans.

3. _____ A stock purchase plan. You are allowed to buy company stock at a discount.

4. _____ Health insurance coverage. Rates vary depending on your family status—single, married with children, single parent, for example—and on the type of plan.

5. _____ Disability coverage. Your employer may offer separate policies for the short term (less than six months) and for the long term (till you retire).

6. _____ Legal services (legal consulting as well as modest fees to pay for drafting a will, adoption, etc.).

7. _____ Auto insurance (may or may not be less expensive than buying a separate policy).

8. _____ Accidental death. Decline it; you don't need extra coverage if you die in an accident.

9. _____ Life insurance: often some multiple of your salary. If you are younger than 40, you may be able to buy a separate policy more cheaply.

Employee Benefits Worksheet
(continued)

10. _____ Vacation pay.

11. _____ Sick pay.

12. _____ Tuition reimbursement.

13. _____ Child care at work. Chances are you must pay most or all of the fees, but the convenience makes this benefit attractive—especially if the facility can care for a sick child.

14. _____ Flextime. Do you have a choice of the hours you work each day?

15. _____ Long-term care insurance coverage. This is a new benefit that progressive employers are offering.

16. _____ Financial planning. All employers should provide this service so that employees would make better use, and be more appreciative, of employer-provided benefits. Benefits include education workshops, one-on-one counseling, software, an 800-number question line, and written financial plans.

The value of these benefits may add another 25 to 40 percent to your basic salary. A growing number of employers offer benefits packages popularly known as cafeteria plans. Employees are offered a fixed dollar amount that each employee can spend on employer-provided benefits. Employees select the benefits they want. Usually, there is not enough money to buy all the benefits the employee wants, so the employee pays part of the cost of the benefit package.

Retirement Plans

You have little chance of adequately funding your retirement unless your employer contributes to a retirement account in your name. What is really important is the percentage of your annual salary that your employer contributes. A growing number of firms are deciding not to offer both defined benefit and defined contribution plans. Check Chapter 13 for an explanation of the plans discussed here if you need to. Contact your benefits office so you can answer the following questions:

- What percentage of your salary is contributed to a defined benefit plan?
- What percentage of your salary is contributed to a defined contribution plan, such as a 401(k)?

One way to rate your employer is by the percentage of your salary contributed to your retirement plan account(s) by the employer. Your employer may offer a pension plan, a 401(k) plan, and a stock purchase plan; be sure to add all retirement contributions made by the employer before checking the chart shown below.

Percent Contributed	*Evaluation of Employer*
Less than 4%	Stingy
4% to 7%	Inadequate
8% to 10%	Acceptable
Above 10%	Generous

If your firm is contributing less than 4 percent of your salary to your retirement plan(s), you will have a difficult time accumulating the nest egg you'll need to fund your retirement. While your employer's contributions are only one factor when evaluating your satisfaction with your job, it is an important one that you cannot ignore.

Investing the Dollars in Your Retirement Account

Both employees and employers contribute to most retirement plans. You will not make investment decisions for the funds in your defined benefit pension since such pension benefits are strictly a function of the number of years you work for your employer and your salary level. However, you are highly likely to be responsible for deciding how funds are invested in your defined contribution plans—(401(k) and a profit-sharing plan, for example.

You probably have the option to invest in one or more of the following three investment alternatives: (1) annuities, (2) shares of your company's stock, and/or (3) mutual funds.

Reject all annuity options if you have other choices. (I will explain why in Chapter 16.) Shares in your employer's company can be an attractive option if you

Figure 9.1 Mutual Funds That Invest in the S&P 500

Dreyfus S&P 500	800-645-6561
Fidelity Spartan	800-544-8888
INVESCO S&P 500	800-424-8085
Schwab S&P 500	800-266-5623
Scudder S&P 500	800-225-2470
Strong Index 500	800-359-3379
T. Rowe Price Equity Index	800-638-5660
Vanguard 500 Portfolio	800-662-7447
USAA S&P 500 Index	800-382-8722

would be interested in investing in the company were you not an employee. Most people should not invest more than 25 percent of their retirement money in their employer's company. For most people, mutual funds are the best alternative and are discussed in greater detail in Chapter 15.

Mutual Funds

Your employer will provide you with a list identifying as few as three mutual fund investment options or as many as several hundred. If you do not have the time or the investment expertise to explore all the options, I hope the following choice is on your list. Check to see if you can invest in an *index* mutual fund that invests in the companies of the Standard and Poor's 500 (S&P 500) index or the Wilshire 5000 index. Below is a list of some of the more popular mutual funds that do invest in the S&P 500. If none of these funds are on your list, look for another fund with the word *index* in its name. Call the mutual fund company and ask if it invests in the S&P 500. If your employer does not include an index fund as an investment option, ask to have one added to the list.

125 Plans

These plans are popular because you pay for certain expenses that are subtracted from your income and are not subject to federal income or Social Security taxes.

Are you able to pay for your health insurance premiums with before-tax dollars? If you can, taxes are computed on your income after health insurance premiums have been paid. For example, Ilene's gross monthly income is $3,000; her employer charges her $300 a month for health insurance that covers her spouse, her children, and herself. Ilene is only taxed on $2,700. Paying her health insurance premiums with pretax dollars will save her at least $70 a month in federal taxes (Social Security and income). If your employer does not offer this benefit, known as *premium conversion,* recommend that you be given this option for paying your health insurance premiums.

Flexible Spending Accounts

Flexible spending accounts enable employees to spend untaxed income to pay for medical and dependent care expenses with dollars that have not had federal income and Social Security taxes withheld. There are actually two separate accounts, health care and dependent care.

If your employer offers such a plan, you can have money withheld from your paycheck that is contributed to a medical reimbursement account. This is how it works: Jamie, whose gross income is $2,000 a month, contributes $100 a month to a medical reimbursement account. Each month Jamie is not taxed on the $100, thus saving $15 a month in federal income tax. Jamie also saves nearly $8 in Social Security taxes. Suppose Jamie has a medical bill for $300 that is not covered by her employer's medical insurance. She sends the medical invoice to the firm handling her medical reimbursement account. The firm sends Jamie $300. Jamie can be reimbursed up to the amount she will contribute to the medical reimbursement account over a 12-month period. In this example, Jamie can be reimbursed for up to $1,200 in medical bills.

Two drawbacks exist to medical reimbursement accounts, however. First, Jamie must spend the entire $1,200 during the 12-month period; any dollars not used to reimburse Jamie for medical expenses

> **Hot Tip**
>
> Every dollar contributed to a dependent care reimbursement account reduces the dependent care credit offered by the Internal Revenue Service (IRS). Lower-income workers are better off taking the IRS's dependent care credit; higher-income persons (adjusted gross income in excess of $24,000) will find the dependent care reimbursement account more attractive. Compute the savings both ways or ask your tax preparer for advice.

are lost to her. Second, Jamie will probably be eligible for slightly less in Social Security benefits as she is not paying Social Security taxes on $100 of her monthly income.

The dependent care reimbursement account works much like the medical reimbursement account. It covers costs incurred caring for dependents, such as children under the age of 13 or elderly parents whom you claim as dependents when you file your federal income tax return.

If your company does not offer either the medical or the dependent care reimbursement account, ask your employer to consider offering such accounts. Employers benefit by being able to reduce what they pay in Social Security taxes.

> **Hot Tip**
>
> The maximum contribution anyone can make to a dependent care reimbursement account is $5,000. It is against federal law to be reimbursed for dependent care expenses if you do not pay Social Security taxes on wages earned when the caregiver works in your home.

Before you accept any new position, carefully check out the benefits offered. A higher salary from one firm that offers few benefits may offer less total compensation than another firm that offers a more attractive package of benefits.

Insurance

You may be spending more than 10 percent of your take-home pay on insurance; after all, you probably need the following policies:

- Life
- Health
- Disability
- Auto
- Homeowners or renters
- Dental

You may need an umbrella and a long-term care policy as well.

Your employer has access to policies that are usually less expensive than indi-

> **Hot Tip**
>
> Any time you discontinue working for an employer, you have the right to continue your health insurance for 18 months. However, your former employer can require you to pay 100 percent of the health care premiums (which may be dramatically more than you paid as an employee).

vidual policies; and such group policies usually offer better coverage. While you may want to take advantage of most coverages offered by your employer, you may want to reject one or more of the following benefits:

- *Accidental death.* Your beneficiaries do not need extra cash because you died as the result of an accident. Make sure you have enough traditional life insurance but decline accidental death.
- *Life insurance.* You may be surprised to see this listed here. Life insurance offered by your employer may be far more expensive than a separate policy you buy. This is almost always true if you are younger than 40, and the premium is the same for each employee regardless of age. Far too often, premiums are too high; the insurance company thinks they can get away with such costly premiums because employees are a captive audience.
- *Short-term disability.* If you have to pay for this benefit, check to see how many sick days you have accumulated. It makes no sense to have $30 a month withheld from your paycheck to purchase a three-month, short-term disability policy when you have accumulated 70 days of sick pay.

> **Hot Tip**
>
> Insurance policies at work are rarely portable. In other words, when you change jobs, you lose the coverage. Before you say goodbye to your present employer, make sure your new employer offers similar coverages, or consider getting a personal policy.

Vacation and Sick Pay

Some employers now combine vacation and sick pay. You need to answer two questions:

1. How many hours of vacation and sick pay are you eligible for each year?
2. Can you carry sick pay or vacation hours that you do not use this year over to the next year?

Many employers who let you accumulate vacation and sick days cap those hours, forcing you to use or lose the hours. The bottom line is to keep track of the hours you use for both vacation and sick time. Before the close of your employer's year, check to make sure your records agree with your employer's.

Educational Benefits

Chapter 20 focuses on keeping your career on the cutting edge. Before accepting any employment offer, find out about the firm's education reimbursement policy. Education benefits fall into four categories:

1. *College degrees (undergraduate and graduate).* How much financial support does the employer offer?
2. *Certification.* So many certifications have sprung up lately that there's probably one for you. How much of the expenses needed to earn the certification will your employer pay?
3. *Continuing education.* Once you become certified, you must earn so many hours of continuing education each year. Will the employer pay for these courses, including books and tuition?
4. *Skill enhancement.* Everyone's job is constantly changing. Will your employer pay the bill to send you to courses so you can update your skills?

Quality-of-Life Benefits

Is your company family friendly? Your answers to the following questions will enable you to decide if your company is.

- Does it have on-site child care? If it does, is this a service available to most employees or just a token effort? The length of the waiting list is the real test. If you need to reserve a place in the child care center before conception, your firm is not really serious about this benefit.
- Are you allowed to work at home? Given the hectic nature of most work environments, many times employees can get far more work done at home in less time. Traditional employers resist letting employees work at home because of fear that the employees won't work. Fortunately, a period of enlightenment may be on the horizon. Some employers are starting to pay employees for what they accomplish instead of the hours they keep.
- Are you offered flextime? Given your family demands as well as traffic congestion, you need to be able to select when your workday starts and ends.
- Can you take time off to take your child to the doctor or watch your child perform in a school activity? Too many employers for too long have been insensitive about this issue. One wonders if the owners of such firms were ever parents.

I have heard all the excuses employers use to try and explain why they are not able to offer family-friendly benefits. When confronted on this issue, I refer them to any list of the best 100 firms to work for. The vast majority are considered family-friendly firms (FFF).

Annual Benefit Statement

Several weeks after the end of their business year, many firms send an individual statement to each employee that shows the employee's benefits provided by the firm. This statement focuses on the benefits programs in which the employee has enrolled. For example, it may indicate what your monthly disability benefit would be, the balance in your retirement account, and the number of vacation and sick days that you have accumulated. Unfortunately, many employers do not see the advantage of generating such an annual statement. Often, the statement generated by firms is not comprehensive. Employers spend thousands on each employee's benefits but have no interest in generating a benefits statement that could cost them no more than $2 or $3 per employee to produce.

Too often, too many employees fail to understand or appreciate the benefits provided by their employers. Too many employers do a poor job educating employees about using their benefits. Take full advantage of the benefits you are now offered before requesting benefits not yet available.

Financial Checkup Checklist

- Determine the percentage of your gross salary that your employer contributes to a retirement plan for you.

- Review every benefit offered by your employer, and enroll in any that would benefit you.

- Review the investment options provided by your employer's retirement plan(s) and switch investments as appropriate.

- If you are currently not making maximum contributions to the retirement plan, increase the percentage withheld from your paycheck by at least 1 percent annually.

- Carefully review the last annual benefit statement provided by your employer.

10 Update Your Auto and Property Insurance

Evaluate your auto and property insurance, improving coverage and reducing premiums.

I made it through the maze of hospital corridors and reached Wing Suet's office at about the time her husband Chun arrived. I was glad to see him. Physicians are so busy that I rely on their spouses to handle much of the work involved in implementing the financial tasks I assign. During my first visit with a client, I like to review his or her insurance policies. If a sound insurance program is not in place, all the rest of the planning and implementing can be for naught if a major problem occurs that should be covered by insurance. While reviewing the Suets' auto policy, I was surprised to discover that a young surgeon earning $300,000 a year had only the state's required minimum liability coverage. I explained the problem to the doctor and her husband and asked them to call their agent right then and increase their coverage. I could just see Wing Suet involved in a car accident. Some court might decide she was the responsible party and award the defendant $500,000 or even more in damages.

We are all risk takers. Risk is a part of every aspect of our life. Much of our success depends on how well we handle the risks we encounter. The risk is minimal that you will drown in your bathtub, but every year a few people do. The risk is much greater that your home will be burglarized while you are at school or work. Auto accidents are so common that someone you know is likely to be hurt or die in an auto accident this year. Tens of thousands will fall victim to cancer or have a heart attack before this year ends. This year, and every year hereafter, many people will lose large sums when their investments fail to perform as expected. This chapter discusses how to manage the financial risks involved in owning and operating a motor vehicle and in insuring your home and property.

Coverages in Your Auto Policy

Find your auto policy; locate the declaration page (the invoice); and evaluate the adequacy of each coverage. Liability coverage is stated two ways: single limit and split limits. If Jack has single-limit coverage, he may have $50,000 in liability protection. Jack's liability coverage is more likely to be stated as 20/40/25 (split limits), meaning the maximum that Jack's policy would pay for medical bills for one person that he hurt with his vehicle is $20,000; the most his insurance company will pay for medical bills for everyone he hurt in one accident is $40,000 (Jack's liability coverage will not cover the medical bills of his immediate family members); and the maximum his insurance company will pay for property damage to other cars or to other peoples' property caused by Jack's vehicle in one accident is $25,000. Suppose that Jack is responsible for an accident in which he destroys a new Toyota Camry, and the passengers in the Camry have the following medical bills: Elizabeth, $18,000; Sherri, $24,000; and Tom $15,000.

	Claims	Jack's Policy Pays	Additional $ That Jack Owes
Medical bills:			
Elizabeth	$18,000		
Sherri	24,000		
Tom	15,000		
Total	$57,000	$40,000	$17,000
Camry	$22,000	$15,000	$ 7,000
Total Claims	$79,000		
Insurance pays		$55,000	
Jack owes			$24,000

How will the injured collect the $24,000 still owed them by Jack? They are likely to sue Jack. If the judge or jury decides against Jack, liens will be placed on property he owns, such as bank accounts, his car, and his house. In most states, but not Texas, his wages are likely to be garnished to collect the judgment.

Collision insurance covers damages that occur to the car when it is moving and impacts another vehicle, a tree, a fence, or rolls over. *Comprehensive insurance* covers damages to the vehicle that usually occur when the car is stationary, such as vandalism (broken window) or theft or damages that result from an earthquake, water, hail, or a windstorm.

Do you need collision and comprehensive coverage? Do you drive an older car that is paid for? Consider dropping both collision and comprehensive (also known as other than collision) if you could not sell your car for more than $4,000. If your car is destroyed, the most you will receive from any insurance company is the car's retail (book) value. An insurance company will usually subtract the salvage value of the car (usually 20 percent of the car's value before the wreck) from the car's book value before it cuts you a check. It is rarely cost-effective to pay $150 or more a year for any insurance on the slight chance that you might collect $3,000 from an insurance company.

Hot Tip

Your auto insurer only covers you and your car in the United States and Canada—not Mexico!

Medical coverage in an auto policy: Are you covered on someone else's medical policy, or do you have your own medical policy? If you have excellent health insurance, any medical coverage duplicates coverages you already have. Medical coverage included in an auto policy only covers expenses associated with an auto accident. If you are covered under an excellent health insurance policy, consider dropping the medical coverage in your auto policy. If you do not have excellent medical insurance, get it immediately. The amount of medical coverage provided in most auto policies is limited.

Personal injury protection (PIP) is disability insurance plus the same medical coverage discussed above. You may not need PIP. If you are not employed or if you have excellent disability and medical insurance elsewhere, consider dropping PIP, although you may not be able to drop it in some states. In other states, such as Texas, you can carry both medical insurance and PIP. If you have both, drop one as you do not need both.

Uninsured motorist coverage may pay for medical bills, rehabilitation expenses, and/or a funeral if an uninsured motorist hurts you or a passenger in your car or if you are struck by a hit-and-run driver. This may be duplicate coverage *if* you already have excellent health insurance for your family. However, uninsured motorist insurance also provides "pain and suffering" coverage. For example, Julia's uninsured motorist coverage is $20,000. An unin-

Hot Tip

Carry liability coverage equal to twice your net worth or five times your gross income, whichever is higher.

sured motorist hit Julia when she was crossing the street. Her medical bills came to $12,000. How much will she receive for "pain and suffering"? She still has $8,000 in coverage that she has not used; but her pain and suffering may be significantly more than that amount. However, her insurance company is the one that will decide how much to compensate her for pain and suffering. If Julia asks to be compensated for her pain and suffering, her insurance company will probably pay her less than $1,000.

Uninsured motorist-property damage insurance is collision coverage for your car if it's hit by an uninsured motorist. This coverage probably duplicates the previously discussed collision coverage. If you have both, ask your agent to explain under what circumstances uninsured motorist-property damage coverage would pay you when your collision coverage would not. Uninsured motorist-property damage insurance should duplicate your collision coverage, but it is not as good as your collision coverage, which pays when your car is damaged no matter who's responsible for the damage. Uninsured motorist coverage only pays if an uninsured motorist damages your property.

Towing/emergency road service coverage is usually low (less than $50), but it will pay for a short tow, part of a more expensive tow, or jump-starting a dead battery. Usually this coverage is less than $5 a year and is must coverage on older cars.

Rental car coverage pays about $15 to $20 a day. It's not recommended unless you have only one car in your household and don't live near public transportation.

Saving Money on Auto Insurance

Whom do insurance companies least like to insure? A single male under the age of 25 who has roommates, drives a sports car, has received tickets, has been involved in at-fault accidents, and wants only mini-

> **Hot Tip**
>
> You can save money on your auto insurance by increasing the deductibles. Your premiums may drop by 10 to 20 percent if you increase your deductible from $100 to $250, $500, or higher.

> **Hot Tip**
>
> Insurance agents don't like clients to drop any coverage because they are afraid they may be liable if a client has a claim but lacks proper insurance coverage. Before dropping any coverage, explain to your agent what you plan to do and why. If the agent disagrees with what you want to do, call your state's department of insurance and ask for its opinion about your planned changes in coverage.

mum coverage. Males between the ages of 16 and 25 have far more accidents than any other group. Girls in that age group have more accidents per miles driven but drive significantly less than do males.

You can reduce what you now pay for auto insurance by focusing on these three areas:

1. The car you drive
2. How the insurance company rates you
3. The insurance company that sells you coverage

> **Hot Tip**
>
> The cheapest way to insure someone under age 25 is to add him or her as an occasional driver to an older model, large car that is not registered to the under-25 driver. Any time a single male under the age of 25 owns his own car, rates will be expensive.

The car you drive. Before you buy your next car remember that sports cars, especially convertibles, are expensive to insure. Instead, consider a car with antilock brakes, air bags, antitheft devices, and automatic seat belts. Finally, check with an insurance company to compare rates before buying your next car. Cars with a history of lower repair costs are much less expensive to insure.

How the insurance company rates you. You will want to remember some of the following bits of information about car insurance rates:

- Tickets and accidents during the past five years dramatically raise premiums.
- Rates may drop when you turn 21 (if you are a girl) and especially 25 (for guys) if you have a driving record free from tickets and accidents; rates are much lower for younger women than for their male counterparts.
- Rates should drop for married males.
- Rates in some states, such as Texas, are lower if you complete a defensive driving class.
- You may be offered lower rates for good grades in school.

> **Hot Tip**
>
> When comparison shopping, ask if the insurance company pays policyholders dividends at the end of the policy year. A policyholder may receive dividends if the company's losses are much smaller than expected. Factor in expected dividends when comparing premiums.

- You may be offered lower rates if you do not smoke or drink. This is often a meaningless gimmick to trick you into thinking the company offers lower rates when it doesn't.
- You will pay lower rates in most states if you don't drive your car to and from work (or drive less than 7,000 miles a year).

Ask for a multicar discount when you and your family insure more than one car with the same company. You may qualify for a discount if you insure your house and car with the same company. And you can save 15 to 20 percent or more if you pay premiums once a year, not monthly or quarterly.

> **Hot Tip**
>
> The premium you pay is calculated in part on the basis of where you garage your car. If you move from the city to the country or to a different town, let your insurance company know your new address. If you fail to do so and are responsible for an accident, the company may cancel your policy.

The insurance company that sells you coverage. Rates from different companies can vary by more than 300 percent for identical coverage. Since you pay insurance year after year, savings really add up. You will usually receive more competitive quotes from local agents when you visit their offices than when you call for quotes. Before you arrive for your appointment, clean and wash the car; dress as you would for a job interview. Get quotes from at least three different companies. Companies can use 30 or 40 variables when calculating your rate. Call your state's department of insurance to see if it has information about rates.

If you have celebrated your 25th birthday, are married, have a clean driving record (no tickets or at-fault accidents during the last five years), live in town, and drive a sensible car, check these Web sites and call the following 800 numbers to see if they offer lower rates before you renew a policy.

Insweb	www.insweb.com (You can find quotes for auto, home, health, etc.)
Insurance News Network	www.insure.com (You can find current news articles on a range of insurance topics as well as links to sites where you can get auto, home, health, etc. quotes.)
Amica	800-242-6422
American Express	800-842-3344
Geico	800-841-3000
USAA	800-531-8080 (active duty, or child of military parent)

✓ Financial Checkup Checklist

- After reviewing your current coverage, request quotes from three companies (your current insurer plus two other companies).

Although auto insurance can be costly, the real issue is whether you have the proper amount of coverage. No coverage is more important than liability. You can't afford the financial risk of driving a car if you don't have adequate insurance protection.

Property Coverage

I could tell that Denise and Michael were angry and upset. Last night their freshman son Tim called from college to tell them that someone had broken into his room and stolen his new computer system, CD player, TV, and VCR. Michael estimated that it would cost him at least $4,000 to replace all these items. I asked the couple if they had proof that Tim actually owned these items. Denise replied that she and Michael had purchased these items for Tim a couple of months before he left for college and she still had the receipts. Denise and Michael seemed somewhat relieved when I told them that their homeowners policy would cover most of the loss.

Various coverages found in the typical homeowners or renters policy are discussed in this section. The major difference between the two is that a homeowner must also insure the house. Owner and renter policies both insure personal items and provide medical and liability coverage.

You have two types of property: real and personal. Real property is permanently attached to the earth. Personal property is portable, such as a VCR or CD player. Your house is real property, as is a bookshelf if it is attached to a wall, floor, or ceiling. An identical bookshelf would be personal property if it were not attached. Your policy covers personal items that are lost, destroyed, or stolen whether you are at home or away.

Personal items such as your television or computer are traditionally insured for what you could get if you sold them "as is" (a concept also referred to as "actual cash value"). When discussing insuring your property (real or personal), the key concept is "replacement cost." You want to replace the missing item with a new one. The check from the insurance company will be large enough to buy a new item if you insure your possessions at their *replacement cost*, not their actual cash value. Does this sound a little like trading in an old lamp for a new one? Well, there is a string attached. Because you must prove you owned the missing item, do the following:

- Record the serial number of each major item on the purchase receipt.
- Staple this receipt on the warranty card or booklet before putting it in your Guarantee/Warranties folder.
- Take photos of expensive items. Better yet, make your own video of the items. Keep one copy at work and put the other in a safe place away from home. Make the video a talkie; explain when and what you paid for expensive items. Update the video annually. If you don't have access to a video camera, make a list of your possessions in each room. Include the cost to replace each item and store the list in a fireproof safe.
- Engrave your driver's license number on the back of expensive items if it won't decrease their value. (Put the initials of your state first.) The police will need your driver's license number to find you if your stolen items are recovered. Sometimes items are recovered in a different state.

When your property is lost, stolen, or destroyed the insurance company will reimburse you for the amount of your loss less your deductible. For example, Melanie made sure that she had replacement cost coverage on her personal items. Melanie's deductible is $100. She lost a $300 coat. The insurance company sent Melanie a check for $200 ($300 less the $100 deductible).

Hot Tip

If you have anything of value (especially items that appreciate in value), such as jewelry, prints, paintings, coins, or collections, ask your insurance agent if the loss of these items is covered on your policy. Most policies limit such coverage (especially for jewelry and coin and stamp collections). You must ask to have additional protection, called a *rider* or *floater*, added to your policy. A rider will increase the amount of coverage you have. For example, Sidney owns expensive jewelry worth $10,000. Her basic policy covers only $500 of jewelry, so she asks her agent to add a rider to the policy increasing the coverage on jewelry to $10,000. In Denise and Michael's case, they had increased the coverage limits in their policy. Had they not done so, in most states the insurance company would have paid significantly less than 50 percent of their loss. Send your agent a detailed list of each valuable item you own and include a photo of each one. Some insurance companies require the installation of a burglar alarm and/or an appraisal before they will insure valuable personal items.

If you own any expensive items, you or your insurance company may want them appraised. Keep the appraisal in the same folder with receipts and warranties. Do not use appraisers whose fee is a percentage of the item appraised. If you cannot locate a reputable appraiser contact:

American Society of Appraisers   800-272-8258
P.O. Box 17265   www.appraisers.org
Washington, DC 20041

Appraisers Association of America 212-889-5404
386 Park Ave., South
Suite 2000
New York, NY 10016

Hourly fees range from $50 to $150 an hour. Always ask about minimum fees.

Homeowners Policies

Houses in most states are insured as follows:

- Basic, or HO2, protects you against a limited number of perils.
- Broad, or HO3, provides protection from a broader range of perils.
- Comprehensive, or HO5, insures against the largest number of perils.

Note: In some states, such as Texas, policies are identified as A or B; B is similar to an HO3. The basic policy, known as an HO4 or renters policy, does not cover real property (the apartment itself).

In addition to basic coverage for both real and personal property, liability, medical costs, and loss of use, your policies should also cover the following:

- Plants and trees damaged by fire, lightning, and so forth
- Debris (what is left of your property) that will be removed following a loss
- Reasonable repairs to protect property from further damage

Liability insurance protects you and your property. If your dog bites someone, you are liable. If a teenager hits a golf ball through your window, the teen's parents are liable. If you trip a friend playing handball, you could be responsible for your friend's medical bills. Your homeowners or renters policy's liability coverage will pay for these damages up to your policy's limits. Standard liability coverage is often $25,000. Carry at least $100,000. Remember to obtain liability coverage that is the greater of two times net worth or five times your gross income. The cost of improving your liability coverage on a homeowners or renters policy is usually less than the cost of a meal at your favorite fast-food restaurant.

Medical coverage protects anyone who visits your property except immediate family members who live with you. Check your policy. Chances are the medical coverage is $5,000 or less. Your medical coverage is no-fault, which means that it pays even if the guest is at fault. Medical coverage does not require you to satisfy a deductible before your insurance company pays the guest's medical bills. If it is your fault that someone was seriously hurt when visiting you, your liability coverage takes over after your medical coverage has paid to the limit. For example, Bubba Jones slips on a newly waxed floor in Sal's bathroom and hits his head on the tub. Sal's renters policy has medical coverage up to $2,000. Bubba's bills come to $6,000. Sal's medical policy (on his renters policy) pays the $2,000, and the remaining $4,000 comes from his liability coverage in his renters policy.

Owners Only: *Houses* are usually insured for replacement cost. Owners often do not carry enough coverage. When a person buys a house, the mortgage lender wants it insured for the amount of the loan, so that is the amount most people buy. Unfortunately, the amount of the loan has little or nothing to do with the amount of insurance someone should carry. Ask a builder, "What would it cost to replace this house?" Your insurance company may do a free replacement cost analysis. Ask for a copy of the report. Does the cost to replace the house include complying with changes to the building code since the house was built? It should! The value of the land the house sits on should be excluded from coverage since it cannot be insured. (The value of the land is included in the loan, so many people carry too much coverage.) It probably costs thousands of dollars more to replace the house than what it sold for. Below are several values for the same house.

> **Hot Tip**
>
> Most experts suggest that you do not file small claims with the insurance company that issued your homeowners or renters policy. For example, Jan had a small fire in her kitchen. The repair job cost $300; her deductible was $250. Had she filed the claim, the most she could collect was $50. Unless her agent encourages her to file, she is wiser not to. After two or three claims (of any size), many insurance companies increase your premiums or cancel your policy. Always ask your agent if filing a specific claim will result in the insurance company's taking either action. Taking out a higher deductible reduces the likelihood that you would want to file small claims and also saves you money.

Purchase price	$100,000
Mortgage balance	70,000
Appraised value	80,000
Market value today	120,000
Net equity	50,000 (market value less mortgage balance)
Replacement cost	140,000

This house should be insured for $140,000.

At a minimum, insure your house for at least 80 percent of the cost to replace it. If you don't, the insurance company won't pay 100 percent of any partial loss you may have, such as a fire in the kitchen. You are wise to insure the house for 100 percent of replacement. A trap that you can get caught in if you fail to insure your house for at least 80 percent of the cost to replace it can be seen in this example: Astrid's house would cost $100,000 to replace; she has insured it for $60,000; it should be insured for at least $80,000. She has a $20,000 fire in the kitchen. Her insurance company will determine how much of the fire loss to reimburse her by using the following formula:

$$\frac{\text{Current coverage}}{80\% \text{ of replacement cost}} = \frac{\$60,000}{\$80,000} = .75$$

Multiply the loss by .75 to find out how much the company will pay. In the above example the company will send Astrid a check for $15,000. Since Astrid did not insure her house for at least 80 percent of its replacement cost, the company pays only $15,000 of her loss.

Many older homes are insured for their actual cash value because it would cost too much to insure the house for its replacement cost. If an older house that is insured for its actual cash value is destroyed, the owner may receive enough dollars to buy a similar home in a different location. When a house insured for replacement cost is destroyed, the owner receives the dollars to replace the house on the existing lot.

A city's building code may have been significantly upgraded since your house was built, so you need to make sure your

> **Hot Tip**
>
> You can improve your replacement cost coverage by asking for guaranteed replacement cost coverage. With such coverage, the insurance company may pay up to 50 percent more than the current coverage on your home. If you have only replacement cost, the policy will pay only up to the limits of the coverage. You may not be able to get such coverage if your home is more than 20 years old.

policy includes a "law and ordinance" clause that provides enough money for you to rebuild your home to be in compliance with these higher code standards.

A policy should contain an inflation-guard clause. This policy provision increases the amount of coverage annually on the house as inflation increases the cost to rebuild it.

Double-check to see that you have replacement cost coverage on personal items. Do you own jewelry, computer equipment, camera equipment, guns, collections, art works? Check to make sure that you have adequately insured each item. Do you live away from home for significant periods during the year? Check with your insurance agent before you leave. Make a video tape of what you take with you; leave receipts and serial numbers of valuables like computers, jewelry, and the like with a family member or friend.

> **Warning!!!**
>
> Many insurance companies have basically limited the amount they will pay to replace your house. Often the amount is capped at 125 to 200 percent of the amount that it cost to build it. Your insurance company may have sent you a notice (that you probably did not read) indicating these new limits in your policy. Call your agent today to see how much it would cost to replace your home and to find out if you have adequate coverage.

Coverage for Special Situations

Earthquake insurance. Can anyone afford it? Premiums are high, and the deductible is often $10,000 or 10 percent of the amount of the coverage on the home, whichever is higher. Such coverage is an endorsement added to a homeowners policy except in California where an owner must purchase a separate policy. Expect earthquake coverage to add at least 50 percent to the cost of insuring your home.

Flood insurance. Because a standard homeowners policy does not include coverage for flood damage, you need to be sure that the house's locale has never had a flood. A lot of people in Iowa thought there had

> **Hot Tip**
>
> Every time a home is remodeled, the owner should let the insurance company (and the property tax appraiser) know about the improvements.

never been a flood in their area before the summer of 1993; the people in one part of North Dakota thought the same thing before the spring of 1997. If you need flood insurance, call the National Flood Insurance hot line in Houston, Texas, at 800-638-6620. You can't wait until the flood is lapping at the door to call. There is a 30-day waiting period after the policy is purchased before it becomes effective. A $350 annual premium should buy about $100,000 in protection.

> **Hot Tip**
>
> Ask your agent how much you would save in premium dollars if you increased your deductible. As a minimum, I recommend that your deductible be the larger of $1,000 or 1 percent of the cost to replace the house.

Saving Money on Homeowners and Renters Insurance

New homes receive substantial discounts—from 15 to 30 percent—on insurance premiums. Homes built in the last ten years receive a discount if the owner asks. Brick homes cost about 15 percent less to insure than wood homes. The closer your house is to a highly rated fire department, the lower your premium.

Increase the deductible (the amount you pay when you have a loss) to $1,000 (or 1 percent of the cost to replace the house if that amount is larger). Expect to save 20 to 35 percent of the premium if your current deductible is $100.

Owners may be eligible for a 5 to 20 percent discount if they have

- dead bolt locks;
- burglar alarms;
- smoke detectors;
- sprinklers; and
- fire extinguishers.

Additional tips for saving money on insurance, whether you're a homeowner or a renter, include the following:

- Owners can often save about 15 percent of the premium by insuring both their house and cars with the same company.
- Owners and renters need to ask for discounts if no one in the house smokes.

> **Hot Tip**
>
> Buy fire extinguishers with a metal, not a plastic, head. Plastic heads lose pressure, and the extinguisher cannot be refilled after use.

- Owners should ask for discounts if they stay with the same company for five years or more.
- Ask if the insurer has paid dividends to policyholders in recent years. Find out what it expects to pay this year.
- When you get your next premium notice, contact three other insurance companies and compare rates.

> **Hot Tip**
>
> Owners and renters should always ask, "What discounts do I qualify for?"

Rates of different companies can vary by more than 300 percent. If you're an owner, you may want to compare your rates with those offered by the following companies:

Amica	800-242-6422	www.amica.com
American Express	800-842-3344	www.americanexpress.com

Also check these two Web sites:

Insweb	www.insweb.com (You can find insurance rate quotes for auto, home, health, etc.)
Insurance News Network	www.insure.com (You can find current news articles on a range of insurance topics as well as links to sites where you can get insurance rate quotes.)

> **Hot Tip**
>
> You may need an umbrella liability policy if two times your net worth or five times your gross income is greater than $300,000. An umbrella policy provides liability coverage in million-dollar units. Many people buy a liability policy with coverage of $1 million, $2 million, or $3 million. The deductibles on such policies are large and usually equal the maximum coverage on a basic homeowners or auto policy. For example, Lucy has $300,000 maximum liability coverage on her auto policy. She has an umbrella policy with coverage of $1 million and a $300,000 deductible. Last year she was responsible for a major auto accident with medical and property damages totaling over $500,000. Her basic auto policy paid $300,000, and her umbrella policy paid the remaining $200,000. You can expect to pay between $125 and $200 annually for a million dollars' worth of coverage. Umbrella policies also cover defamation of character, libel, slander, wrongful eviction, false arrest, and so on.

If you have questions about your renters or homeowners policy, call the National Insurance Consumer help line at 800-942-4242 or your state's insurance department, usually located in the state capital. Ask either group if it has any publications that would help you find the most cost-effective homeowners or renters policy.

Financial Checkup Checklist

- Call your current insurer plus two or three other companies and compare rates.
- Have at least one fire extinguisher with a metal head.
- Have expensive items appraised.
- Make a video of your personal possessions.
- Keep a copy of warranties plus purchase receipts in a file stored away from home.
- Complete a home inventory and store it in a safe place away from your home or apartment.
- Apply for earthquake or flood insurance if needed.
- Try to improve your insurance coverage and at the same time lower your premiums.

11 How Healthy Are Your Health and Disability Policies?

Learn how to get the best coverage for the least cost.

> Ronda and Elroy had a problem. Ronda was diabetic and Elroy was self-employed. It was impossible for them to get health insurance coverage because of Ronda's diabetes. The only option was for Elroy to get a job with a fairly large employer so that the family could obtain health insurance. A small employer would probably not hire Elroy because Ronda's medical expenses would force the employer's health insurance company to raise premiums. If premiums were raised for everyone at the company because of Ronda, the firm would likely find reasons to let Elroy go. Ronda's medical expenses would be buried in a large firm because many employees and their families would have expensive medical problems. Elroy had a good income working for himself and refused to consider working for anyone else. As far as I know, the family never obtained health insurance but paid thousands in medical bills.

Understanding your auto and renters policies is child's play compared with medical insurance. Health insurance is expensive and often complicated. There are many different types of policies and a variety of coverages. Basically, health care is separated into two groups: fee for service and managed care.

Fee for Service

These are the basic types of fee-for-service coverage:

Hospital insurance. This covers you for costs related to hospitalization, including room and board, laboratory expenses, nursing services, drugs, and supplies. It is not adequate if it is the only coverage you have.

Surgical insurance. This covers services provided by surgeons and anesthesiologists. Again, such coverage is inadequate by itself.

Medical expense insurance. This covers fees associated with your visits to doctors' offices and related outpatient fees. It should be purchased only in combination with other coverages.

Major medical insurance. This coverage is similar in concept to an umbrella liability policy. It may pay your medical bills up to $1 million (or higher), but it carries a high deductible. This type of coverage is often sold in conjunction with hospital, surgical, and medical expense policies that have dollar ceilings on the coverages they provide. Besides deductibles, major medical policies include copayment clauses. After you satisfy the deductible, you pay 20 percent of the remaining bills and your major medical policy will pay 80 percent.

Avoid major medical polices that do not include stop-loss limits, which put a cap on the out-of-pocket dollar amount you pay each calendar year. For example, your major medical policy has a $2,000 deductible and an 80/20 coinsurance clause on medical expenses between $2,000 and $10,000. If you have a $15,300 medical bill, you must pay the first $2,000 of medical expenses to satisfy the deductible. You also owe an additional $1,600 (20 percent of $8,000). The policy will pay $11,700.

Comprehensive major medical insurance. This includes major medical, hospital, surgical, and medical expense policies with deductibles much lower than major medical deductibles. The policy coverage may function like the one described above, but the deductible might be as low as $300. Such a policy will be more expensive than traditional major medical policies that come with much larger deductibles.

The best known of the fee-for-service plans are offered by Blue Cross/Blue Shield (often known as the Blues). Such policies can include a combination of hospital, surgical, medical expense, and major medical insurance. Blue Cross contracts with doctors and hospitals; all parties agree to a set of fees. Participating doctors and hospitals accept the Blues' reimbursement as payment in full. Nonparticipating doctors and hospitals charge higher fees and require you to pay the difference between what the Blues pay and their charges.

Private insurance. Private insurance policies often reimburse doctors and hospitals much like Blue Cross/Blue Shield pays nonparticipating doctors and hospitals, but these policies usually have more exclusions than the Blues' policies. Many times, private insurance policies have internal limits that cap the amount the policy will pay for the cost of a semiprivate hospital room as well as the amount it will reimburse you for each fee charged by the doctors and the hospital.

The drawbacks to fee-for-service insurance are the costs you incur when you receive medical care. You usually have to satisfy a deductible and make copayments. Some doctors who operate on a fee-for-service basis are guilty of overuse, subjecting patients to treatments that are not needed. On the positive side, many people have more options when selecting doctors and hospitals with fee-for-service plans.

Managed Care

Managed care usually means a health maintenance organization (HMO). HMOs are not actually health insurance (where the insured pays premiums and the insurance company reimburses medical providers for services rendered). Patients who belong to an HMO prepay for medical services. Other than small fees for an office call, you are not charged for services when medical benefits are provided. So HMOs have a built-in incentive to keep clients healthy. As a result, HMOs focus much more on preventive care (unlike most insurance companies that often do not even cover annual physical examinations). Since no revenue is generated when a member receives medical attention, some critics believe that the quality of many HMOs' services suffer because of their cost-cutting procedures. In many HMOs, you see whatever doctor is available during an office visit. Some HMOs do allow you to select your own primary care physician (PCP). HMOs usually require you to first see a general practitioner or the PCP with any problem before visiting a specialist. When the problem is complicated, the general practitioner or PCP is likely to refer you to a specialist. Many people have complained that their general practitioner has refused to send them to a specialist, preferring to treat their problems, sometimes with unsatisfactory results.

Hot Tip

A reputable HMO will allow a woman to select a gynecologist or obstetrician as her primary care physician.

11 / How Healthy Are Your Health and Disability Policies?   147

There are several drawbacks to HMOs. A major one is coverage when you incur medical costs away from home. HMOs often cover emergency room expenses for you and your family only when you cannot be treated in the city or town where you live. HMOs are commonly accused of underuse, failing to provide a service or treatment that patients needed.

You can check out your HMO with the National Committee for Quality Assurance, which has evaluated the quality of care at hundreds of HMOs. Call it at 888-275-7585 or visit its Web site: www.ncqa.org.

There *is* a middle ground between fee-for-service health care and managed care, the most common form being the preferred provider organization (PPO). PPOs are similar to the participating relationship Blue Cross has with doctors and hospitals. Under a PPO, you must first visit your primary care physician (either an internist or family practitioner) who is associated with the PPO. If you visit an "out-of-network" doctor or are not referred to an "in-network" doctor by your PCP, fees are significantly higher.

Under each of the above services, you may select your own doctors (and will usually see the same doctor every time a medical problem requires attention).

> **Hot Tip**
>
> When referred to a specialist, make sure you get a referral in writing and keep a copy. Often the referral is only good for two or three visits to a specialist. If you need to see the specialist again after the two visits, another referral is needed from the primary care physician or HMO doctor. Read the fine print in any policy before ever visiting a medical doctor, clinic, or hospital.

Finding a Policy

If you are not covered by a policy at work, you have to buy one. Consider the following options:

- Contact an insurance broker where you live. A local broker is familiar with the most competitive rates for a policy that best fits your needs.
- Contact a firm that specializes in selling medical insurance; such a firm often maintains a database of 20 to 50 different policies. You can get information about more companies than you can from a single broker.
- Check a Web site that provides insurance information, such as QuoteSmith, www.quotesmith.com.

It is much more difficult to find an adequate medical insurance policy at a competitive price than it is to purchase an auto or renters policy. Your state insurance department may be able to supply a list of the most competitively priced policies.

Before any company provides you a medical insurance policy, it will want to know some things about you. Do you smoke, drink, or have a history of substance abuse? Are you overweight? What previous medical problems have you experienced, particularly during the past 12 months? Expect a health insurer to charge you a higher premium than you initially expected to pay if you have any of these

Compare Policies Worksheet

Insured	_____	_____	_____
Company	_____	_____	_____
Policy #	_____	_____	_____
Type	_____	_____	_____
Agent	_____	_____	_____
Telephone	_____	_____	_____
Deductible	_____	_____	_____
ER deductible	_____	_____	_____
Coinsurance	_____	_____	_____
Stop loss	_____	_____	_____
Internal limits	_____	_____	_____
Exclusions	_____	_____	_____
Premiums	_____	_____	_____

problems. Maybe you have never heard of the Medical Information Bureau (MIB), but it has probably heard of you. When you apply for life, disability, or health insurance, the insurance company checks your record at MIB. You can obtain a copy of your MIB report by calling 617-426-3660 or write to P. O. Box 105, Essex Station, Boston, MA 02112.

> **Hot Tip**
>
> If you find errors in your report, MIB will correct them. You want those errors corrected. If they are not, your insurance can cost much more.

How to Reduce Your Medical Insurance Costs

If you have an individual health insurance policy, you can dramatically reduce your premiums by increasing the size of the deductible. If you can afford to self-insure for $1,000 or even $2,000, ask about rates for policies that have larger deductibles.

Does your employer offer a premium conversion option? Premium conversion lets you pay health insurance premiums with pretax dollars. In other words, your tax liability is assessed against your income *after* health insurance premiums have been paid. Suppose you earn $22,000 a year, and your medical insurance costs you $150 a month, or $1,800 a year. Your top marginal tax rate is 15 percent.

> **Hot Tip**
>
> Before you apply for any health insurance policy, contact your state's insurance department and ask the following questions:
> - How long has the insurance company been doing business in the state?
> - How many complaints have consumers filed during each of the last three years against the company? The insurance department may tell you the exact number of complaints filed or give you a rating that is usually the number of complaints per 10,000 policyholders.
> - What can they tell you about the financial strengths of the company?
> - What can they tell you about the company's rates? (Are they below or above average? How often do they increase rates?)

If you can choose a premium conversion option, your income will be taxed on $20,200 ($22,000 less $1,800), and you will save $270 in income taxes.

Does your employer offer a medical reimbursement account? Such an account works much like a premium conversion option as far as income taxes are concerned. You decide at the start of the year how much you think you will pay in out-of-pocket medical expenses. One-twelfth of that amount is withheld from your paycheck each month. When you incur medical expenses, the medical reimbursement account sends you a check. Many people use medical reimbursement accounts because the amount withheld from their paycheck is not subject to federal income taxes. There is one major drawback to money kept in a medical reimbursement account: *If you do not use it during the year, you lose it.* For example, Louise has $40 withheld from her paycheck and deposited into her medical reimbursement account each month. Her taxable income for the year was reduced by $480. Since she pays taxes at the rate of 15 percent, she saved $72 in taxes by using a medical reimbursement account. As long as she leaves less than $72 in her account by the end of the year, she is dollars ahead using the medical reimbursement account.

If you are married and both you and your spouse are employed, are you both covered under health plans at separate employers? Married couples may be able to save money if one spouse can be covered for less under the other spouse's policy than if each pays for a separate policy at work. But check out the following before canceling one policy:

- Does each employer pay 100 percent of one spouse's insurance premiums?
- Does either spouse have a preexisting condition that would prevent immediate coverage if added to the other spouse's policy?
- Compare deductibles for both policies.
- Compare stop-loss limits for both policies.
- Compare the ability to select doctors.
- Compare coverages (dental, optical, etc.).
- Identify medical problems that are not covered in each policy.
- What is the net premium savings by putting both spouses on one policy?
- How secure is the job of the person whose policy insures both spouses?
- Does the spouse with the best policy plan to stay with his or her employer for an extended period of time?

> **Hot Tip**
>
> If you have a serious medical problem, you need to read all you can about it. Do not assume that your doctor is an expert or that he or she will recommend all current treatments. The more you know about your problem, the better the treatment your doctor can provide.

When shopping for a policy, remember that rates depend on the

- number of members of the family;
- the size of the deductible;
- the coverages required; and
- the doctor and hospital options. The least expensive policies limit your choices of both hospitals and doctors. The next most expensive limits your choice of doctors. The most expensive policies have no restrictions on either doctors or hospitals.

Paying the Doctor or Hospital Bill

Paying the bill means you should be able to read and understand it. Research has demonstrated that a large majority of hospitals overcharge. Most hospitals only send out summary bills. So how can you cope?

Before going to see a doctor or before going to the hospital emergency room (except in a life threatening situation), read your medical insurance policy first. Once you have received treatment, insist on an itemized bill (fewer and fewer doctors and hospitals provide them). Check each medical bill carefully. Billing errors are common, especially on hospital bills. Look for double billing or billing for services not provided. Keep a diary of visits, medicines, and services provided as many hospitals routinely pad bills with services not provided.

Review the bill with the hospital's financial counselor housed in the accounts receivable department before your discharge. Go over the bill with your insurance company, and remember to log phone calls with your insurance companies and medical providers.

Do not send any money to the hospital or doctor until after your insurance company has paid everything it plans to. Why? Insurance companies often catch double and triple billings as well as overcharges. The insurance company may also tell you what your share of the bill is (which is often less than the amount the hospital originally billed you).

If your health insurance company doesn't pay as much on your claim as you think that they should, find out why. Often

> **Hot Tip**
>
> Increasingly, policies require second opinions before major surgery; if you fail to get one, the policy pays significantly less or nothing at all. Check with your insurer to make certain that the policy pays the costs of obtaining a second opinion. If the second opinion disagrees with the first, either have both doctors confer or seek a third opinion.

the insurance company needs more documentation or the hospital or doctor must submit a certain form. Initially, respond in writing to both your insurance company and the hospital or doctor asking them to reevaluate.

If your claim is again not paid as you expected, call the insurance company and ask the appropriate person to explain. If you believe that the insurance company is not reimbursing you according to the terms of your policy, ask to talk with the appropriate person's supervisor. If you are still unable to resolve the problem, contact your benefit specialist at work. Explain the problem carefully and bring in copies of all documentation.

> **Hot Tip**
>
> If you still think errors exist in your bill, contact Medreview, 3429 Executive Center Dr., Suite 258, Austin, Texas 78731 at 800-397-5359. For a modest fee, it will review your bill and even contact your doctor or hospital about overcharges.

If you are still not satisfied with the results, do the following:

- Send a letter to the president of the insurance company; send a copy to the person in charge of benefits at your company; and send another letter to the chairperson of your state's insurance commission. Send all three letters certified.
- Explain exactly why you sought medical treatment as well as the treatment that you or a member of your family received. Include copies of all of your previous letters, copies of all letters sent to you from the insurance company, and copies of all medical bills.
- Ask to have an administrative hearing so that the facts in your case can be reviewed.
- If you are still not satisfied, consider talking with an attorney. On small claims, consider taking the insurance company and/or hospital to small claims court.

> **Hot Tip**
>
> Never buy medical insurance through the mail, newspaper, or television! Coverages are expensive and many procedures are not covered. Trying to get a company that is not licensed in your state to pay your medical bills is often a nightmare. If the insurance offer seems too good to be true, it is!

The federal government offers two types of medical care. Medicare, provided by Social Security, is a hospital and surgical program primarily for persons 67 and older. To be eligible for Medicare, you must apply during the 12 months following your 65th birthday. Medicaid (financed by both the federal government and state governments) pays medical bills for low-income individuals and families. Primary users include single parents on welfare and aged individuals, especially residents of nursing homes.

Two Policies to Avoid

Two policies you should avoid are discussed below.

> **Hot Tip**
>
> Check your doctor's credentials by calling the American Board of Medical Specialists, 800-776-2378, or check its Web site: www.certifieddoctor.org. Is your doctor who he or she claims to be?

Accident insurance. This type of policy pays a certain amount for every day you stay in a hospital. The premiums are high and the coverage poor. You do not need such duplicate coverage if you already have adequate medical insurance.

Dread disease insurance. Again, this policy pays only if you develop a certain type of cancer specified in the policy. Premiums are high relative to the poor coverage provided. Assuming you have adequate medical insurance, this duplicate coverage wastes money.

Health insurance is both expensive and necessary. Be grateful if your employer pays some, most, or all of your premiums. Read your policy. Become familiar with the types of coverages you have. Follow the rules carefully before seeing a specialist. If you have a serious problem, read all you can about it. Discuss with your doctor treatments that he or she has not recommended. Carefully check all medical bills. Medical care gets better every day, but the cost of that care gets higher. Do not let anyone pressure you into paying a bill before you are sure you owe it. You cannot ever become financially fit if you lack adequate medical insurance.

✓ Financial Checkup Checklist

- Read your policy thoroughly and be sure you are intimately familiar with your coverages. If you don't understand something, query your agent or insurance company.

Disability Insurance

Denise told me the earliest clue anyone had of Bob's problem was the first time he fell down in the pharmacy while making his rounds as a drug salesman. After three or four more falls over a period of ten days, Bob went to see his doctor. His multiple sclerosis progressed so rapidly that in less than three months, he could no longer work. Denise and Bob's finances were a mess now that Bob was no longer employed. Bob's monthly Social Security check, combined with Denise's income as a teacher, couldn't handle the increased costs resulting from Bob's illness. Denise mentioned how often she wished that Bob had taken out a disability policy. Before his illness, he often talked about doing just that. However, he felt that since he was only 36, he really didn't need to just yet.

Where would you get the money to support yourself and your family if you were unable to work because of accident or illness? You and I are four or five times more likely to be disabled for at least two years than we are to die before our 65th birthday. Do you have adequate disability coverage? Will your policy provide the benefits you expect and need?

There are three sources of disability income:

1. *Workers' compensation.* Workers' comp, as it is often called, provides coverage when you are injured while employed (and may cover injuries that occur commuting to and from work). Coverage includes medical expenses and partial replacement for lost wages. The key is to file as soon as you know that an injury or sickness is work related. Contact your state's industrial commission or department of labor.
2. *Social Security.* Your Social Security Earnings and Benefit Estimate Statement outlines your eligible benefits. If you have not sent for Form SSA-7004 yet, do so immediately. To receive Social Security disability benefits, you must be expected to be totally disabled for 12 months or die from the disabling injury or sickness. Benefits do not start until 6 months after the disability. Most people who file for Social Security disability benefits are turned down the first and second time. Most people must appeal to be awarded benefits, and such an appeal often requires the assistance of an attorney.

Hot Tip

If your employer pays disability premiums and you become disabled, you must pay income taxes on your disability benefits. If you pay premiums and become disabled, you do not pay taxes on your disability benefits.

3. *Disability income policy.* Employers often provide two types of disability policies. One covers short-term illnesses of a few weeks or months. The more important long-term policy covers disabilities resulting from sickness and/or accident until you reach retirement age. If you can afford only one policy, buy the one that offers long-term coverage. Employer-provided coverage is usually less expensive than buying a separate individual policy. Employers often require employees to pay part of the premiums. If you are self-employed, you will need to buy an individual policy.

Hot Tip

Obtain enough income from a disability policy to cover any deficit.

To figure out how much disability coverage you need, complete the Analysis of Disability Needs worksheet.

Although an analysis of your disability needs may be helpful, the bottom line is simply this: buy as much coverage as you can get. For example, don't assume

Analysis of Disability Needs Worksheet

1. Household's gross monthly income   _____

2. Less

    spouse's income   _____

    Social Security   _____

    other income   _____

        Total   (_____)

3. Surplus (deficit)   _____

that you will be able to collect Social Security. You can usually buy a policy that will cover up to 60 to 70 percent of your gross monthly income (wages). If you earn more than $100,000 a year, you may have a difficult time covering that large a percentage of your income.

Many policies are integrated with Social Security. For example, Ross earns $4,000 a month. Were he disabled, his company's disability policy would pay him $3,000 monthly. Because his benefits are integrated with Social Security, once he qualifies for Social Security, his income would be as follows:

Social Security	$1,000
Disability policy	$2,000
Total	$3,000

Some policy benefits are not integrated with Social Security. Policies that merge their benefits with Social Security are less expensive than those that don't. Why? Because Social Security benefits are indexed to inflation. Every year Social Security pays more and the policy pays less. For example, Ross's policy is integrated with Social Security. Next year Social Security will pay Ross $1,040, so his insurance payment will be $1,960, or $40 less.

What coverages should you buy when purchasing a disability policy? Chances are that a policy purchased through your employer will not include partial or residual disability coverage. Consider adding a residual benefits rider that will pay benefits if you are unable to work full-time. You could become disabled but still able to work part-time. Without a residual benefits rider, you will not receive any disability income for the hours you do not work.

> **Hot Tip**
>
> If you want to cover 100 percent of your income, first take out an individual disability policy before signing up for group coverage. It is possible that both policies will pay 100 percent of promised benefits. However, if you purchase an individual policy after enrolling in a group policy, group benefits are likely to be reduced by the amount of the benefits paid by the individual policy.

> **Hot Tip**
>
> If you buy a policy whose benefits are not merged with Social Security, maximum benefits paid by an insurance company will be lower than if such benefits were integrated. Why? Because the insurance company assumes that you will eventually qualify to receive Social Security benefits. To protect yourself in case you never qualify for Social Security, ask the agent to add a rider to your disability policy that will increase your benefits to be equal to expected Social Security benefits.

Inflation slowly increases the cost of living, yet most policy benefits do not increase. If you are permanently disabled for an extended period of time, the buying power of your disability income will decline. Seriously consider adding a cost-of-living-adjustment rider to your policy.

Length of coverage. Buy a policy that will pay benefits until you reach retirement age (65). If you are still disabled at 65, Social Security and your retirement benefits should support you. If you do not expect to have enough retirement income from sources other than Social Security, you may want to find a company that offers lifetime coverage. When such coverage is available, it is much more expensive than coverage to age 65. Make sure the coverage includes disabilities as a result of sickness and for accident. Some policies cover only one or both causes of disability for five years.

> **Hot Tip**
>
> Make sure your policy will pay benefits if you are unable to work at your present occupation, not the occupation you held when you took out the policy.

Elimination period. This is the time between the start of a disability and the time when the insurance company starts paying benefits. The longer the elimination period, the lower the premiums for the disability policy. If you are shopping for a policy, get quotes on one that has at least a 90-day waiting period before benefits start. Policy premiums based on elimination periods longer than 180 days are not much cheaper than policies with 180 days. Whatever elimination period you end up with, make sure that you have the financial resources to pay your bills until coverage starts. Check to see if your employer also offers a short-term policy. You may need that coverage if you have not accumulated very many sick days.

> **Hot Tip**
>
> Newer and better policies are termed "income-replacement." They cover loss of income if you're unable to work at all, but they also make up the difference between your former wage (before you were disabled) and your new wage because your disability prevents you from returning to your previous job.

Definition of disability. Many definitions exist, but there are two primary definitions: "unable to work" and "unable to work at present occupation." Look for a policy with the second definition. Many policies assume that you are unable to work at your present occupation if you are unable to perform one of your major job responsibilities. However, some policies will only consider you disabled if you are unable to perform several (or all) of your primary duties. If the definition of disability in your policy is "unable to work," you may not be eligible for benefits if you could flip burgers at Micky D's. Unfortunately, most policies that include the definition "unable to work at present occupation" switch to the definition "unable to work" after you have received disability benefits for two years.

Rehabilitation. A policy should provide rehabilitation benefits and provide financing so you can train for a new job. This is essential coverage if your policy's definition of disability is "unable to work."

Waiver of premium. You pay extra for this policy feature, but you want it. Without this clause in your policy, if you are disabled, you must continue to pay policy premiums. Request that premiums be waived as soon as benefits start.

Noncancelable. Try to find a policy that is noncancelable, meaning the insurance company cannot reduce benefits, raise premiums, or cancel your policy. Many companies no longer write noncancelable policies. Do not settle for a policy unless it is at least guaranteed renewable. The insurer cannot cancel guaranteed renewable policies either, but it can raise premiums for all insureds in a specific class or category of insureds.

> **Hot Tip**
>
> List the names and phone numbers of all of your previous doctors on the application form. Then it is up to the insurer to check with each one. And put in as much detail as you can about your job when filling out the application.

Buying a Policy

The three major disability insurers are: Provident Life, UNUM, and Paul Revere. Check your yellow pages for a local agent. Before purchasing any disability policy, match that policy's benefits and premiums with one available from either the Wholesale Insurance Network (800-808-5810) or TermQuote (800-444-8376).

As you complete the disability application, answer all questions honestly and

> **Hot Tip**
>
> Never go back to the office—even once, after your injury! Your insurance company will argue that you are not disabled as you returned to work.

Comparing Your Policy Worksheet

Except for the questions about benefits marked with an asterisk, answer yes or no. If you are self-employed, get a quote from two other firms.

Insurer _____ _____ _____

Agent _____ _____ _____

Phone number _____ _____ _____

Benefits	Current Coverage	Improved Coverage	Quote	Quote
*Monthly policy benefit	_____	_____	_____	_____
*Monthly premium	_____	_____	_____	_____
Integrated with Social Security	_____	_____	_____	_____
Covered to age 65	_____	_____	_____	_____
Policy covers accident and sickness	_____	_____	_____	_____
*Elimination period in days	_____	_____	_____	_____
Partial disability coverage	_____	_____	_____	_____
Income replacement coverage	_____	_____	_____	_____

(continued)

Comparing Your Policy Worksheet
(continued)

Benefits	Current Coverage	Improved Coverage	Quote	Quote
Rehabilitation coverage	_____	_____	_____	_____
Noncancelable	_____	_____	_____	_____
Guaranteed renewable	_____	_____	_____	_____
Waiver of premium	_____	_____	_____	_____
How disability is defined				
unable to work	_____	_____	_____	_____
unable to work at my job	_____	_____	_____	_____

completely. Insurers have access to information about you that goes back many years. Any misleading or fraudulent statements usually result in the insurance company's terminating coverage. *Don't conceal any prior medical problems.*

Women. Disability rates are higher for women. If you're a woman trying to find a policy, see if you can find a company that offers unisex rates.

Self-employed. If you're self-employed, try to get a better rate from your professional or trade organization before you buy an individual policy. These associations

Hot Tip

Ask your attorney to review all your paperwork before you send in your claim form. Let your attorney check all the fine print in the policy before the insurance company sees your claim. The insurance company knows your policy; expect it to challenge your request for benefits unless your claim is carefully prepared.

often offer group policies that are competitively priced.

Before you purchase any policy, check with A. M. Best (908-439-2200) or visit its Web site: www.ambest.com/rating.html to obtain a report that evaluates the financial strength of any insurance company. You would not want to buy disability insurance from a company that became financially disabled and unable to pay you benefits if you needed them. You may also save on premiums if you have a permanent medical problem and are willing to buy a policy that excludes (will not provide benefits) if you become disabled because of this problem.

Think twice about replacing an old disability policy with a new one. Many older policies offer better coverages than their newer cousins.

Financial Checkup Checklist

- Complete the disability needs analysis form to determine the amount of coverage that you need.

- If you own a personal disability policy, compare your coverage and premium with two other policies.

- Improve your disability coverage if needed.

12 Update Your Life Insurance

Make sure your life insurance coverage is adequate and cost-effective.

> When I first met JoAnn, she could hardly hold back the tears. Two weeks before, she and her husband, Doug, had returned from a European vacation. He walked into the house, laid down on the couch, and died. The flowers were still fresh on the grave when JoAnn realized that Doug had left her with an unreal mess. Yes, he had insured his life for $100,000 and she was the beneficiary of his policy, but he also owned real estate all over town. The problem? Most of the real estate was worth less than the mortgages on it, and JoAnn's name was listed as a joint owner on each piece of property. She was also listed as a guarantor of each mortgage. When we figured JoAnn's net worth, the result was a negative figure. Although she had graduated from college, JoAnn had stayed home the last 25 years raising the children. In today's job world, she had no marketable skills. Her feelings for Doug quickly turned into a love/hate affair. Too bad the deceased can't hear what their loved ones say about them when they leave behind such messes.

Life insurance is designed to create an instant financial estate when a person dies before he or she had the chance to build one. Before making any life insurance decisions, you need to come up with answers for each of the following four questions:

1. Do I need life insurance?
2. How much do I need?
3. What type of policy should I buy?
4. Whom should I purchase the policy from?

Do I Need Life Insurance?

If no one will suffer financially by your death, then you really don't need life insurance. However, you may want to purchase enough to pay for your funeral and such debts as credit card balances and student loans. It's hoped that the sale of your car generates enough cash to pay off the loan on it.

How Much Life Insurance Do I Need?

To find out the dollar amount for which to insure your life, complete the nine-step Life Insurance Needs Analysis Worksheet. If you have a significant other, then complete the analysis for your partner as well. Completing forms can be intimidating. Before you try to complete the worksheet using your data, first try to complete the worksheet using the hypothetical data that follow. Compare your results with how I filled in the blanks on the sample worksheet.

Hypothetical Data

Linda Chow is a single mother of two children, three-year-old Denise and five-year-old Kelly. Linda does not have any savings. She decided to order her earnings and benefit statement from the Social Security Administration. According to information in the statement, Social Security will provide her children $350 a month at her death. Currently, Linda brings home $1,600 a month. She thinks that it would cost her mother, Jackie, about $1,200 a month to raise both children.

Record Linda's information on the appropriate lines of the Life Insurance Needs Analysis worksheet:

Lines 1a–1e. Linda does not want more than $4,000 spent on a funeral. She owes $9,000 on a car loan, $14,000 on a student loan, and $5,000 on credit cards. The stop-loss limit in her medical policy is $2,000 (a stop-loss limit defines the maximum out-of-pocket medical expenses one person would have to pay in a year). Because her estate is small, she does not expect her attorney's fees to be more than $3,000. She would like an education fund of $60,000 created to send her two children to college.

Line 2.   Add together amounts on lines 1a–1e.
Line 3.   Annual income needed to support dependents. Be sure to adjust budget to reflect absence of insured.
Lines 4a–4d. Available income
Line 5.   Total amount of lines 4a–4d. This amount is the annual income that needs to be replaced.
Line 6.   Subtract total on line 5 from amount on line 3.
Line 7.   Divide as indicated. This is the amount needed to generate the shortage in the annual income on line 6.
Line 8.   Add together amounts on lines 2 and 7. These amounts are the financial resources not earmarked for other goals.
Lines 9a–9b. Resources available to support dependents.
Line 10.   Add together amounts on lines 9a and 9b.
Line 11.   Subtract the total on line 10 from the amount on line 9. This is the amount of life insurance needed.

Compare your numbers with the numbers on page 166 that I filled out.

If your numbers differ from those in the sample, the following explanations should help:

1a. Funerals cost between $4,000 and $10,000, and that doesn't cover burial plots. You may want to budget between $7,500 and $10,000.
1b. The total for credit card balances, car loans, and other personal debts is listed here.
1c. Review your health insurance policy. What is the most that you would have to pay in one year for medical expenses? The better policies have stop-loss provisions that do not require the insured to pay more than $2,000 to $3,000 a year.
1d. These expenses can range from less than $1,000 to more than 5 percent of the net worth of the person who died. If you are not sure, put (in the blank) 5 percent of your net worth.
1e. List here what you plan to pay to educate your children. Today, the cost of attending four years of college at a state university averages about $40,000; double the amount will be required if you plan to send your child to a private college or university.
2. Total immediate needs that would have to be met at Linda's death.
3. Linda thought that the children would need about $1,200 a month to cover their basic needs and wants.
4a. Linda does not have a spouse.
4b. Social Security will send a check for $350 each month at her death. This monthly payment is indexed to inflation, so it will increase every year.
4c. Linda has no pension that provides dependents with a monthly income.
4d. Linda has no other source of income.

Life Insurance Needs Analysis Worksheet

1. Immediate needs at death:
   a. Funeral _____
   b. Debts _____
   c. Medical _____
   d. Estate settlement costs _____
   e. Education _____
2. Total _____
3. Annual income needed to support dependents _____
4. Less:
   a. Spouse's annual salary _____
   b. Social Security annual payments (refer to your Personal Earnings and Benefit Estimate Statement) _____
   c. Annual pension benefits _____
   d. Other _____ _____
5. Total (_____)
6. Subtract the total on line 5 from the amount on line 3. _____
7. Divide the amount on line 6 by .05. _____
8. Add the amounts on lines 2 and 7. _____
9. Available resources
   a. Savings _____
   b. Investments _____
10. Total (_____)
11. Amount of life insurance needed: _____

Sample Life Insurance Needs Analysis Worksheet

1. Immediate needs at death:
   a. Funeral $ 4,000
   b. Debts 28,000
   c. Medical 2,000
   d. Estate settlement costs 3,000
   e. Education 60,000
2. Total $ 97,000
3. Annual income needed to support dependents $ 14,400
4. Less:
   a. Spouse's annual salary 0
   b. Social Security annual payments (refer to your Personal Earnings and Benefit Estimate Statement) 4,200
   c. Annual pension benefits 0
   d. Other _____ 0
5. Total ($ 4,200)
6. Subtract the total on line 5 from the amount on line 3. $ 10,200
7. Divide the amount on line 6 by .05. $204,000
8. Add the amounts on lines 2 and 7. $301,000
9. Available resources
   a. Savings $ 0
   b. Investments 0
10. Total (0)
11. Amount of life insurance needed: $301,000

5. The total for numbers on lines 4a through 4d.
6. The amount of annual income that dependents need after subtracting income sources from dependents' needs.
7. This is the amount of money needed to generate the income deficit on line 6. If this amount can be invested at 5 percent, it will yield the amount on line 6. In reality, an investment adviser should be able to invest this amount so that it earns more than the amount on line 6.
8. The total of the amounts on lines 2 and 7 is the amount of income the dependents need to meet their basic needs and wants.
9. List resources here that the insured may have earmarked to support dependents if the insured died. If you already have life insurance, then you face a decision. Should you keep your present policies? If so, list the amount of each policy here. If you plan to replace your present policies, make sure the new policy is in place before you cancel any existing policies.
10. This is the total amount of all available resources including current life insurance policies.
11. This is the amount of life insurance that needs to be purchased. Most policies are sold in $50,000 units. For example, if the amount on line 11 was $223,000, the person buying the policy would need to choose between a $200,000 policy and a $250,000 policy.

> **Warning !!!**
>
> Never cancel an existing policy until a new policy is in place.

Now fill in the form using your own data. If you have a partner copy this form.

You may prefer to put your data in an interactive life insurance needs calculator. There are dozens on the Web but most are terrible. Try these two: http://www.rightquote.com/ and www.quicken.com/insurance/ (click on the family needs planner that you will find under Planning Tools).

> **Hot Tip**
>
> When putting your data into any needs analysis on the Web, always complete two different analyses. Do not feel comfortable with the amount of life insurance you need unless figures from two analyses are fairly close. Most calculators on the Web are so inaccurate that they are worse than useless.

Your Life Insurance Needs Analysis Worksheet

1. Immediate needs at death:

    a. Funeral _____

    b. Debts _____

    c. Medical _____

    d. Estate settlement costs _____

    e. Education _____

2. Total _____

3. Annual income needed to support dependents _____

4. Less:

    a. Spouse's annual salary _____

    b. Social Security annual payments (refer to your Personal Earnings and Benefit Estimate Statement) _____

    c. Annual pension benefits _____

    d. Other _____ _____

5. Total (_____)

6. Subtract the total on line 5 from the amount on line 3. _____

7. Divide the amount on line 6 by .05. _____

8. Add the amounts on lines 2 and 7. _____

9. Available resources

    a. Savings _____

    b. Investments _____

10. Total (_____)

11. Amount of life insurance needed: _____

What Type of Policy Should I Buy?

The insurance industry has created hundreds of different life insurance policies. Your family probably doesn't care what type you buy, but they do care that you buy enough coverage. All policies can be separated into the following three groups: term, whole life, and universal life.

Term. Term insurance is pure life insurance and does not include a cash value or investment account as do universal and whole life policies. The premiums for a term policy are much lower than for the other two kinds of policies as premium dollars go to buy insurance only. None of the premium dollars are deposited into a savings or investment account. The insurance industry likes to say that term insurance is not permanent, but you can buy term coverage up to age 65 and beyond. You shouldn't need life insurance once you reach retirement. By then, your investments should be large enough to support your partner without life insurance. If you decide on term, I suggest that you buy a policy with a level premium (meaning that premiums do not increase for 5, 10, 15, 20, 25, or even more years).

Do *not* buy the following types of term policies:

- *Decreasing term insurance.* Premiums do not increase, but the amount of insurance coverage declines every year. For some reason, life insurance companies charge much more for each dollar of coverage for this type of policy than they do for more traditional term policies.
- *Annual renewable term.* Insurance coverage stays level, but premiums increase every year. The first year's premium is often a teaser rate and is artificially low to tempt you to buy.
- *Mortgage insurance.* This is the same as decreasing term insurance.
- *Credit life or disability.* This type of coverage is extremely expensive. If borrowing money causes you to be underinsured, buy more level term coverage.
- *Flight insurance.* Buy enough life insurance so that your dependents will not need more if you die in a plane crash.
- *Accidental death rider.* This pays double the amount of your policy if you die in an accident. Your dependents do not need twice as

> **Hot Tip**
>
> Consider buying a level premium policy with coverage lasting at least until your youngest child celebrates his or her 25th birthday. In Linda's case, she needs to buy a policy that would last for at least 22 years.

much if your death is accidental, and it is often difficult to collect from such policies.
- *Waiver-of-premium rider.* If you become disabled, the policy pays the premiums. Buy enough disability coverage so that this coverage is not needed.

Whole life (also called permanent insurance). Such coverage is a combination of term insurance and a savings or investment account. Most people cannot afford whole life if they plan on buying all the life insurance coverage they need. Don't be distracted by the insurance company's promise to pay dividends. Companies inflate the premiums you pay so they can pay you dividends if their expenses are not excessive at the end of the policy year.

Universal life. These policies also combine term insurance with either a savings or investment account. Universal life differs from whole life because in a universal life policy the savings account does not come with a guaranteed rate of return as it does with a whole life policy. When interest rates are high, buying a universal life policy can be risky. As interest rates drop, you can expect premiums to increase. With high interest rates, the savings component generates enough cash so there is enough money to pay the expenses the insurance company incurs in handling the policy. When interest rates drop, the insurance company often has to increase the premiums on its universal life policies because the investment accounts are not generating enough income.

Because the interest rate on a universal life policy is not guaranteed, the premium for universal life policies is lower than for whole life. If you consider purchasing a universal life policy, then investigate those that are referred to as variable universal life policies. Such policies combine term insurance with mutual funds. Part of your premium buys term coverage; the rest is invested in a mutual fund. Many different life insurance companies sell variable universal life policies; each company should give you a choice of several different mutual funds in which to invest. Universal life policies work well for people who lack the discipline to put money away for retirement. If you die before retirement, the life insurance part supports your dependents. If you reach retirement, the dollars in the mutual fund can be tapped to help support you during retirement.

The numbers in Figure 12.1 clearly show the range of costs for four types of policies at different ages for men and women. Annual premiums will increase for annual renewable term policies, so I suggest that you do not buy such a policy.

Buy Term and Invest the Difference

Should you buy term and invest the difference between premium costs for a term policy and a whole life policy? In the following example, let's suppose we are insuring a 35-year-old male for $100,000. Note the differences in premiums by

Figure 12.1 Annual Premiums for $100,000 of Coverage from Four Types of Life Insurance Policies*

		Annual Renewable Term	20-year Level Term	Whole Life	Universal Life
Age 25	Female	$100.00	$155.00	$608.00	$239.24
	Male	100.00	170.00	731.00	289.72
Age 30	Female	100.00	155.00	737.00	280.96
	Male	100.00	175.00	894.00	231.05
Age 35	Female	100.00	167.00	905.00	341.45
	Male	100.00	186.00	1,114.00	402.75
Age 40	Female	110.00	199.00	1,123.00	435.14
	Male	120.00	266.00	1,405.00	508.06
Age 45	Female	120.00	247.00	1,401.00	583.38
	Male	134.00	320.00	1,787.00	682.00
Age 50	Female	138.00	325.00	1,766.00	777.08
	Male	170.00	443.00	2,299.00	938.00
Age 55	Female	166.00	431.00	2,252.00	1,051.97
	Male	225.00	634.00	2,958.00	1,271.19

*Quotes supplied by TermQuote: 800-444-8326.

buying a whole life policy and purchasing a term policy (with a 20-year level premium). We're assuming that the 35-year-old male can invest the difference between the two premiums and earn an annual return of 10 percent:

Whole life premium	$1,114
20-year level term	– 186
Difference	$ 928

Whether this 35-year-old male buys the whole life or the level term policy, his life will be insured for $100,000 if he pays the premiums for 20 years. If he has the discipline to invest the $928 each year in a mutual fund, that amount could grow to over $50,000 if the fund he selects earns on average 10 percent a year (which most funds have done for the past 20 years). (See Figure 12.2.)

However, if he lacks the discipline to invest the $928 difference each year, he may be better off buying a variable universal life policy, which includes an investment account with funds invested in shares of mutual funds.

Figure 12.2 Whole Life versus Term Plus Investment Account

End of Policy Year	Whole Life Benefits	Investment Account	Term Benefits + Investment Acc't
1	$100,000	$ 1,020	$101,020
2	100,000	2,142	102,142
3	100,000	3,376	103,376
4	100,000	4,733	104,733
5	100,000	6,227	106,227
6	100,000	7,869	107,869
7	100,000	9,675	109,675
8	100,000	11,662	111,662
9	100,000	13,848	113,848
10	100,000	16,252	116,252
11	100,000	18,897	118,897
12	100,000	21,860	121,860
13	100,000	25,007	125,007
14	100,000	28,528	128,528
15	100,000	32,400	132,400
16	100,000	36,661	136,661
17	100,000	41,347	141,347
18	100,000	46,501	146,501
19	100,000	52,171	152,171
20	100,000	58,408	158,408

Suggestions for Buying Life Insurance

- Do not buy term and plan to invest the difference if you have thus far been unable to put money away regularly for retirement. If you have lacked discipline in the past, then strongly consider buying a variable universal life policy.
- Do buy term and invest the difference if you have a track record of regularly investing funds every month. You will be more successful if you set up an automatic purchase program with a mutual fund so that you are investing the difference between premium costs monthly.

Whom Should You Buy Your Policy From?

Rates for the same coverage vary drastically among companies. Shopping around can save you hundreds, even thousands, of dollars over the life of the policy. I suggest that you compare the annual premium quoted by a local insurance agent with the rates available by checking the Web sites listed below or by calling the 800 numbers listed below. Before you call, fill in these blanks:

- Dollar amount of coverage you desire _____
- Number of years for which you need coverage _____
- Type of policy you want _____

You will find dozens of policies at the following Web sites or by calling the 800 numbers:

Fee for Service		874-5662
InsuranceQuote	www.iquote.com	972-1104
LifeRates of America		457-2837
MasterQuote	www.masterquote.com	337-5433

Hot Tip

Before buying a new life insurance policy, check with your employer's benefit office to see what coverages it has available. An employer may be able to offer you term insurance coverage that is two to three times more than your wages. On the other hand, some problems with buying life insurance at work include these:

- The coverage is not enough, so you will still need to buy a personal policy.
- When you leave the firm, the coverage will stop.
- The cost of the coverage may be significantly less expensive than buying your own policy; but life insurance purchased at work often costs more than a personal policy if you are in your 20s or 30s.

Quotesmith	www.quotesmith.com	431-1147
Select Quote		343-1985
TermQuote	www.rcinet.com/~termquote/	444-8376
Wholesale Insurance Network		808-5810

If you phone the firms listed above, each will send you quotes on three to five policies that fit your criteria. If you call five numbers, you may end up with 25 quotes. Record the three most competitive quotes in the Shopping for a Policy Worksheet. Several of the sites display prices for dozens of policies.

Instructions for Filling in the Worksheet

1. *Insured:* you if you are taking out a policy on your life. The company that you ask to insure your life is probably going to require you to complete a physical, which it pays for. If the company's doctors find a health problem, the premium will be raised to offset the increased risk resulting from your health condition. Do you need to quit smoking and/or lose weight? You will save a bundle if you can do either or both; as a bonus, you are likely to live longer. The life insurance company is betting that you will live longer, which is why your premiums will be lower.
2. *Owner:* who should own the policy? If you are married, your spouse probably should own the policy on your life. Let your spouse pay the premiums as he or she will receive the policy benefits at your death. If you own the policy, the face amount of the policy will be included in your taxable estate at your death, making the proceeds subject to federal estate taxes.
3. *Beneficiary:* the person who will receive the proceeds of the policy. Companies also ask the insured

> **Hot Tip**
> You may be more satisfied buying a policy from a financial adviser if you know little about life insurance.

> **Hot Tip**
> You definitely want to own the policy on your spouse if you anticipate a divorce so that you can continue the coverage if it's needed. If you are single and your net worth plus the face amount of the policy exceeds $1 million, you need to see an estate planning attorney.

Shopping for a Policy Worksheet

Life Insurance Policies

1. Insured: _____ _____ _____

2. Owner: _____ _____ _____

3. Beneficiary: _____ _____ _____

4. Company: _____ _____ _____

5. A. M. Best rating: _____ _____ _____

6. Face amount: _____ _____ _____

7. Type: _____ _____ _____

8. Years of coverage: _____ _____ _____

9. Annual premium: _____ _____ _____

10. Agent: _____ _____ _____

11. Agent's phone: _____ _____ _____

to select a contingent beneficiary, someone to receive policy proceeds if at the death of the insured, the primary beneficiary has already passed away. Most husbands select their wives, and wives select husbands as beneficiaries. This is often not the wisest choice, however, especially if the spouse is young and has had little experience managing large sums of money. Too often the proceeds of a life insurance policy are spent in less than two years. This is especially painful when the deceased has left behind small children. If you have any reason to think that your beneficiary would promptly spend the policy proceeds after your death, consider making the beneficiary a trustee in a trust that you create. A trustee

spends the money providing for your spouse and dependents. (This is discussed in greater detail in Chapter 21 on estate planning.)
4. *Company:* record the company name here.
5. *A. M. Best rating:* an assurance that the company selling the policy is financially sound after you have identified three of the lowest-priced policies. The company that sent you the quote on a life policy probably included a rating of the insurance company by a firm known as A. M. Best. If not, then visit your neighborhood library, and ask the reference librarian for a copy of Best's. Look up the company whose policy you are considering buying. Only buy from companies rated A, A+, or A++ by Best. If your library doesn't have a copy, call 908-439-2200 or visit Best's Web site at www.ambest.com/rating.html to obtain the same information (you will be charged a modest fee). Remember, life insurance companies do go broke!
6. *Face amount:* the dollar amount of coverage you purchase. Policies are usually sold in $50,000 units. Typical amounts are $100,000, $250,000, and $500,000.
7. *Type:* the hundreds of variations on the three major types of policies. The bottom line: how much must you pay each year for the amount of life insurance coverage you need? For most readers a level term or variable universal life policy is the only affordable option.
8. *Years of coverage:* how many years will people depend on you for financial support? How long will it take you to accumulate enough funds to become finan-

> **Hot Tip**
>
> When getting quotes for level term premium policies, insist on policies in which the premium is guaranteed not to increase for the term of the policy. Some insurers only guarantee the premium for five years, then require the insured to take a second physical (and often raise rates for the rest of the term).

> **Hot Tip**
>
> In three or four years, complete the needs analysis again to compare rates. Premiums have been dropping for years. You may find that the same coverage purchased three years from now may cost significantly less than it does today.

cially independent? You may want the term of the policy to extend until your youngest child turns 25 or your spouse reaches retirement age.

9. *Annual premium:* the amount you are charged each year for coverage. You want a policy in which the premium is guaranteed to remain level over the life of the policy.
10. *Agent:* the person who gets paid for selling you the policy. When using the 800 numbers or Web sites to find a policy, you may never meet the agent.
11. *Phone number:* the number you call when buying the policy or when you have questions about policy service.

Have an old life insurance policy that you would like to have evaluated to see if you should keep it or replace it? Contact the Consumer Federation of America at 202-387-6121; for a small fee it can tell you if your policy is cost effective.

Do you live in Connecticut, Massachusetts, or New York? You can purchase term insurance at your neighborhood savings bank or call 800-438-4252 for more information about buying insurance in these states. Rates are extremely competitive.

If you need to insure your life, buy the coverage you need. First check the life insurance coverage available at your job. If you have the discipline to invest regularly, term insurance is the way to go; if not, buy a variable universal life policy. Make sure that the beneficiary you select can properly manage a large sum of money for all of your dependents. No one can be considered financially fit without having purchased adequate life insurance protection.

 Financial Checkup Checklist

- Complete a life insurance needs analysis.

- Obtain quotes from three companies for the type and amount of coverage you need.

- Purchase the desired coverage.

13 Funding Financial Independence

Determine the amount you need to be investing each month to achieve financial independence.

When Mr. and Mrs. Chaves came to see me, both were in their middle 40s, and together earned about $200,000 a year. They wanted to retire when the younger turned 60, which was about 15 years off. So far they had not put away a single dime for retirement. I asked them: "How much do you want to spend each year once you retire?" They responded, "We think that we can get by on $100,000 a year." I ran their numbers based on this information. To become financially independent at 60, they would need to invest $75,000 a year. Not a realistic amount for a couple who had not put away any money for their retirement.

People who achieve financial independence will never again need to receive a paycheck to support themselves and their dependents. Technically, a person who is financially independent may be different from someone who has retired. A retired person no longer receives a paycheck but may lack enough money to meet basic wants and needs. A person who is financially independent may continue receiving a paycheck but doesn't need any of that income for support. Financially independent individuals are thought to live more satisfying lives than retirees. Much of a person's self-esteem is tied to the productive work he or she does. When the paycheck stops, many people sense that their value as human beings has diminished.

Planning for retirement can seem a daunting task with lots of numbers to crunch. Discipline is required to make adequate monthly investment payments. You must know enough about investing to make proper investment decisions. To become financially fit, any preretiree must understand the basic constraints of the emerging retirement crisis. As you read through this chapter, keep asking yourself, "Am I on track for funding my retirement?"

The Retirement Crisis Facing You

Before discussing exactly what you need to be doing now to fund your financial independence, consider how the current retirement crisis affects you.

The vast majority of Americans employed today who survive into their 80s are likely to live in poverty during retirement in the 21st century unless they attain millionaire status prior to retirement. A growing number of retirees are expected to outlive their retirement resources. As a result, government and private researchers predict that more and more retirees will depend on welfare benefits to survive. Because the welfare system is not expected to adequately support these increasing numbers of welfare recipients, the federal government is currently taking proactive measures to encourage employers and their employees to invest more now to reduce the likelihood of needing public assistance later. In 1997 Congress passed both the Savings Are Vital to Everyone's Retirement (SAVER) Act and the Tax Simplification Act; both pieces of legislation were designed to encourage employees to put more away for retirement, but this legislation is not enough to stem the tide of a growing crisis.

Most seniors will not immediately live in poverty after they retire, but the majority will exhaust their personal savings and company pensions during their first 10 to 15 years of retirement. Today, the group of individuals with the highest percentage living in poverty is the group of those 75 and older. The situation will continue to worsen for the following three reasons:

1. Individuals are living longer. According to the U.S. Census Bureau, 2,000 U.S. citizens had celebrated their 100th birthday in 1960. By the year 2050, the bureau predicts there will be more than 1.25 million centenarians.
2. Social Security will be less generous in the 21st century than it has been in the 20th century. During most of this century there has been an average of ten workers for every retiree (currently there are about three); early in the 21st century that average is expected to drop to two workers for every retiree. Currently, most employees contribute nearly 8 percent of their wages to Social Security and Medicare. Realistically, employees cannot be expected to pay too much more in Social Security taxes, so benefits will be cut.

3. Increasing numbers of public and private employers (including the federal government) have switched from defined benefit pensions to defined contribution plans. A defined benefit pension pays a retiree a monthly income for life. Many of those pensions were indexed to inflation with a cost-of-living-adjustment (COLA) that increased monthly payments annually. With the downsizing and cost cutting that began in the 1980s, employers switched to less expensive defined contribution plans. For employees covered by a defined contribution plan, available benefits at retirement depend directly on how well the employees invest the funds in their company-sponsored retirement account. Employers prefer defined contribution plans for two reasons: (1) they are less expensive to fund than defined benefit pensions; and (2) employer liability is limited to the annual contribution the employer makes to each employee's account. With a defined benefit pension, the employer must come up with the funds to make pension payments until the employee (and often the employee's spouse) dies, often 15 to 30 years after the employee retires.

These three factors together—individuals living longer, potentially less generous Social Security benefits, and employers' shift to defined contribution plans—forecast a life of poverty for millions who are expected to outlive their retirement resources.

Conclusion: When it comes to financing retirement, you are basically on your own!

These three factors negatively impact a retiree's income, and inflation makes financing retirement even more difficult. Many in the labor force have short memories; they forget what inflation did to prices in the recent past. In 1973 a postage stamp cost eight cents; the average price of a new car was approximately $3,000 to $4,000. In the early 1970s the price of a new house cost what an average-priced car costs today. While the inflation rate today is low when compared with historical standards, prices still continue to climb. The inflation rate is expected to increase at a faster rate than it does now. Anyone who retired 20 years ago needs nearly three times as much money today to buy the same basket of goods as they bought then. Someone retiring today should wisely assume that prices will be two to three times higher 20 years from now.

How much should you accumulate before you can retire with confidence that you will not outlive your income? That answer depends on a number of factors. The most important is *how much income do you want to spend each year?* While some believe they can get by on an annual income of $20,000, others don't see how they could make do with less than $200,000.

The numbers in Figure 13.1 show the number of dollars in millions you will need to fund your retirement. In creating this chart, I have made two assumptions:

Figure 13.1 Millions of Dollars Needed to Fund Retirement

(numbers represent millions)

	Annual retirement income desired (in today's dollars)				
Current age:	$30,000	$40,000	$50,000	$60,000	$70,000
55	$ .7	$1.0	$1.2	$1.5	$1.7
45	1.1	1.5	1.8	2.2	2.6
35	1.6	2.2	2.7	3.3	3.8
25	2.4	3.2	4.1	4.8	5.7
18	3.2	4.3	5.4	6.4	7.5

(1) inflation will average 4 percent annually for the foreseeable future as it has done during the past 100 years; and (2) people will want to continue to retire about the time they reach 65 years of age. Read the chart as follows: Find where the row closest to your age intersects with the column headed by the annual income you desire. For example, Jane is 45 years old and she wants an income of $50,000 a year (in today's dollars) when she retires. At her retirement, Jane needs approximately $1.8 million. Jack, who is 35, wants to live on $100,000 (in today's dollars) at retirement. He will need more than $5 million (add together the 1.6 under the column labeled $30,000 plus the 3.8 under the column labeled $70,000).

How Much Should You Be Investing Each Month?

In today's dollars, how much annual income do you need to be financially independent? To help you answer that question, complete your retirement budget by filling in the blanks below. The first and second columns in the worksheet are similar to the spending plan that you are currently using.

Myth: At retirement you will need only 70 percent of the income you are earning prior to retirement. You may want less or a whole lot more.

Jack retired last Wednesday after work; on Thursday Jack began life as a retiree. Does he incur substantial savings because he no longer goes to work? With

Retirement Budget Worksheet
(in today's dollars)

Spending Categories	Annual Expenditures (today)	Annual Expenditures (at retirement)
_____	_____	_____
_____	_____	_____
_____	_____	_____
_____	_____	_____
_____	_____	_____
_____	_____	_____
_____	_____	_____
_____	_____	_____
_____	_____	_____
_____	_____	_____
_____	_____	_____
_____	_____	_____
Total	_____	_____

more free time on his hands, might Jack spend even more money than he did before he retired? Some expenditures will decrease or be eliminated by retirement; others will increase. Your situation is unique. Estimate carefully how each expenditure will change at retirement.

Expenditures that should decrease or be eliminated at retirement include:

- The mortgage, which should be paid off
- Social Security taxes, which you'll no longer pay unless you remain employed
- Costs of raising children, including college costs

Expenditures that are likely to be more costly at retirement than before include:

- Recreation and travel
- Hobbies
- Medical care

Now you can answer the question posed at the beginning of this section: "In today's dollars, how much annual income do you need to be financially independent?"

At what age do you want to retire? If you are married and both you and your spouse do not wish to retire in the same calendar year, you each need to perform separate retirement calculations.

What average annual rate of return do you want to earn on all investments earmarked to fund retirement? Below is a list of average percentage returns since the 1920s:

	% return
Stocks	10.7%
Mutual funds	10.2
Corporate bonds	6.9
Government bonds	4.8

What will be your top marginal tax bracket? Your top bracket is the tax rate that you pay on the last dollar you earn during the tax year. Check your tax return or ask the person who prepared your return what your top tax bracket is. The different tax rates are 15 percent; 28 percent; 31 percent; 36 percent; and 39.6 percent.

What do you expect inflation to average during the rest of your life? Below are the average inflation rates for different periods of time:

1927 to today	3.7%
1971 to today	5.6
1981 to today	4.9
1991 to today	3.2

How much are you and your employer together currently putting away each month for your retirement? Dollars earmarked for financial independence often come from three sources:

- Your contribution at work to a 401(k) or 403(b) plan
- Contributions your employer makes on your behalf
- Your personal contribution to an IRA or other investment program

How much are you putting away in a company-sponsored retirement plan such as a 401(k) or 403(b)? Usually, your taxable income is reduced by the amount of such contributions. How much are you currently contributing each month to a retirement plan at work?

How much is your employer putting away for you each month? As discussed previously, employers fund two different types of plans: defined benefit pensions and defined contribution plans. Under a defined benefit pension plan, a retired employee is typically sent a check each month. The amount of the check is often a function of the number of years the employee worked for the employer and the employee's average salary during the last three or five years that the employee worked for the employer. For example, Charlene Wells taught school for the state of Texas for 25 years. Her average salary for the last three years she worked was $30,000. For every year that Charlene taught, she will receive 2 percent of that average salary, or $600. Since Charlene taught school for 25 years, her pension will be $15,000 a year.

A defined contribution plan is more like an investment account. Each year the employer contributes funds to an account bearing the employee's name. Employers offer their employees from 3 to as many as 300 options for investing these dollars in their defined contribution account. Each employee must select how he or she wants the dollars invested.

> **Hot Tip**
>
> An annual average rate of return is computed in two different ways. First, it is the average rate of return for all your investments for the past 12 months. For example: Jo has $50,000 invested in stocks and $50,000 invested in bonds. Last year her rate of return on the stocks was 12 percent; Jo earned 8 percent on her bonds, giving her a 10 percent average rate of return. The second rate of return is the mathematical average year after year after year. For example, Jo earned 7 percent three years ago, 9 percent two years ago, and 17 percent last year to give her an average annual return of 11 percent over the last three years.

Two Issues of Concern

Vesting. Vesting refers to your ownership of employer contributions. Each employer selects one of the following two vesting schedules for its retirement plans. Employers can offer more generous vesting schedules than those that federal law requires, as explained below. With *cliff vesting,* an employee does not own employer contributions during the first five years of employment but owns 100 percent of the employer's contributions after five years of employment. With *graded vesting,* an employee does not own employer contributions during the first two years of employment, but after the third year owns 20 percent of the employer's contributions. Employee ownership grows at 20 percent a year until after seven years the employee owns 100 percent of the employer's contributions.

Pension indexing. Are pension benefits indexed to inflation? For example, George Pyle's pension includes a COLA (cost-of-living-adjustment). Last year inflation averaged 3 percent, so at the start of this year, his pension check was adjusted upward by 3 percent. Defined contribution plans do not have COLAs, but some defined benefit pensions do. The best example is Social Security whereby pension checks are adjusted annually based on the previous year's inflation rate.

How much are you regularly setting aside each month in an account that is not part of your employer's retirement plans? Your funds could be going into the following accounts:

- A traditional individual retirement account (IRA)
- A Roth IRA
- An annuity (discussed in Chapter 27)
- An investment portfolio

A traditional IRA lets you and your spouse contribute up to $4,000 annually. The maximum contribution to one IRA is always $2,000. With a few exceptions, you will pay a 10 percent penalty on dollars withdrawn before you turn 59½.

Funds in an IRA can be used for a wide range of investments. You can open an IRA at a bank, a brokerage firm, or an insurance or mutual fund company.

Will your contributions reduce your adjusted gross income? Yes, they will if you and/or your employer do not contribute to a pension at work, or if your gross income is less than the lower number in the ranges listed below. If your income falls

Hot Tip

You have until April 15 of this year to make an IRA contribution for last year.

within the ranges, you will receive a partial deduction (but you are better off contributing to a Roth IRA).

Year	Range for Joint Filers	Range for Single Filers
1999	$51,000 to $61,000	$31,000 to $41,000
2000	$52,000 to $62,000	$32,000 to $42,000
2001	$53,000 to $63,000	$33,000 to $43,000
2002	$54,000 to $64,000	$34,000 to $44,000
2003	$60,000 to $70,000	$40,000 to $50,000
2004	$65,000 to $75,000	$45,000 to $55,000
2005	$70,000 to $80,000	$50,000 to $60,000
2006	$75,000 to $85,000	$50,000 to $60,000
2007	$80,000 to $100,000	$50,000 to $60,000

If your contribution to an IRA reduces your adjusted gross income, you will defer paying income taxes until you withdraw funds from your IRA. If your contributions to an IRA do not qualify as a reduction to your adjusted gross income, you should open a Roth IRA. The maximum contribution of $2,000 to a Roth IRA is reduced if you file a joint return and your adjusted gross income is between $150,000 and $160,000, or you file a single return and your adjusted gross income is between $95,000 and $110,000. You will not be taxed on money withdrawn from a Roth IRA after you turn 59½, and you are not required to start taking money out of a Roth IRA once you turn 70½. Check out *Maximize Your IRA* by Neil Downing for details regarding whether a traditional or Roth IRA is best for you.

Depending on the value of your estate, as much as two-thirds of the value of your IRA could be paid in taxes at your death. To save on income and estate taxes at your death, you need to select your beneficiary long before your 70th birthday (and the sooner the better). Even if the balance in your IRA is less than $50,000, whom you select as your beneficiary has a major impact on taxes assessed against your IRA after your death. As a general rule, the younger the person you name as a beneficiary, the less the IRS will get of your IRA. If the balance in your IRA is currently more than $100,000, seek competent professional help concerning whom you should name as the beneficiary of your IRA.

Your Investment Portfolio

Most financial advisers recommend that you take advantage of all tax-favored investment options open to you to fund financial independence before you put money away in any other investment account. If you are already making maximum contri-

Warning!!!

Pick the *right* IRA beneficiary.

butions to your employer's retirement plan and to an IRA but still need to put more dollars away each year, remaining dollars will be invested without the tax benefits previously discussed. Each year you will be required to pay income taxes on the dividends you receive from such investments. When you sell these investments at a profit, you will be required to pay capital gains taxes in the year of the sale. While you may not receive any immediate favored tax treatment, your funds will increase in value as you fund your retirement and other goals.

Pension Plans for the Self-Employed

Most self-employed people set up one of the following pension plans:

- Keogh
- Simplified Employee Pension (SEP)
- Savings Incentive Match Plan for Employees (SIMPLE)

A key issue with all retirement plans set up by the self-employed is that they must cover their employees in the plan they adopt. Both SEPs and SIMPLEs are IRAs with one huge difference: A self-employed person who makes contributions for his or her employees may be eligible to contribute up to $6,000 to a SIMPLE and up to $24,000 to a SEP. Fewer of the self-employed are setting up Keogh plans because the paperwork is too demanding. SEPs are the preferred plan because they are relatively simple to administer and are similar to profit-sharing plans. An employer does not have to make contributions to a SEP every year. Any self-employed person should explore retirement plan options thoroughly with his or her tax adviser before setting up any pension or retirement plan.

Now that you know the amount that you and your employer are setting aside each month, you are ready to determine if that amount is adequate to achieve your financial independence goals.

Your retirement needs analysis should answer the following questions:

- Are you on track for funding retirement?
- How much do you (and your employer) need to invest each month to fund retirement?
- At what age can you afford to retire?

> **Hot Tip**
>
> If you are middle-aged, self-employed, and have not yet put any money away for retirement, you may want to consider a Keogh plan (which can be either a defined contribution or a defined benefit plan). Unlike SIMPLEs and SEPs, which are only defined contribution plans with contribution caps, you may be eligible to contribute significantly more than $24,000 to a defined benefit Keogh.

Retirement Needs Analysis Worksheet

Many variables are involved in calculating a retirement needs analysis, but without one you have no way of knowing if you are on track for funding your retirement. Any decent computer program or Web site analysis will include the following variables:

- Your current age or birth date
- The age at which you want to retire
- How long you expect to live during retirement (The average retiree lives 15 to 20 years; unless you have serious medical problems, try to fund your retirement for 30 years.)
- Expected annual income from Social Security
- Expected annual pension income from former and current employers
- Current balances in your retirement accounts that are sheltered from taxes (such as your RIA)
- Current balances in your retirement accounts that are not sheltered from taxes
- Any other assets, such as real estate or a business, that you plan to use to fund retirement
- The rate of return you are trying to earn on investments before retirement
- The rate of return you want to earn on investments after you retire
- What you expect the inflation rate to average for the next 20 years
- The amount that you can invest each year
- Your current salary
- Any other income you currently receive
- The expected annual percentage increase in your salary
- Expected future inheritances (not all programs ask this)

You should receive a printout like the one in Figure 13.2 showing at what age your retirement funds will be exhausted.

You can determine if you are on track for funding retirement in four different ways described in the following. Complete at least two of them. If the numbers from the first two are not close, try a third.

Figure 13.2 Sample Printout for Hypothetical Worker of Age at Which Retirement Funds Will Be Exhausted

Year	Your Age	Spouse's Age	Your Portfolio	Total Income	From Portfolio	Social Security
1999	57	56	$362,000			
2000	58	57	410,000			
2001	59	58	464,000			
2002	60	59	523,000			
2003	61	60	568,000			
2004	62	61	660,000			
2005	63	62	739,000			
2006	64	63	827,000			
2007	65	64	923,000	$72,000	$42,000	$30,000
2008	66	65	1,025,000	75,000	44,000	31,000
2009	67	66	1,082,000	78,000	46,000	32,000
2010	68	67	1,143,000	82,000	48,000	34,000
2036	94	93	5,594,000	217,000	128,000	89,000
2037	95	94	6,021,000	226,000	133,000	93,000
2038	96	95	6,484,000	235,000	138,000	97,000

Observations: The worker did not have a defined benefit pension. In this example, the retired couple's portfolio balance is expected to continue growing during the rest of their life, but they will have an estate tax problem well before they turn 70. While this portfolio continues to grow at 8 percent each year, in a real situation the total value of the portfolio will decline some years. In other years it will increase at a rate significantly above 8 percent. The person retires at age 65.

Software. Buy a software program like Quicken Financial Planner.

Hire a financial planner. Chapter 3 discusses how to find a competent planner. *The Baby Boomer Financial Wake-Up Call* by Kay R. Shirley (Dearborn Financial Publishing, 1999) discusses specific strategies based on your age (40, 50, or 60).

Check Web site www.money.com/ This is an excellent site with information about a wide range of financial topics, including several retirement calculators. To find the one that I like best, look on the left side of the home page for Goals. In the text immediately below Goals, click on Retirement. When you get to the next page, click on Retirement Savings Calculator; on the following page, click on Retirement Calculator.

If you will not become financially independent at the age you have selected, you have the following five choices:

1. Reduce the amount of monthly income that you think you need at retirement.
2. Try to earn a higher return on your invested dollars.
3. Invest more each month.
4. Plan to postpone retirement for one or more years.
5. Plan to work for several years *during* retirement.

Using the Retirement Calculator at the Web site noted above makes it easy for you to do "what if" experiments. When Jackie first ran her numbers, her funds were exhausted at age 79. Jackie comes from a family in which relatives often live into their

> **Hot Tip**
>
> **I**f you are married, most computer programs assume that you and your spouse will retire together. The better programs allow each spouse to enter his or her own data.

> **Hot Tip**
>
> **J**ust before you finish entering all your data, you will come to two boxes: select Year by Year Cash Flow Statement in the first box and Show Results in Future Dollars in the second box before clicking on Calculate.

> **Hot Tip**
>
> **C**heck any printout carefully. You do not want the total value of your portfolio to start to decline before you turn 85. If it does, your portfolio will likely be exhausted before you reach 95 (and you may live that long).

80s and 90s, so Jackie did not want to run out of money before she reached her 80s. She decided to postpone retirement for two years, giving her investments a longer time to grow while reducing the numbers of years they would have to fund her retirement. Because of this adjustment, her retirement funds were now projected to last until she turned 86. Well, Jackie really wanted to make it into her 90s, so she reduced the amount of money she wanted to spend by $2,000 a year. Sure enough, with this additional change, her funds were projected to last until she turned 92.

Compute the needs analysis below. You have seen needs analyses similar to this one in numerous articles about planning retirement. These are helpful *if* retirement is more than 15 years away, but they lack the precision of one using more complex mathematical modeling. No matter when you plan to retire, I recommend that you work through this one. Doing so does indicate if you are currently on track for funding your retirement.

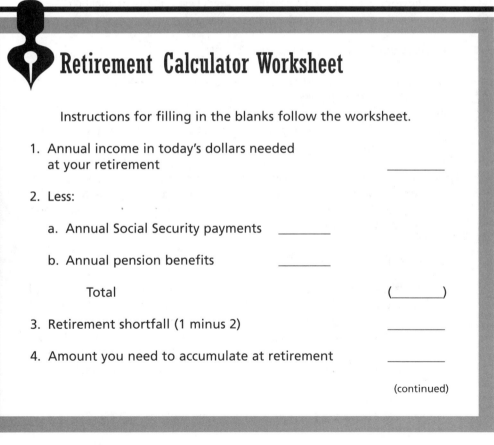

Retirement Calculator Worksheet

Instructions for filling in the blanks follow the worksheet.

1. Annual income in today's dollars needed at your retirement   _____

2. Less:

    a. Annual Social Security payments   _____

    b. Annual pension benefits   _____

    Total   (_____)

3. Retirement shortfall (1 minus 2)   _____

4. Amount you need to accumulate at retirement   _____

(continued)

Retirement Calculator Worksheet
(continued)

5. Current balances in retirement accounts _____

6. Future value of current balances in your retirement accounts _____

7. Retirement surplus (deficit) _____
   (Note: If you have a surplus, ignore step 8.)

8. Annual contribution needed to fund deficit on 7 _____
   (Note: You will probably need your employer's help with this contribution.)

Instructions for filling in the worksheet:

1. Obtain this amount from the retirement budget you completed earlier in the chapter.

2a. Obtain this amount from your Social Security benefit statement; if married, include both spouses' benefits.

2b. You will need to get this amount from any employer who sponsored a defined benefit retirement plan. You should be able to locate this amount on the annual benefit statement your employer should send you.

3. Subtract the amount on line 2 from the amount on line 1.

4. Multiply the amount on line 3 by your factor from Table 1. Find your factor by seeing where the column titled "Years till you retire" intersects with "Your life expectancy after you retire." For example, Roger wants to retire in 30 years and expects to live 25 years after he retires. His factor is 49. Jane wants to retire in 27 years and expects to live 28 years after she retires. Her factor is 55.

Retirement Calculator Worksheet
(continued)

Table 1

Your life expectancy after you retire

	5	10	15	20	25	30	35	40	45
15	13	16	19	24	29	35	43	52	63
20	16	19	24	29	35	43	52	63	77
25	19	23	27	33	40	49	60	73	89
30	21	25	30	37	45	55	67	81	99
35	22	27	33	40	49	59	72	88	107
40	24	29	35	43	52	63	77	93	114

(Columns labeled "Years till you retire")

5. Add together the amounts that you have in your 401(k) or 403(b) account, your IRA balances, your investment accounts, your net equity in real estate earmarked for retirement, and the current market value of your business.

6. Multiply the amount on line 5 by your factor from Table 2. Will does not want to retire for 30 years. He can earn 9 percent on average on the dollars he has invested, so his factor is 13.27.

Table 2

Rate of return — Years till you retire

Rate of return	5	10	15	20	25	30	35	40	45
7%	1.40	1.97	2.76	3.87	5.43	7.61	10.68	14.97	21.00
8%	1.47	2.16	3.17	4.66	6.85	10.06	14.79	21.72	31.92
9%	1.54	2.37	3.64	5.60	8.62	13.27	20.41	31.41	48.33
10%	1.61	2.59	4.18	6.73	10.83	17.45	28.10	45.26	72.89
11%	1.69	2.84	4.78	8.06	13.59	22.89	38.57	65.00	109.53
12%	1.76	3.11	5.47	9.65	17.00	29.96	52.80	93.05	163.99

7. Subtract amount on line 6 from amount on line 4.

(continued)

Retirement Calculator Worksheet
(continued)

8. Divide amount on line 7 by factor in Table 3.

Table 3

Rate of return	Years till you retire								
	5	10	15	20	25	30	35	40	45
7%	5.75	13.82	25.13	41.00	63.25	94.46	138.24	199.64	285.75
8%	5.87	14.49	27.15	45.76	73.11	113.28	172.32	259.06	386.51
9%	5.98	15.19	29.36	51.16	84.70	136.31	215.71	337.88	525.86
10%	6.11	15.94	31.77	57.27	98.35	164.49	271.02	442.59	718.90
11%	6.23	16.72	34.41	64.20	114.41	199.02	341.59	581.83	986.64
12%	6.35	17.55	37.28	72.05	133.33	241.33	431.66	767.09	1358.23

Are you on track for funding your retirement? You have been exposed to four different methods you can use to answer this question. If your answer is a definite *no,* then you need professional help now.

The Soft Side of Retiring

The primary focus of this chapter has been the financial side of retiring. If, however, retirement is less than 20 years away, you need to think about the quality of the life you are seeking when you retire. I always ask my clients, "How do you want to spend your time after you retire?" I specifically want to know the activities that interest them. Responses usually include traveling, golf, volunteer work, education, and often a passion for a special project. I want them to tell me which of these activities they do not plan to engage in until they retire.

Too many times, people look forward to retirement as a time when they can do things they lacked the time to do when raising a family and working. Next to underfunding retirement, this is the second biggest mistake people make. Don't save yourself for retirement. Do not put off your involvement in any activity until you retire. You may currently not have all the time right now you want to devote to that activity. No matter what that pastime is, you can find some time this year to participate in the activity.

Clients always have one of the following three excuses: (1) I don't have the money; (2) I don't have the time; or (3) I really don't know how to begin. I respond: People always find time for what interests them. Most people also seem to be able to get their hands on the money needed. I remind clients that three people out of ten never live long enough to reach retirement. If an activity is saved for retirement, you may lose the chance to participate.

Start on a hobby or activity now, and you will enrich your life. Only a fool puts off living life until after retirement.

Besides wanting to know how clients plan to spend their time, I am also interested in knowing where they want to live. The happiest retirees seem to live near family and friends. People who move away from everyone they have spent a lifetime getting to know find they take an emptiness with them that takes a long time to fill. It is understandable that most retirees want to live where there is less winter, close to excellent medical services, and in an area where the cost of living is bearable. Retirees planning on living in a place they have only read about in books should wisely spend at least three weeks in that fantasy world during each of the four seasons of the year before they make a permanent move. People who retire smart do three things well:

1. They do not retire until they have accumulated the needed funds.
2. They are currently involved in every activity that will interest them at retirement.
3. If they move to a new place, they have thoroughly checked it out several times before moving there.

The real retirement all-stars are the people who engage in work that they love so much that they never plan to retire. Promise yourself that you will start at least one activity this year that you were saving for retirement. You will enrich your life now. Planning for tomorrow is smart; getting the most out of this day is wise.

Financial Checkup Checklist

- Complete your retirement budget.

- Be confident that you have selected the appropriate beneficiary for each retirement plan or account.

- Complete at least two different retirement needs analyses.

- Know the amount that you need to invest each month to fund retirement.

- Start participating in at least one activity that you had planned to save for retirement.

- Visit any new place you plan to retire to at least once during each season before buying a place to live.

14 Investing in Stocks and Bonds

Understand the basics of investing in stocks and bonds.

> Ethel and Henry wanted to know when they could retire. I went through the basic questions, including at what age they wanted to retire, and, at retirement, how much they wanted to live on a month. Ethel and Henry were children of the depression. When they started stashing money away for retirement, they bought bonds. When they came to visit me, their entire investment portfolio was made up of bonds. My calculations showed that if they would continue to put money away as they had, they could retire in ten years. However, to do so they needed one change: they needed to switch 50 percent of their investments from bonds to stocks. They were disappointed that they had to wait ten more years before they could retire. I did not tell them that had they bought stocks all those years instead of bonds, they could retire now with much more money than they wanted.

Today, there is a place for bonds in a portfolio but not when retirement is decades off. In the short run, stocks are riskier than bonds; however, in the long run, bonds carry the greater risk. Investing is for the long haul. The farther away the goal you are trying to fund through investments, the more likely you are to be successful if you buy stocks. While there are several different types of investments, such as real estate and owning a business, in this chapter I examine only stocks and bonds.

How Comfortable Are You with Investment Risk?

Yes, you can buy an investment and lose all your money, but that rarely happens when you pay cash for the types of investments discussed in this chapter. All investments change in value each day. Such short-term price movements are not important. Wise investors expect to leave their money in investments for several years. Most people who are afraid of losing their money when they invest really know very little about investing. You can dramatically reduce your fear of investing by educating yourself about it. The more you know, the more you will not only increase your comfort level with risk but the better the job you'll do investing. If you have never invested or if you become upset when your investments decline in value, read at least one of the following books before you invest another dime. Peter Lynch has written two of my favorites: *One Up on Wall Street* and *Beating the Street*. No one explains investing any better.

Anyone who buys a share of stock is a part owner in the company that issued the stock. Owners can benefit in two ways:

1. The stock may pay dividends to shareholders. Dividends are a share of the profits of the company.
2. The stock market demonstrates the economic concept of supply and demand. When people want to own more shares of a company's stock than the amount the company has issued, the price of the shares goes up. This often occurs when the company's profits grow at an increasing rate each year. When profits, sometimes called earnings, are going down or are expected to go down, the price of each share of stock drops because fewer people want to own the shares.

Anyone who buys bonds issued by a company or government is a lender. Bonds are evidence of debt. A bond owner may benefit two ways:

1. A bond pays interest. The company or government that issued the bonds uses some of its income or tax revenues to pay interest to bondholders.
2. The value of the bond may go up or go down depending on the direction interest rates are headed. When interest rates are climbing, bond prices are declining. Why? Suppose you bought a bond several years ago for $1,000 that paid 5 percent interest or $50 a year. Suppose that interest rates are climbing and new bonds recently purchased now pay 7 percent interest annually. Is anyone going to give you $1,000 for a bond that only pays 5 percent interest, or $50, a year when a new bond pays $70? Now that bond interest rates are 7 percent, the price of your bond must drop until it yields 7 percent. Here's how it works:

$$\frac{\$50}{\$710} = 7\%$$

Believe it or not, you can pay $1,000 for a bond issued by the United States government, but when interest rates rise, you could get no more than $710 for the bond if you wanted to sell it several years before the government redeemed it. Almost any bond sold has a redemption date—that's the day when the company or government that issued the bond will buy it back. If you bought the 5 percent bond from the U.S. government and held it until it was redeemed, you would get $1,000 for it. Because of inflation, however, that $1,000 would buy significantly less than it could have when you first bought the bond. Anyone who buys bonds must live with interest rate risk, the risk that the value of bonds will decline as interest rates rise.

Historically, stocks have increased in value about 10 percent annually, whereas bonds have returned less than 5 percent. Over the long run, your money will grow much faster invested in stocks.

Buying Stocks

Everyone wants to help you manage your investments. The more you know about investing, the more successful you will be, with or without professional help. Educate yourself before you seek professional help and before you invest your money. While I recommend that you start investing by first purchasing mutual fund shares (discussed in the next chapter), you need to know something about buying stocks before you ever invest. People who buy stocks can be sorted into three groups:

1. *Traders.* They follow the movement of the market all day, every day. Traders often buy and sell the same security the same day. Few traders actually make money, and watching the market all day long is an easy way to develop ulcers.
2. *Timers.* These people actually think they can predict market highs and lows. Few can, so almost no market timers make money owning stocks.
3. *Buy and holders.* Almost anyone who has ever made money in the stock market holds stock for the long term. Peter Lynch, the once longtime manager of the Fidelity Magellan mutual fund, states that he learned early it usually took a stock two or three years after he bought it before the stock started to move up the charts. Warren Buffett believes that one should own a stock for at least ten years. You are saved from the traps that snare traders and timers if you lack the expertise, experience, and time to play their games.

Stock prices change constantly, but over the longer term, the trend is definitely up. For almost any ten-year period you select (except the 1970s), the return on common stocks has ranged between 10 and 12 percent or higher. I want to discuss three different approaches that you might use to buy stocks, but I want to discuss two issues first.

Did you find it hard to believe that most traders and timers don't make money most of the time? Let me tell you why. Three of the most respected names in investing—Warren Buffett, Peter Lynch, and Sir Isaac Templeton—not only recommend that you invest for the long term, but they suggest that you stay fully invested all the time. They seem to know what the traders and timers do not. In the short run, investor psychology moves market prices. If traders and timers think a depression is coming or that interest rates or inflation is headed higher, they sell. However, the market often moves in the opposite direction from the one conventional wisdom suggests, so traders and times are often left with large losses. *No one can correctly predict what the stock market is going to do over a few days or weeks.* If someone could, he or she could turn $1,000 into $1 million in less than a year.

The second issue I want to discuss is that the name of the game is the number of shares you own, *not* the value of each share. Everyone wants stock prices to rise, but unless you own shares of Berkshire Hathaway, you are never going to own a stock whose price goes through the glass ceiling. Why? Most companies want to keep the price of their stock shares between $20 and $100. When the price of a company's stock goes above a certain value, such as $100, the company will often split its stock, which results in each shareholder receiving more shares. For example, the value of ABC's shares has reached $100, so for every share a person owns, ABC sends that shareholder another share of stock—this is a 2-for-1 split. Now the person owns two shares, and naturally the value of each share drops to $50. Before the split, the shareholder owned one share worth $100, but now owns two shares that together are worth $100. Is the shareholder better off? Maybe not initially, but it's hoped and is probable the price of the shares will go back to $100 again as ABC continues to make more profits.

Only two ways are available for you to increase the numbers of shares of a stock you own: buy them or own shares of

> **Hot Tip**
>
> Before you buy shares of a stock that pays a dividend, find out if the company offers a dividend reinvestment plan (DRIP). A stockbroker can answer this question for you as can a company's shareholders' services office. You can also buy stocks directly from over 1,000 companies. To check on both programs, check www.netstockdirect.com, which lists companies whose stocks you can purchase directly from the company and those offering DRIPs.

a company that provides you with additional shares without a purchase through a dividend reinvestment plan or as the result of a stock split. Many companies participate in a program that allows you to take the dividends your stock pays and buy more shares of that company's stock without paying a commission. Some popular stocks that offer such a dividend reinvestment plan, more commonly referred to as a DRIP program, include AT&T, General Electric, IBM, Kellogg, Merck, and Procter & Gamble.

> **Hot Tip**
>
> Most people who have ever made significant profits in stocks have owned shares for a considerable period of time, long enough for their stocks to have split several times.

A more dramatic way to increase the number of shares you own is to buy stocks of companies that periodically split their shares as discussed using the ABC example.

Three Approaches to Buying Shares of Stock

There are many more approaches than the three discussed here. Two common ones are known as the technical and the fundamental approaches. Space doesn't allow a discussion of these two strategies, but any book devoted to investing in stocks typically discusses these two approaches. My three approaches follow.

1. Make a list of companies whose products and services you use and like.

These may be products or services that you use as a consumer or as an employee. Consider buying stocks of companies that have a factory or store close enough so that your local paper will follow the fortunes of the company. Add to your list companies whose products and services have been recommended by friends and family. Many professional stock pickers poke fun at this idea. Such pros would be thrilled to have owned McDonald's, Coke, The Home Depot, Wal-Mart, The Gap, MCI Worldcom, Southwestern Bell, Southwest Airlines, and Microsoft since they started investing. Most of what they have recommended (and owned) have not performed nearly as well as did these stocks. Build your list until you have the names of 25 companies who make or offer products and services you like and use.

Turn on your computer or head for your nearby library and ask the reference librarian to help you find the Value Line Investment Survey and Standard and Poor's Stock Report. Stocks are bought and sold on exchanges like the New York Stock Exchange and the Nasdaq. In its list of stocks, Value Line does not separate stocks by the exchange on which they are traded. Standard and Poor's does, so they have a separate reference service (set of books) for stocks traded on each exchange. Look up each of the 25 stocks on your list in Value Line first so you can tell on which exchange the stock is traded. You will find one page devoted to each of the stocks on your list.

Research any company at these Web sites:

- www.hoovers.com
- www.personalwealth.com
- www.zacks.com
- www.investorama.com

After you have read summaries about a stock in both Value Line and Standard and Poor's, assign the stock a priority from 1 (the best) to 10 (avoid).

Now focus on those stocks which you rated 1. Prioritize these stocks in Group 1 by giving the most attractive stock an A, next most a B, and so on. Begin buying shares of the stock you ranked 1A until you own 100 shares. Next start buying 100 shares of the stock ranked 1B. Continue until you own 100 shares of five different companies. *You really never get to know a company until you own its stock.* When you have additional money to invest, you will know which of your five stocks is doing the best. In fact, you may want to sell the shares of one or two stocks so you can buy more shares of one of the other companies.

2. Buy stocks of companies that have a history of increasing their dividends each year. The dividends of most companies, much like interest on savings accounts, pay a low return between 2 and 4 percent. But the dividends of many companies, unlike savings interest, increase each year. Look for companies that have a history of increasing their dividends at least 6 per-

Hot Tip

Never buy a share of stock when the stock's price-earnings (PE) ratio is higher than the expected annual percentage growth in profits for the foreseeable future. A price-earnings ratio is computed as follows: divide the current market price of the stock by the earnings (the amount of profit per share). For example, if the company has 1,000 shareholders and earned a $10,000 profit, the earnings (profit) per share would be $10. If shares were selling at $120 a share, the company's PE ratio, or PE, would be 12 ($120 divided by $10). If the company expects profits to grow 15 percent a year for the next several years, then the stock has a place on your list since its PE is 12. However, suppose that Fliget Company's PE was 45 compared with an expected annual increase in profits of 32 percent for the next several years. Right now Fliget shares are too expensive to buy. Wait to buy until Fliget's PE is lower than the expected annual percentage increase in profits.

cent a year for the past several years. Many companies do not pay dividends. Refer to your list of your 25 favorite companies and check to see which ones have a sound record of paying dividends. Paying dividends is not a criteria for owning stocks unless you need the dividend income to support you. However, eight to ten years before you retire, it makes sense to start buying shares of stocks of companies that do pay dividends.

3. Start an investment club. Get together a group of friends or fellow employees. Contact the National Association of Investors Corporation, P. O. Box 220, Royal Oak, MI 48068; phone 248-583-6242, fax 248-583-4880; its Web site is www.better-investing.org. It will be happy to provide information on setting up a club. With several people looking for investment opportunities, you can easily expand your investment horizons while learning more about investing at the same time. Many clubs meet once a week or once a month. Members often contribute between $20 and $100 a month. If you have never bought stock before, this is an excellent way to learn the ropes.

Buying Shares of Stock

When you are ready to buy stocks, you will need to open an account. All you need do is phone a company like Merrill Lynch and ask to talk with a broker. While most brokers are competent and honest, they make a living only when you buy and sell shares; expect them to call fairly often suggesting that you sell one stock so that you can buy another. Commissions can eat up most of your profit if you are not careful.

If you do not need all the benefits of working with a full-service broker, consider opening an account with a discount broker like those listed below. You should benefit in two ways:

1. Commissions charged by discount brokers are lower than full-service brokers. You can trade 1,000 shares and pay a commission of $30 or less at a discount broker. A full-service broker may charge significantly more to buy 100 shares of a stock.

> **Hot Tip**
>
> Rarely consider giving a broker blanket permission to buy and sell shares in your account without first receiving your permission to execute every specific transaction. Far too many brokers churn such accounts by buying and selling shares so often that brokers earn excellent incomes, but the commissions eat up clients' profits.

2. No one will call you and try to talk you into buying the hot stock of the day. Brokers primarily like to sell cyclical stocks (stocks whose prices are expected to go up for several months and then are likely to go down for several months). Most brokers cannot make a living selling stocks that a client holds for a long time. Basic message: brokers prefer traders and timers to buy and holders.

Discount brokers who deserve a call:

Bidwell	800-547-6337
Charles Schwab	800-435-4000
Fidelity	800-544-6666
T. Rowe Price	800-225-5132

> **Hot Tip**
>
> Some people think that low-priced trading sites may not execute orders fast enough (although I think they are faster than humans most of the time). You can go to www.quicken.com and find a list showing how much each stock traded for at one-minute intervals during the day. You can then compare what you paid for the stock with the price at the time you placed your order.

Also find out about making trades in your account using the Internet. For example, Shirley has an account with Charles Schwab. Whenever she wants to buy or sell stocks or shares of mutual funds in her accounts, she does the entire trade once she has accessed her account on the Internet. Shirley also pays less in commissions than if she had talked with a human. Trade stocks using the Internet and no broker will call. You can place an order 24 hours a day, 7 days a week (although it will only be executed during the day Monday through Friday). Trading on the computer is one more way to simplify your life.

Here are two low-cost trading sites on the Web:

E*Trade	www.etrade.com	800-786-2575
AmeriTrade	www.ameritrade.com	800-454-9272

When Should You Sell?

You should sell

- when your invested dollars have grown large enough to fund the goal you set;
- when the company is not operating as profitably as before; or

> **Hot Tip**
>
> At some Web sites, you can execute trades for as little as $8.

- when you would prefer having your dollars invested in the stock of a company other than the one you now own.

How do you know when the company is not operating as profitably as before? You may have received clues as a customer. Service or product quality may have declined. Quarterly or annual reports from the company may have reported disappointing earnings (profits) per share. If you purchased shares of a firm with a store or factory nearby, an article in your local paper may have fingered the problem.

> **Hot Tip**
>
> **C**ongress has made the tax computations of selling securities somewhat complicated. Unless you know the tax law concerning capital gains and losses, consult a certified public accountant who specializes in personal income taxes before filing your return if you made several sales during the year.

When Not to Buy

- Don't buy anything from anyone who calls you on the phone. Most calls are from novices who may know less than you do about investing—maybe a lot less.
- Don't buy anything based on someone's hot tip unless he or she has made a fortune investing in stocks.
- Don't buy on hot tips from an employee about a pending, but unknown-to-the-public deal involving his or her company; it is illegal to invest in a stock if you receive such insider information before the public knows.

Keep an Accurate Record of Your Stock Transactions

Check your monthly statements carefully (and keep the statements). Keep a separate log of all transactions as a check against the statements.

When Goals Are Less Than Ten Years Away

Invest in stocks to fund longer-term goals such as retirement, education, and starting a business when such goals are at least five or six years away (ten is better). As you get closer to the time when the goal is to be funded, you need to monitor your investments more closely. Consider selling more speculative investments. Bonds can be less risky in the short run than stocks. Here are the basics that you need to know about bonds.

Stock Transactions Worksheet

Name of Company	Date Bought	# of Shares	Amount Paid* per Share	Date Sold	# of Shares Sold	Amount Received* per Share

*Include sales commissions

Corporate bonds are sold in $1,000 units; government bonds can be sold in $1,000, $5,000, and $10,000 units. Most bonds carry fixed rates of interest. For example, a corporation issues a $1,000 bond with a 6 percent fixed coupon rate. Each year the bond will pay $60 in interest until the corporation buys it back. If the bond does not make the interest payment, it is in default. (When the company that issues the bonds is liquidated, bondholders may receive back some of their money.) Some newer bonds' interest rates are variable, with the interest rates tied to indexes that measure inflation.

Rating services evaluate bonds based on the financial health of the company. The most common rating services are Moody's and Standard and Poor's. If you have a computer check out both Web sites: Moody's is www.moodys.com/ and Standard and Poor's is www.stockinfo.standardpoor.com/.

Bonds face two types of risk:

1. *Business risk.* The company or government that issued the bonds goes broke, so it is unable to pay interest income to bondholders and to buy back the bonds. The rating services provide the buyer with a fairly reliable assessment of the likelihood that the issuer will go broke.
2. *Interest rate risk.* When interest rates go up, new bonds carry a higher interest rate; the value of old bonds declines as previously discussed. Bond interest rates climbed dramatically during the 1970s, reaching peaks in the early 1980s. During the 1970s, bond owners took a beating as rising bond interest rates pushed down the value of bonds in their portfolios. Beginning in the early 1980s, rates started coming down. That decline lasted through the 1990s. With rates coming down, new bonds were issued with lower rates, but the value of previously issued bonds increased.

What can you expect to happen to bonds? Interest rates may continue to decline a little longer, but interest rates are getting close to the bottom. Rates may (or may not) stay low for a long time, but eventually they will start to go up again. People who buy a new bond will receive a low rate of return; when rates do start back up, the value of their bonds will decline unless the bond's redemption date is close.

Real After-Tax Rate of Return for Bonds

Many bonds today pay about 5 percent interest. How much of the 5 percent really benefits the owner? Consider a bond that pays $50 a year.

Bond interest	$50
Less: inflation	(30)
Less: taxes at .28%	(14)
Bondholder's real benefit	$ 6

The bondholder paid $1,000 for the bond; however, inflation reduced the buying power of the bond by 3 percent, or $30 on average each year. So the bondholder gets the $30 back from the interest the bond pays. Uncle Sam also gets paid taxes on the interest. Since this bondholder pays 28 percent of her income in taxes, $14 of the $50 is sent to the IRS. The bondholder is ahead $6. Not much of a return, especially since the bondholder faces the risk that the value of her bond will drop when interest rates start back up.

If you must buy bonds during the foreseeable future, purchase bonds with short-term maturities (less than a year). Because a government or corporation will redeem its bonds in a few weeks or months, you have basically eliminated both business and interest rate risk. While you can buy individual bonds, most people find it more convenient and less expensive to buy shares of mutual funds that invest in bonds (discussed in the next chapter). Shares of mutual funds whose portfolios mirror short-term interest rate indexes are popular.

Consider the following portfolio adjustments when goals are less than ten years away:

- *Between five and ten years away.* Eliminate the vast majority of speculative investments such as small companies and international companies. Increase your ownership of blue chip companies like those in Standard and Poor's 500 index. This is also an excellent time to increase your holdings of utility stocks. You may want to include bonds and shares of bond mutual funds in your portfolio.
- *Less than five years away.* Focus on owning shares of companies that have a long history of paying dividends, especially companies whose dividend payments have been increasing. Increase your ownership of bonds and mutual funds that invest in bonds; the maturity date for these bond investments should be short term.

There is a place in your portfolio for bonds under the following three conditions:

1. You have more money than you know what to do with and you do not want to risk losing your principal (so you buy bonds with short-term maturities).
2. You are trying to fund a goal that is less than ten years away.
3. You are retired and are concerned about not risking all of your prin-

> **Hot Tip**
>
> When retirement is less than ten years away, you may want to include some bonds in your portfolio. However, at retirement most of your investment dollars should still be in stocks or mutual funds that own stocks.

cipal so you own bonds with short-term maturities. Fifteen or 20 years from now, when interest rates start rising again, you can switch to bonds with much longer maturities.

Fund goals that are more than ten years away with stocks and mutual funds that invest in stocks. Read Peter Lynch's book *One Up on Wall Street* and Harry Dent's book *The Roaring 2000s,* published by Simon and Schuster. If you have never invested before, these books should be required reading before you do.

If seeing the value of your bonds or shares of stock drop significantly causes an anxiety attack, stick with mutual funds (discussed next). While the value of fund shares can also drop, at least your investment risk is spread over dozens, perhaps hundreds, of different investments. Mutual fund shares will eventually rebound; this is not true for the price of all shares of stock. You can make more money owning shares of stock, but you can also lose more. Stock and bond ownership is not for everyone.

Financial Checkup Checklist

- Become more educated about the stock market—read at least one of the books mentioned above.

- Make a list of 25 companies whose products and services you use and like—these are potential investment opportunities.

- Open a brokerage account.

15 Buying and Selling Mutual Fund Shares

Understand the basic steps in creating a mutual fund portfolio.

When the Youngs came to see me, I asked how I could help them. They replied: We want to retire within ten years. We put all our money with a company in Arizona that told us it would invest it for us in its mutual funds to enable us to achieve our retirement goals. The company had earned 7 percent on average a year for the last nine years. Somehow its financial advisor had selected a portfolio of some of the worst-performing mutual funds in the industry. While I was familiar with the company to whom they had entrusted their money, I had never heard of the funds that made up their portfolio. Needless to say, the Youngs were behind in their plan to retire in ten years. Had they obtained a 10 percent return during the past nine years, they would have been right on target for achieving their retirement dream (and a 10 percent average return would have been significantly below what the average mutual fund returned in the 1990s).

What Is a Mutual Fund?

Mutual funds are companies that own stocks and bonds of corporations as well as bonds issued by governments. Some mutual funds own only stocks of companies headquartered in the United States. Some mutual funds just own stocks and/or bonds of companies in a certain region of the world, such as Europe. Owning mutual fund shares offers many advantages over owning shares of individual stocks. The following sections examine some of the characteristics of mutual funds.

Portfolio diversification. Mutual funds pool the money of their investors so they can own a variety of stocks and bonds. A person who buys one share of a mutual fund is indirectly the part owner (or creditor) of many different companies and/or governments. Owning mutual fund shares reduces the risk of only owning shares in one company and then losing all your money if that company goes broke.

Professional management of invested dollars. Many investors lack the time, knowledge, or interest to select and manage individual investments, so they let professional stock pickers, who work for—actually manage—mutual funds make the choices. Mutual funds that primarily buy stocks of technology companies and are creating the information highway have performed well over the past several years. Yet few investors feel comfortable investing in these companies, many of which have only been in business for a short period of time. For example, Ty knows that many technology companies have seen their stock prices skyrocket; Ty expects many of these companies to continue to do well. However, Ty does not feel comfortable selecting individual stocks, so Ty buys shares of a mutual fund that invests in the information highway. He believes that the fund's managers can do a better job selecting stocks than he can.

The dollar amount required to open and add to an account. This amount varies greatly from mutual fund to mutual fund. The amount may be as low as $25 or as high as $10,000 to open an account with a mutual fund company. The dollar amount required to make additional purchases also varies. In a few funds, there is no minimum, but most require additional purchases to be at least $25. Some funds require that additional purchases be at least $1,000.

The ability to open an account through the mail or on the Internet. For example, Sally opens an account in a mutual fund that will accept an initial deposit of $100. Once the fund receives Sally's check, the fund sends Sally a confirmation. When Sally makes additional purchases, she will receive a statement showing the price she paid for each share she bought with her latest check, the total number of shares she owns, and the total value of her account.

Dollar Cost Averaging

Almost all successful investors share one characteristic: they regularly purchase shares each and every month.

Hot Tip

The best way to buy mutual fund shares is to give the mutual fund authority to automatically send its check for a predetermined amount to your checking account once a month to buy shares. You have almost no bookkeeping to do, and you buy shares every month. Many mutual funds require that minimum purchases must be $100 or higher. However, if you check the fine print in the fund's literature, such funds will often allow you to set up an automatic purchase plan that allows the fund to make minimum purchases of $25 or $50 a month for you. Some fund families, shown below, allow you to make monthly purchases for as little as $25 a month for most funds in their family. A fund family is a group of mutual funds managed by one company; for example, Fidelity manages several dozen different mutual funds. Most of the funds on the following list are load funds, meaning they charge a sales commission to cover the cost of handling such small transactions. If you are interested in learning more about the funds in one or more of these families, call the 800 number:

Fund Families	800 Numbers
Alliance	221-5672
Franklin	342-5236
Oppenheimer	525-7048
Putman	225-1581
Templeton	292-9293
Van Kampen	421-5666
Waddell & Reed	366-5465

Have you ever heard the advice, "Buy low and sell high"? Too many people do just the opposite. They buy when a security is selling at a high price, hold it for awhile until its price has dropped significantly, get tired of waiting for the price to go back up, and then sell low.

Avoid the trap of buying when the price of a security is high and selling when it is low by buying the same dollar amount every month. This strategy is known as dollar cost averaging, and has two benefits:

1. Your portfolio is growing because you are making regular monthly purchases.
2. The average price of the shares is likely to be higher than what you actually paid for them.

Here's how dollar cost averaging works. JoAnn makes the following purchases:

Month	Purchase	Price per Share	Number of Shares Bought	Number of Shares Owned
March	$100	$10	10	10
April	$100	12	8.33	18.33
May	$100	8	12.50	30.83
June	$100	10	10	40.83

Dollar amount invested $400
Value of portfolio $408.30

Dividends and capital gains distributions are automatically reinvested to buy you more shares of the fund. When you buy shares of a stock, most companies will send you a dividend check every three months (this is your share of the profits the company earned). Most people make the mistake of spending their dividend income. When a mutual fund receives dividends from the shares it holds, the fund must send the dividends to its fund shareholders. Funds give shareholders an option. They can send dividends to the shareholder or reinvest a shareholder's dividends to buy more shares.

Mutual fund companies are always selling and buying stocks and bonds. They hope to sell the stocks and bonds in their portfolio at a profit. The profit, known as capital gains, must also be sent to the shareholder, who has the option of receiving a check for his or her share of the capital gains or having the fund use the gains to buy more shares for the shareholder.

The chart in Figure 15.1 assumes that an investor initially invested $10,000 in December 1988. Years later the $10,000 grew to $24,030 if the investor received the capital gains and dividends in cash from the mutual fund. Had the shareholder let the mutual fund use the capital gains and dividends to buy more shares of the fund, the value of the account would have grown to $37,243. Be sure to notice that the original $10,000 grew by $14,030 ($24,030 − $10,000). However, by reinvesting the dividends and capital gains, the account grew an additional $13,213 ($37,243 − $24,030). That increase is nearly as much as the original $10,000 grew. Anyone who received the dividends and capital gains in cash and spent that income failed to earn the additional $13,213.

When you buy and sell fund shares, you deal directly with the mutual fund by letter, phone, fax, or over the Internet. This often saves you money by eliminating a third party and often makes transactions possible 24 hours a day, 7 days a week.

You can buy shares of many mutual funds without paying a sales commission (such funds are known as no-load funds). Sales commissions can run as high as 8 percent on fund shares known as load mutual funds. Jane invests $100 into a no-load fund; her $100 buys $100 worth of shares. Jack invests $100 in a mutual fund that charges a sales fee of 8 percent; only 92 of his dollars go to work for him.

Figure 15.1 Fund Value of $10,000 Investment

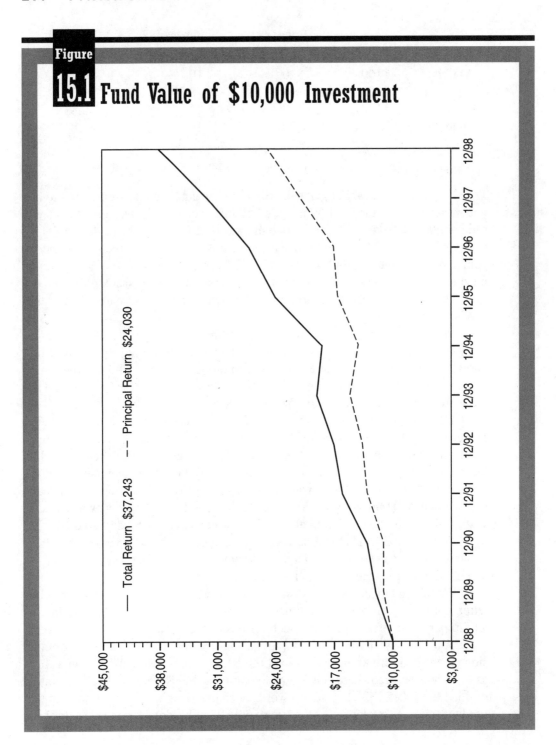

Should you buy only no-load mutual fund shares? A sales commission is only one factor in selecting a mutual fund. If your top-ranked fund charges a sales commission, buy the shares and pay the commission. Whether you initially paid a commission to buy shares will have little impact over the long haul (more than ten years) on the value of your fund shares.

Once the market value of your shares in a specific mutual fund exceeds $10,000, that fund can send you a check each month (if you ask). Of course, the mutual fund must sell some of your shares each month. Obviously, this is a strategy you will want to refrain from using until you become financially independent.

> **Hot Tip**
>
> Take advantage of the mutual fund's reinvesting dividends and capital gains to purchase more shares of the mutual fund. As the chart in Figure 15.1 shows, the reinvestment of dividends and capital gains is a powerful way to achieve financial independence.

Because each fund is part of a family of funds, you can sell one fund with a single phone call and use the proceeds to buy another fund in the same family. Suppose you think that the stock market is going to crash and you own an aggressive growth fund (a fund whose share price can be expected to dive if the market crashes). Funds make it convenient to phone the fund and transfer your dollars from the growth fund to a money market fund.

How to Select Mutual Funds

Your company's retirement plan probably requires you to decide how the money withheld from your paycheck will be invested. You probably have the option to select from 3 to 300 mutual funds. You may want to include mutual fund shares in your IRA, or start an investment portfolio by purchasing fund shares. Selecting mutual fund shares differs substantially from selecting shares of stock. The questions in the following sections should help you in the process of mutual fund selection.

How much money can you invest regularly every month? If you have between $25 and $50, refer to the previous list of mutual fund families. If you have several hundred dollars a month, you may wish to invest $100 into each of several different funds.

What rate of return do you want to earn on the dollars you invest? The higher the return you seek, the greater the investment risk you must assume. The higher the return you try to earn, however, the fewer dollars you may need to invest to fund a certain goal. For example, Jane needs to invest $300 a month and earn 10 percent annually to reach her investment goal. Gloria, who is trying to fund the same goal, does not feel comfortable with the risks associated with trying to earn 10 percent. Gloria settles for a rate of return of 7 percent, but Gloria must invest $500 a month to reach the same goal as Jane. If you accept less risk, expect to invest more dollars than someone taking more risk to fund the same goal. Once in a while the person who assumes more risk will not do well. But if that person chooses an investment wisely and gives the investment enough time (over ten years), the greater initial risk is usually neutralized.

What are your investment objectives? Mutual funds are separated based on their investment objectives. These objectives are indicated by the following types of funds:

- *Aggressive growth*—primary goal of skyrocketing appreciation
- *Growth*—goal of above-average share appreciation
- *Growth and income*—goal of respectable growth combined with annual income
- *Balanced*—goal similar to growth and income
- *Bond*—goal of income and safety of principal
- *Sector*—goal whereby each fund invests in a certain industry
- *Global/international*—goal of investing around the world

Do you want to diversify your investment dollars? Diversification is similar to the idea "Don't put all your eggs in one basket." If all you own is Best Buy and the value of its shares drops, you could easily lose 50 to 75 percent of the value of your portfolio. Investors like owning mutual funds because they reduce the negative impact of a single company's stock dropping precipitously. Of course, 20 years ago if you had purchased $2,000 worth of stock in any one of several companies—McDonald's, Disney, Wal-Mart, Coke, Southwest Airlines, or Microsoft—and never sold the shares, you would be a mil-

> **Hot Tip**
>
> Do you wish to become financially independent sooner rather than later? Are you willing to accept the related risks? Then consider <u>aggressive growth funds</u>. Do you want to invest in the information highway? If so, consider a sector fund that does just that.

lionaire today. Diversification protects your downside risk but limits your upside potential.

Do you know how to select mutual funds? Much like ranking college football teams, financial experts compile volumes of data on how different funds perform. I focus on two types of performance data:

1. The annual percentage increase in the value of each fund's shares (known as the rate of return). While the change in the value of a fund's shares can be measured from one day to the next, most measures look at the rates of return for the past 12 months as well as the past three-year, five-year, and ten-year periods.
2. Each fund's risk rating. Risk is a measure that compares how the value of a fund's shares has performed during periods when the stock market both drops and rises. Fund shares that increase in value much faster than the market as a whole often drop farther when the market declines. Such funds are considered to have above-average risk. Funds that underperform the market when it is climbing but also drop less than market averages when the market falls are considered lower risk. You can find funds with above-average annual rates of return that also carry average or below-risk ratings.

The problem with risk and return ratings is that past performance is no guarantee of future performance. Funds that did very well over the past five years may not do nearly so well over the next five years; the opposite is also true.

Ignore return ratings for a single year. The performance of one stock owned by a mutual fund could dramatically push up or down the value of that mutual fund's shares during the previous 12 months. Focus on three-year and five-year performance ratings, a standard that automatically excludes all new funds that don't have at least a 36-month track record.

Who manages the fund? Have you ever noticed that highly ranked college and pro teams always have outstanding coaches? Well, the same holds for mutual funds. Funds that do well have outstanding managers. Peter Lynch became a legend in his own time because of the job he did managing the Fidelity Magellan fund. The media focus too much on fund per-

> **Hot Tip**
>
> Pay careful attention when managers of the funds you own change. Check the new manager's performance record at the fund he or she left. If the fund with new management underperforms the market for two years, sell it.

formance; not nearly enough attention is paid the managers who are responsible for the fund's success.

What expenses can you expect to pay? Some funds have front-end loads, whereby you pay the sales commission when you buy shares. Other funds have back-end loads, so if you sell shares before you have owned them eight years, you will be charged a sales commission as illustrated in the table below:

Back-End Load Commissions

Years You Owned Shares	Commission %
Less than one	8%
One, but less than two	7
Two, but less than three	6
Three, but less than four	5
Four, but less than five	4
Five, but less than six	3
Six, but less than seven	2
Seven, but less than eight	1
Eight or longer	0

Management fees are another expense typically charged by mutual funds. The people who pick the stocks get compensated handsomely for their work. Management fees range from a low of about .20 or 20 basis points (100 basis points is 1 percent) to 2.25 percent (225 basis points). For example, Ralph's mutual fund's management fee is 1.25 percent; Ralph has $10,000 invested in this mutual fund. He pays the fund $125 a year to manage the dollars he has invested with this fund. Look for funds whose management fee is less than 1 percent.

Most funds do not charge 12b(1) fees, which are actually sales charges payable to the salesperson every year for as long as you own that fund's shares. Paying a commission every year you own a particular fund is highway robbery. (Remember that a fund owner already pays an annual management fee to the fund.)

Where do you find performance ratings? Several magazines periodically publish mutual fund performance data. The magazines include:

Money	www.pathfinder.com
Kiplinger's Personal Financial Magazine	www.kiplinger.com
Consumer Reports	www.consumerreports.com
Forbes	www.forbes.com

These magazines make it easy for you to compare fund performance and risk data. Visit your university or local public library to see if the reference section has one or both of the following loose-leaf services:

Morningstar Mutual Funds (top-rated
   funds receive five stars)   www.morningstar.com
Value Line Mutual Fund Survey
   (top-rated funds receive a one)   www.valueline.com

You can find the following information about a fund on a single page in Morningstar and Value Line:

- Fund's performance over the past one, three, and five years
- Fund's risk ratings
- Fund's investment objective
- Fund's sales commission
- Fund's required initial investment
- Fund's annual management fee
- Fund's 800 telephone number.

You can also expect a discussion of the fund manager's performance record and a forecast of the fund manager's expected performance over the next two to three years.

When you find a mutual fund you may want to own, record information about it on the Selecting a Mutual Fund Worksheet. Once you have completed your search, call the 800 number for each fund and request a prospectus. A prospectus is supposed to be easy to read and understand (but many are too detailed and boring). Information in the prospectus should answer all your questions about the fund. It should also include an application so that you can buy fund shares directly from the fund. Call the fund when you have questions or problems.

Tracking a Mutual Fund's Performance

Besides reports sent to you by the fund, each major newspaper carries yesterday's mutual fund net asset values (NAVs) and other information (see Figure 15.2). An abbreviated name of the fund is in the first column under the heading of the mutual fund family to which it belongs.

Remember: Morningstar and Value Line ratings are no guarantee of future performance.

Selecting a Mutual Fund Worksheet

Your investment objective: _____

Fund	_____	_____	_____
Fund's 800 #	_____	_____	_____
3-year return rating	_____	_____	_____
5-year return rating	_____	_____	_____
Risk rating	_____	_____	_____
Management fee	_____	_____	_____
Front-end load	_____	_____	_____
12(b)1 fee (yes or no?)	_____	_____	_____
Back-end load	_____	_____	_____
Min. initial purchase	$_____	$_____	$_____
Min. check plan purchase	$_____	$_____	$_____

What each share of the fund is worth—the NAV—is usually in the second column. The price investors must pay to buy shares is in the third column. If the column has an NL, it means that this fund is a no load, and shares are bought and sold by the fund at the price in column two. Price change from yesterday is in the fourth column. Listing formats may vary from newspaper to newspaper.

Most people know how well their fund did. For example, someone might say, "My Janus Worldwide shares went up 28 percent last year." Certainly, 28 percent is impressive in and of itself. To be really meaningful, you must know how well your fund did against some standard or index, such as the Standard and Poor's 500,

Figure 15.2 Newspaper Table of Mutual Fund Prices

Name	Bid	Ask	Change
Dest1	16.13	17.09	(.06)
DisEqr	16.66	NL	—
Eq Inc	26.70	27.24	(.01)
EQ11	15.20	NL	(.01)
EqIdx	15.14	NL	(.02)
Fidel	18.60	NL	(.07)
FlexB	7.10	NL	.01
GNMA	10.86	NL	—
GroInc	20.91	21.34	—
HIYID	12.53	NL	.01

which reflects how a group of stocks similar to the ones owned by your mutual fund performed over a specific period.

There are many indexes. They measure the change in value of a certain category of stocks or bonds over a period such as a day, week, month, or year. Some of the most common indexes are:

- *Dow Jones Industrial Average.* This index is made up of 30 blue chip industrial giants such as IBM and General Motors. When a news commentator says that the Dow Jones Industrial Average dropped 15 points, it means that altogether on average the value of the 30 stocks in the index went down; however, the price of one or more companies' shares included in the index may have gone up that day.
- *Standard & Poor's 500:* This index includes stocks of the 500 largest companies traded on the New York Stock Exchange.
- *Russell 2000:* This index measures the change in value of 2,000 small capitalization stocks.
- *Wilshire 5000:* This index tracks the changes in prices of over 5,000 companies from the extremely large to the not very big.
- *EAFE:* This index tracks the performance of companies headquartered in Europe, Australia, and the Far East.

Many investors compare the performance of their funds against one of the more popular indexes, such as the Standard and Poor's 500. Make sure when comparing your fund's performance against an index that you select the appropriate index. For example, the S&P 500 would not be appropriate if you owned a global or sector mutual fund. If your fund owns stocks similar to the companies included in the S&P and your fund outperformed the S&P, you did well. For example, if your fund lost 11 percent during the past 12 months, you should not feel too disappointed if the S&P dropped 21 percent for the same period.

> **Hot Tip**
>
> If it bothers you when the price of your shares declines, ignore day-to-day, weekly, monthly, and even quarterly performance data. However, once a year check on how well your fund has done. Performance can be looked at from several perspectives.

Compare your fund's performance with other funds in the same group. For example, if global mutual funds as a group had an average return of 4 percent during the year and your global fund returned 8 percent, you have reason to celebrate.

Monitor your funds' managers. Did your fund change managers during the year? Most funds send out quarterly reports to shareholders. Check to see if your fund recently changed managers. A new fund manager means a new investment philosophy. You need to monitor your fund's performance more closely after a new manager takes over.

Should You Own Index Funds?

Even after reading my advice, does selecting a mutual fund seem a bit overwhelming? Well, you have another alternative. Invest in a fund that owns the stocks of a certain index. The most popular index is the Standard and Poor's 500. Several mutual funds, known as index funds, own the stocks in the S&P. Below are four common index funds whose portfolios mirror an index. You can find more index funds by checking this Web site: www.indexfundsonline.com.

> **Hot Tip**
>
> I previously suggested that you not use one-year performance data when selecting a fund. But, of course, one year of data is meaningful when evaluating the performance of a fund you own against indexes and funds with similar investment objectives.

Index	Mutual Fund	800 Number
Standard & Poor's 500	Vanguard 500 Index	662-7447
	Schwab S&P 500	435-4000
	T. Rowe Price Equity Index	638-5660
Russell 2000	Vanguard Small Cap Index	662-7447
Wilshire 5000	Vanguard Total Market Index	662-7447
	Fidelity Spartan Total Index	544-8888
	T. Rowe Price Total Index	638-5660
Europe, Asia, Far East	Dreyfus International Index	645-6561
	Fidelity Spartan International	544-8888
	Vanguard Total International	662-7447

The Case for Buying Shares of Index Funds

At least four reasons can be offered for investing in index funds.

First, usually no sales commission or load is paid when purchasing the shares. Second, the management fee of an index fund is much lower than fees charged by non-index-funds because the index fund manager has little work to do. Why? Stocks are rarely added to or taken away from the index. An index fund's lower management fee has a big impact on return over ten years or longer. Third, over the past ten-year period, the rate of return for most index funds has been higher than the rate of return of 95 percent of the mutual funds that have similar investment objectives. And finally, index owners experience less stress as an index fund closely mirrors the performance of the market.

Hot Tip

Many mutual funds require a minimum initial purchase of $1,000 to $2,500. However, a beginning investor who elects to use T. Rowe Price's Asset Builder can start buying shares of this fund with a minimum deposit of $50. To open an account with only $50, you must agree to give T. Rowe Price permission to charge your checking account at least $50 each month to buy more shares. This Asset Builder account is an excellent way to take advantage of the benefits of dollar cost averaging while building a portfolio.

Asset Allocation

If you have less than $10,000 to invest, owning shares of one mutual fund is sufficient. The larger the dollar amount of your portfolio, the more important diversification becomes. The buzzword that both academicians and investment experts have promoted to address this topic is *asset allocation*. Investment experts believe that savvy investors reduce their investment risk by owning several different classes of assets or investments. Each class has a different set of risks and rates of return. The following seven asset classes cover most investments (and are sufficient for all investors except individuals with seven-figure portfolios):

1. *Value.* This refers to shares of older, respected companies such as IBM, each with a long history of paying dividends.
2. *Growth.* This refers to shares of companies whose profits grow much faster than typical companies. Microsoft shares are an example of a growth investment.
3. *Small capital.* This class includes shares of young companies whose products and services are often new on the market. Such companies often have yet to earn a profit (like most of the Internet stocks).
4. *Sector.* This refers to shares of a group of companies that are part of the same industry. Well-known sector mutual funds include medical, real estate, computer, banking, and technology.
5. *Government bonds.*
6. *Corporate bonds.*
7. *International securities.* This asset class can include stocks and/or bonds.

Investment experts suggest that investors own mutual funds in several different asset classes. The asset classes you select and the number of asset classes to include depend on your age, the dollar amount of your investments, and your risk preference. For example, a 22-year-old who recently started her first full-time job might invest in only one asset class—for example, growth stocks. An investor in his 50s with a portfolio of several hundred thousand dollars may want to own shares of funds in each of the asset classes.

An investor in his 50s has distributed his portfolio as follows:

Asset Class	*Percent Invested*
Value	30%
Growth	30
Small capital	10
Sector	10
International	10
Bonds (government and corporate)	10

Evaluation Tools

Such an investor may wish to buy shares of traditional or index mutual funds or some combination.

In today's high-tech world, the electronic media make it easy to evaluate mutual funds.

Software:
Your Mutual Fund Selector by Intuit   800-624-5710
Principia by Morningstar   800-735-0700

Web sites:
www.fundfocus.com
www.Quicken.com/investments/mutualfunds/finder/

These sites let you select such criteria as the size of a fund, its investment objectives, its minimum performance over a number of years, its management fees, and so forth.

If you want to keep a log of all your mutual fund purchases, record each one in Mutual Fund Purchases Worksheet.

If the risk of selecting mutual funds makes you nervous, that's natural. You may want to learn more about buying mutual fund shares before you risk any of your money. Check Vanguard's Web site at www.Vanguard.com/educ/inveduc.html. This location includes several courses on investing in mutual funds.

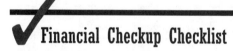
Financial Checkup Checklist

- Set up a program to purchase fund shares every month.

- Compare the performance of each of your funds with the appropriate index for the past three-year and five-year periods. Reallocate your funds if necessary.

- Check to see when each fund last changed managers. Your fund manager should have experience!

- Evaluate each of your funds based on its risk rating and its performance rating.

- Determine the percentage of your funds in each asset class.

Mutual Fund Purchases Worksheet

Mutual Fund	Phone Number	Dollar Amount of Purchase	Share Price	Number of Shares	Date
_____	_____	_____	_____	_____	_____
_____	_____	_____	_____	_____	_____
_____	_____	_____	_____	_____	_____
_____	_____	_____	_____	_____	_____
_____	_____	_____	_____	_____	_____
_____	_____	_____	_____	_____	_____
_____	_____	_____	_____	_____	_____
_____	_____	_____	_____	_____	_____
_____	_____	_____	_____	_____	_____
_____	_____	_____	_____	_____	_____
_____	_____	_____	_____	_____	_____
_____	_____	_____	_____	_____	_____
_____	_____	_____	_____	_____	_____
_____	_____	_____	_____	_____	_____
_____	_____	_____	_____	_____	_____
_____	_____	_____	_____	_____	_____

16 Annuities

Understand the pros and cons of owning annuities.

> JoAnn taught school; her husband, Jack, loved his life as a cotton farmer and planned to farm until he couldn't climb up on the tractor. When he could no longer farm, he wanted the farm to go to their two oldest boys. JoAnn knew that Jack had never put a dime away for retirement; in fact, he owed a sizable amount on a loan at the bank. JoAnn did not pay Social Security taxes. Although her school system did have a retirement plan, it wouldn't provide nearly enough for their retirement. For the past 15 years, JoAnn has been purchasing an annuity. She wanted to know if they could live off her teacher's retirement plus her annuity.

What You Need to Know about Annuities

Annuity payments are the reverse of life insurance payouts. A life insurance policy pays off when you die, at which time someone else gets the policy proceeds. At some point in your life after you buy an annuity, you are supposed to get a check once every month. In most cases, those payments will continue as long as you live. Annuities are classified as fixed or variable.

Many people who buy annuities are lenders, their money being used to buy bonds. Millions of people, just like JoAnn, are trying to fund their retirement by buying fixed annuities. They are loaning money to the insurance company and receive low, fixed rates of return on their money. At retirement these people would have enjoyed a higher level of living had they purchased variable annuities during their working years. People who buy variable annuities purchase shares of mutual funds that invest in stocks. Over the long haul, variable annuities will outperform fixed annuities. So why do so many people own fixed annuities? Because fixed annuities guarantee fixed, albeit low, rates of return. People are afraid to tie the performance of their annuity to the performance of the stock market. Because in some years, for a short period of time the value of a variable annuity may decline, too many people purchase fixed annuities.

Annuities come in four varieties:

1. A *fixed (immediate)* annuity is one that pays a fixed low rate of return. It starts to send the purchaser a monthly check immediately.
2. A *fixed (deferred)* annuity pays a fixed rate of return, but the monthly payments do not start until several years in the future—for example, after the purchaser celebrates his or her 65th birthday.
3. With a *variable (immediate)* annuity, purchasers have their money invested in shares of mutual funds that buy shares of stocks. The insurance company that sold the annuity starts immediately to send the purchaser a check each month.
4. With a *variable (deferred)* annuity, purchasers' money is invested in mutual fund shares, but the owners don't start to receive monthly checks until several years in the future.

Anyone who wants to buy an annuity has the choice of paying the entire cost of an annuity at once, often referred to as a "lump sum" purchase. For example, Mrs. Phillips spends $100,000 to buy an annuity, which will begin sending her monthly payments. Because most people don't have that much cash on hand, they purchase annuities on an installment basis. Most annuities are sold this way. Elizabeth just

Hot Tip

With a variable annuity you usually have a choice of mutual funds in which to invest. Dollars invested in mutual funds are not accessible to creditors of the insurance company that sold the variable annuity if the insurance company runs into financial trouble. Owners of fixed annuities could lose all or part of their funds if the insurance companies that sold the annuities get into financial trouble, because creditors of the insurance companies could claim the assets in fixed annuities.

started work with MEDCAP; as part of the company's retirement program, employees have 5 percent of their wages withheld from their paychecks; that 5 percent is used to buy an annuity on the installment plan.

Annuity Payout Options

If you are buying a deferred annuity on the installment plan, years will go by before you start to collect from the annuity. When you do reach the age at which your annuity starts to send checks each month, your annuity contract will probably include the following payout options:

- *Single-life option.* This is appropriate for a single person only. When a married person receiving the annuity dies, payments stop and the remaining partner is left with nothing.
- *Life with a period certain option.* Single persons may select this payment option if they would like the payment stream guaranteed for a minimum number of years. With a single-life option, a retiree might die after receiving one payment and no one else would receive the rest of the money used to purchase the annuity. With a period certain option, payments go to the beneficiary if the person initially receiving the payments dies before the minimum number of payments have been made. This option is not recommended for married couples because payments will stop at the end of the period selected, yet the remaining spouse is still likely to need income. For example, Bonnie selects the life with period certain payment option. She selects a payment period of ten years. She dies after receiving payments for three years; her husband, Jack, is the beneficiary and continues to receive payments for the remaining seven years. At the time of the last payment, Jack is 77 and still needs that discontinued monthly check.
- *Joint-and-survivor option.* Because payments cover two lives (usually the husband and wife), the monthly payments under this option are lower than the two options previously discussed when payments covered only one life. This option is strongly recommended for married couples. If you purchase the

Hot Tip

When you purchase an annuity, you will be required to select a beneficiary. A beneficiary is someone who will receive the annuity proceeds after you die.

annuity at work, federal law requires you to select this option unless your spouse surrenders his or her right to be covered by your annuity.

Should You Own Annuities?

People too often fail to ask the right questions when investing. Too few people ask, "Is putting my money into annuities the best way for me to fund financial independence?" You would be wrong in thinking that this is a question interesting only to elderly people. Anyone employed full-time may be forced to choose from among several savings and investment options, including fixed and variable annuities. Since one of these options is likely to be an annuity, you need to know about them.

Pros and Cons of Annuities

The advantages of annuities include the following:

- If you are already making maximum contributions to your IRA and your company's retirement plan, then an annuity contract may be your next best option. Why? Because taxes are not paid on any earnings generated by the dollars placed in an annuity until the dollars are withdrawn during retirement. You must pay taxes on the dollars deposited to the annuity unless the annuity is part of a qualified retirement plan like a 401(k). For example, Jack makes maximum contributions to his company's retirement plan; he buys an annuity so he can put even more money away for retirement. Jack contributes $1,000 annually to purchase the annuity. The income generated by the $1,000 is not taxed until Jack starts to withdraw money from the annuity.
- There is no limit on the amount of dollars you may deposit in an annuity in any one year, but there *are* limits on deposits to IRAs and 401(k)s.
- When you retire, you have several options for withdrawing your money from an annuity. Almost all of them include payments to you for the rest of your life. In other words, with most payout options you cannot outlive annuity payments.
- Unlike a traditional IRA or 401(k) plan, you are not forced to start withdrawing your money when you turn 70½.

The disadvantages of annuities are the following:

- Management fees are often twice those of mutual fund shares. The company that sold the annuity earns a management fee; so does the firm that manages the mutual fund included in the annuity.

- Annuities come equipped with surrender or withdrawal charges. Suppose you decide to take your cash out of an annuity before you've owned it seven to ten years. You may pay as much as 7 to 10 percent of the amount invested in surrender charges to get the cash. For example, the value in Bill's annuity is $20,000; however, if he were to cash the annuity in today, the insurance company that sold it would refund only $18,000. He is paying $2,000 in surrender charges. Make sure you clearly understand how this charge is assessed before you purchase an annuity.
- When you cash in an annuity, you will also be subject to income tax on the capital gains and income earned inside the annuity. For example, if Larry, age 45, put $10,000 into an annuity but received $16,000 when he cashed it in, he will owe taxes on $6,000. He will also have to pay a 10 percent penalty on annuity dollars withdrawn from an annuity inside a qualified retirement plan because he took out the funds before he was age 59½. So Larry will also be assessed a $1,600 penalty if he withdraws his annuity proceeds before he turns 59½.
- Monthly payments from fixed annuities never increase—there is no inflation protection!
- Besides the annual management fee, you also pay an annual mortality charge, which is usually 1 to 2 percent of the value of your account.
- In addition to the management fee and the mortality charge, expect to pay a maintenance fee, or contract charge, between $25 and $75 for handling your annuity account. These three charges together can reduce the return on your investment from 2 percent to 5 percent a year. For example, Elaine has $30,000 in her annuity account; the insurance company could with-

> **Hot Tip**
>
> If you decide to buy a fixed annuity, watch out for the interest rate the salesperson may be promoting. The first year's interest rate on a fixed annuity is a teaser rate, with the annuity paying a far higher rate during the first year than it is likely to pay in succeeding years. A year after you purchase the annuity, the rate will no longer be guaranteed and will usually drop significantly. You may want to get your cash out of the annuity if the rate drops too much after the first year. Never buy an annuity without a "bailout clause." Such a clause allows you to withdraw your funds without paying a penalty if the new interest rate falls below a rate promised in the annuity policy. If you cash out early and there is *no* bailout clause, you will be subject to the annuity's surrender charge.

draw as much as $600 or more each year from her account than a mutual fund would charge for the same investment.
- Unless you are buying an annuity inside a qualified retirement account, your annuity payment is not tax sheltered like a contribution to an IRA.
- Distributions from annuities are taxed as current income, not at the lower capital gains tax rates.

Many financial advisers don't like their clients to fund financial independence by purchasing annuities. They feel that life insurance companies, which sell the annuities, charge fees that are too high. Too many dollars that are paid to purchase annuities go for life insurance company administrative expenses and sales commissions, leaving too few dollars to invest in the annuities. Most financial planners believe that a client is likely to earn a better return by owning mutual fund shares directly than by purchasing a variable annuity.

Before you buy an annuity, you should make maximum contributions to your company's retirement plan, such as a 401(k); and you should make maximum contributions to your traditional or Roth IRA.

If an Annuity Is Appropriate, What Kind Should You Buy?

If retirement is several years away and you are currently making maximum contributions to your company's retirement plan plus an IRA, consider buying a deferred annuity. I recommend that you purchase variable annuities. How much should you spend on purchasing an annuity each month? That depends on the retirement analysis you did in a previous chapter. You should have continued to work your numbers until you came up with the amount that you need to invest each month to achieve your retirement goals. Subtract the amount you contribute to your company pension and your IRA. If you still need to invest more money each month, buy an annuity.

If you are currently putting most of your money into a fixed annuity at work, talk with your benefit people about changing. You face two issues:

1. You should not be putting any money into an annuity that is part of a qualified tax-deferred retirement plan; those dollars should be going into mutual funds that invest in stocks.
2. If you are purchasing a fixed annuity in addition to making maximum contributions as described above, ask the benefits personnel how you can convert from a fixed to a variable annuity.

If you are currently putting most of your money into a fixed annuity that is not part of any program at work, ask your agent about switching from a fixed to a variable annuity.

Do you plan to retire soon? Will you receive a large distribution from a retirement plan? After your tax professional has explained the pros and cons of taking a lump sum distribution from your retirement plan, you may consider purchasing an immediate annuity. You may actually want to purchase two annuities—one fixed and one variable. Everyone's situation is different, but in the long run you are likely to be happier if more money goes into the variable annuity. To help with a decision, you may want to visit with a professional adviser.

Shopping for an Annuity

Before purchasing an annuity, consider performing the following tasks:

- Comparison shop when buying an annuity just as you do when buying everything else. As previously mentioned, the guaranteed rate for the first year means next to nothing.
- If it is a fixed annuity, compare the interest rate the annuity promises with the interest on bonds.
- Insist on a bailout clause and compare minimum guaranteed rates for each annuity.
- Compare the annual charge to administer the annuity.
- Compare the annual charges for mortality expenses.
- Compare withdrawal charges (what an insurance company charges if you cash in the annuity before you have held it seven to ten years). Check for a guaranteed death benefit that pays your beneficiary the amount you deposited into the annuity or its current value at your death, whichever is larger.

To buy low-cost variable annuities, call the following firms:

Fidelity	800-634-9361
Charles Schwab	800-838-0650
T. Rowe Price	800-469-6587
USAA	800-531-8000
Vanguard	800-522-5555

You may prefer calling an annuity shopping service. Firms such as United States Annuities (800-872-6684; www.annuityshopper.com) will try to find you the best buy in an annuity.

The company that issues the annuity should be rated A++ or A+ by A. M. Best, or AA or AAA by Standard & Poor's or Moody's. Check your local library or the business library of a university for these services.

Annuities are not for everyone. If you are in poor health, don't buy one. Before considering purchasing an annuity, make maximum contributions to your company's retirement plan as well as $2,000 a year to an individual retirement account. Avoid buying any annuity if you think there is even a slight chance that you will need the money in less than ten years. If retirement is many years away and you decide to buy an annuity, buy a variable annuity. Don't be sold an annuity by a salesperson. Check out any annuity with Morningstar before you sign a contract and make a deposit. How you invest your dollars for retirement is key in becoming financially fit. Far too many people are putting far too many dollars into fixed annuities. If all you have at retirement is a fixed annuity and Social Security, you will buy groceries with food stamps not long after you retire. Count on it!

> **Hot Tip**
>
> I suggest that before you buy any variable annuity, you compare annuities. Morningstar makes it easy by offering its Morningstar Variable Annuity/Life Performance Report; call 312-424-4288.

Annuities You Own Worksheet

Owner	Monthly payment	Insurer/ Policy number	Beneficiary
_____	_____	_____	_____
_____	_____	_____	_____
_____	_____	_____	_____
_____	_____	_____	_____
_____	_____	_____	_____
_____	_____	_____	_____

✓ Financial Checkup Checklist

- If retirement is more than ten years away and you are purchasing a fixed annuity, talk to a professional adviser about switching to a variable annuity.

- Check Morningstar's ratings for any variable annuities that you own or are considering.

- Check the payout options you have selected. Make changes as necessary.

17 Give Your Money Away

Give back to a society that has given you so much.

> Ken and Barbie went the second mile, some would even say the third, when it came to giving away money. Over the years several of my clients have tithed, but I had never worked with a couple who gave away 30 percent of their income. They said that the more they gave away, the more they benefited. Ken and Barbie were unique in another way—their only debt was their mortgage. Because they had been making extra principal payments each month, they would retire their mortgage in less than five years. I couldn't help but contrast Ken and Barbie with so many other clients who had accumulated piles of debt. Ken and Barbie did seem happier and more at peace with themselves than most clients. They were not self-righteous but seemed to sincerely believe that they had a responsibility to give back because they had been given so much.

We are a generous people, donating trillions of hours and billions of dollars each year to favorite charities. Those who give away their money seem to enrich themselves as much as, or possibly more than, the receiver. Most of us want to donate to a worthy cause that will use our gift in a way acceptable to us. Unfortunately, some organizations take advantage of people's generous spirit.

There are unlimited opportunities to give to needy individuals and groups. Make a list of your most passionate interests. Assign priorities. Decide how many dollars you have to donate. You may find giving more satisfying by focusing on one or two charities than by trying to spread your money too thin by giving to several groups. And check out the charities. Many that sound promising may not spend your contributions as you would like. Too often the cost of fund-raising and charity administration consumes most of the donated dollars.

To check out the charities on your list, contact the following organizations:

> National Charities Information
>   Bureau, Inc.
> 19 Union Square West
> 6th Floor (Department 418)
> New York, NY 10003-3395
> 800-501-6242
> Ask for a copy of its report.

> Philanthropic Advisory Service
> Council of Better Business Bureaus, Inc.
> 4200 Wilson Boulevard, Suite 800
> Arlington, VA 22203
> 703-276-0100

> **Hot Tip**
>
> Decline requests for money that come over the phone, at your door, or through the mail. Instead, take a proactive approach to giving. Check out a charity before giving. Always pay by check when donating money; the payee should be the charity, never the person representing the charity.

You may also want to check a charity with another group; the two groups listed above rely primarily on information volunteered by the charity. The American Institute of Philanthropy depends primarily on information found in IRS Form 990 filed annually by charities and in the charities' audited financial statements. For a modest fee, the organization will send you its charity rating guide and watchdog report. You may contact it as follows:

> The American Institute of
>   Philanthropy
> 4905 De Ray Avenue
> Suite 300
> Bethesda, MD 20814
> 301-913-5200
> www.charitywatch.org

> **Hot Tip**
>
> Once a year *Money* magazine publishes an extensive article ranking the nation's largest charities. This report indicates if a charity is OK with either or both of the two watchdog groups listed above.

Obtain information from your favorite charities. Read the literature carefully, paying close attention to each charity's mission. Study the organization's past accomplishments. Evaluate your donation strategy. With many charities you can insist that your dollars be directed exclusively to one of the charity's specific projects. Will your employer match the dollars you donate? Is your contribution tax deductible? If you aren't sure, call the IRS at 800-829-1040 and ask.

Although there are many deserving causes that can benefit from your generosity, sometimes the most satisfying gifts are made anonymously. Too often when the beneficiary knows who gave the money, he or she feels the donor will judge how the funds are spent. The recipient often feels indebted to the donor. When someone receives a gift from an anonymous donor, the recipient thinks kind thoughts about several people, not knowing who helped. You can find someone you can trust like a minister, bishop, rabbi, or priest to whom you can give your money, indicating whom you want helped.

The form on the next page makes it convenient to keep track of your contributions.

I once knew of a man who gave the university where I taught $1 million. His stockbroker suggested that he sell stock worth $1 million and give the university cash. The man had paid only $100,000 for the stock, so he had to pay capital gains on the remaining $900,000, which cost him over $200,000 in taxes. He should have given the stock to the university so he wouldn't owe any taxes. However, the broker wanted him to sell his stock so the broker could earn his $10,000 commission.

> **Hot Tip**
>
> **W**atch out—many charities try to hide fund-raising expenses by calling them education and program expenses. You will need the help of the three organizations listed here to determine exactly how much the charity spends on its mission; the minimum should be at least 60 percent of receipts.

> **Hot Tip**
>
> **W**hen donations of dollars or discards exceed $250, the IRS requires documentation from the charity that describes your gift. While you cannot receive a tax deduction for the time you donate, you are allowed to deduct 12¢ for every mile that you drive to and from, or for, the charity (but only if you record the trip in a log).

Charitable Contributions Worksheet

Date   Charity   Donation (describe)   Amount   Donor

Donate Time

Donating your time can certainly help others in your community. Take an inventory of your skills and interests. Decide how much time you can share a week, and then look for a way to spend that time so that you are making a difference. If you don't know where to donate your time, call your local United Way office. It can put you in touch with many local organizations that are a match for your skills and interests.

Before you can donate money, check that you have enough to support yourself and your family. People who donate a significant amount of their income know they

Hot Tip

When you buy a ticket to attend a charity event, you are only allowed to deduct an amount that exceeds the fair market value of the benefit you receive. For example, you paid $50 to attend a dinner that would have cost $20 if purchased at a restaurant; your deduction is $30.

need only so much; they have figured out what is enough income for them to meet their wants and needs. Giving is partially selfish; I give because I feel good for having done what I know I should do. I feel good because I have helped someone else. I feel good because other people have given to me, and I am continuing their legacy. While not everyone agreed with the way John Rockefeller conducted his life, he lived by two cardinal rules. He invested 10 percent of his income and he gave away 10 percent of his income. What a much better world this would be if you and I did the same.

Financial Checkup Checklist

- In your budget include donating money to important causes. You get back what you give.

- Investigate a charity *before* donating.

18 Make Your Taxes Less Taxing

Understand the steps to take for reducing the time and stress associated with paying taxes.

> Larry came to see me before the Internal Revenue Service breathed down his neck. He had not filed a tax return for the last three years and was soon to be in trouble. Not only did Larry not have any money to pay taxes, he also had no records of his financial transactions. Since he opened his small business nearly four years ago, Larry hadn't paid income taxes or the Social Security taxes that he had withheld from employees' salaries. Larry could go to jail. I wanted to know why he had come to see me. Larry told me he figured the company would eventually start to make lots of money, but so far it hadn't. He knew that eventually the IRS would catch up with him, so he wanted to approach it first. Luckily, a counselor gets to select his clients. I referred him to someone else who could and did help. I remember thinking at the time how much better off Larry would have been had he kept accurate records during those four years.

Paying taxes is expensive. This chapter discusses steps you can take to make the process less stressful for you. Chapter 19 discusses strategies you can use to pay only what you are legally required to pay.

Filling Out the W-4 Form Correctly

I never could understand why anyone would want to receive a tax refund. Why would you want more taxes withheld than you owe? Are not most people's budgets tight enough already? To make sure that you don't overwithhold or underwithhold, fill out your W-4 carefully. Your personnel office has forms available. Your answers to the questions on the form help your employer withhold the approximate amount that you should owe in taxes at the end of the tax year.

Keep Accurate Records

Unless your financial affairs are extremely straightforward, you may need several folders to hold the necessary tax information. The necessary tax information for you to keep, usually for at least several years, includes the following:

- *Tax returns from four prior years.* Put a copy of each return plus supporting documentation in an envelope; indicate both the tax year and the date to discard. Retain each return you file for a minimum of four years. Unless you have understated your income by more than 25 percent or failed to sign your return, the statute of limitations expires three years after the April 15th filing date. If the IRS suspects fraud, it can go back as many years as it wants when checking your tax returns. For example, if you signed and mailed your 1998 return on February 15, 1999, the IRS must start the audit before April 15, 2002.
- *Proof of income.* Retain each pay stub for the tax year until you file your return (especially W-2s). Keep any paper that documents dividends and interest payments (especially 1099s). And keep any form or paper that indicates income you may have received for any other reason.
- *Employee business expenses.* Business expenses that are not reimbursed by your employer are often tax deductible. Keep receipts and canceled checks.
- *Information about your business.* If your business is small, one folder may hold all important receipts. Of special importance are payroll records and health insurance premiums.

> **Hot Tip**
>
> When the IRS audits someone, it doesn't have to accept canceled checks as proof of a transaction. You need to keep original receipts and invoices for this purpose.

- *Rental income.* All documentation supporting the receipt of income as well as expenses related to renting vacant land, other real estate, and equipment is kept here.
- *Investment gains and losses.* You need detailed records each time you buy and sell an investment such as shares of stocks and mutual funds, bonds, and real estate.
- *Itemized deductions.* This is the file for medical invoices, mortgage interest, a copy indicating payment of state and local income and property taxes, charitable contributions, and property losses. Deductions are discussed in detail in the following chapter.
- *Credits.* This file holds documentation of payments made for child and dependent care, and college tuition.
- *Miscellaneous.* Keep any document you think might save you tax dollars.

> **Hot Tip**
>
> If you receive incorrect information from an IRS employee, you, not the IRS, will be held responsible for any mistakes on your tax return. *If you do get advice from the IRS, get it in writing*—and that is difficult to do.

Tax Preparation

If you hate to prepare your returns, here's how to find someone to prepare your tax return:

- Visit your local IRS office and ask an appropriate employee to help you prepare your return. You will probably be asked to participate in a class taught by an IRS instructor.
- Check your phone book for either Volunteer Income Tax Assistance (VITA) or Tax Counseling for the Elderly (TCE). There is no charge for their services.
- Find an enrolled agent by contacting the National Association of Enrolled Agents at 301-212-9608 (www.NAEA.org). It may (or may not) charge less than a certified

> **Hot Tip**
>
> Tax preparation firms are not the least costly alternative that most people consider them. They may be as expensive, or more expensive, than a CPA yet not nearly as competent because most of their employees work only part of the year and lack the academic and professional training of a CPA.

public accountant (CPA) but is competent for all but the most involved tax problems.
- Contact a CPA, especially when you think your tax problem is extremely complicated. However, make sure you find a CPA who primarily does personal tax work; most CPAs prefer corporate accounting and may not be up to speed handling personal tax problems.
- Search out a tax preparation firm. Most of these firms' staff work only during the tax season. In some firms, there is an inherent conflict of interest. For example, H&R Block employees are paid on a commission basis. The more tax returns they complete in an eight-hour shift, the more they earn. If you do go to a tax preparation firm, ask for someone who has been doing returns for at least five years.
- Use software to prepare your return. The two best programs are Intuit's TurboTax and Kiplinger's TaxCut. You can complete and file your return on-line at these two Web sites: www.turbotax.com or www.taxcut.com. When I couldn't sleep at 3 AM one morning, I decided to prepare and file my tax return. I downloaded one of the software programs. In less than two hours, I was finished and back under the sheets.

Hot Tip

If you want to learn how to prepare your own returns (and it isn't complicated), contact H&R Block and enroll in the same course its staff completes.

Do Not Underwithhold

Ideally, the amount of taxes withheld from your paycheck during the year will come close to equaling your tax liability. If you underwithhold by more than $1,000, you may be charged penalty fees on the difference between the taxes that you owe and the amount that you had withheld from your wages. For example, if your tax liability for the year was $2,200 but you had only $1,000 withheld, you are short $1,200. The IRS is likely to assess late fees on the $1,200. (Anyone underwithholding should complete Form 2210.)

Hot Tip

Caution: You are accountable for the tax return you file! If the software makes a mistake, or if a tax preparer creates an error, *you are responsible!*

If You're Self-Employed

If you are self-employed, the IRS wants you to make four quarterly tax payments on four dates: April 15, June 15, September 15, and January 15 (of the following year).

Dolores, who is single, is self-employed and expects to earn $20,000. Her federal income tax liability for 1999 is computed as follows:

Gross Income	$20,000
Less: Personal exemption	($2,750)
Standard deduction	($4,300)
Taxable income	12,950
Federal income tax:	1,943
Self-employment tax (15.30%)	3,060
Taxes due	5,003
Quarterly tax payment	$1,251

> **Hot Tip**
>
> **M**ake sure the amount of the four payments comes close to the amount of taxes you will owe to avoid having the IRS assess interest on any underpayment.

If You Can't File by April 15

Some years you may just not have the paperwork done. No later than April 15, file Form 4868, Application for Automatic Extension of Time to File U.S. Individual Income Tax Return. *Filing this form does not extend the time you have to pay your taxes.* If you owe any taxes, you must send in a check for the proper amount on April 15. Sounds like a contradiction, doesn't it? You ask for an extension because you haven't finished your paperwork and don't know exactly how much you owe. Well, the IRS wants you to make a pretty accurate guess. If you don't pay the taxes you owe by April 15, you will incur both penalties and interest.

> **Hot Tip**
>
> **E**ven if you don't have any money to send to the IRS by April 15, either ask for an extension or file the proper forms by that date. Fail to submit your paperwork by this famous deadline and the penalties are significantly greater than if you send in the paperwork without a payment.

When the IRS Comes Knocking

Almost everyone gets audited sometime, and some people get audited many times. If you are audited, the better the records you have kept, the better your chances for getting the IRS off your back without paying additional taxes.

> **Hot Tip**
>
> Answer IRS notices and letters on or before the date requested in its letter.

Follow these steps to avoid an audit:

- Keep accurate records.
- Deposit all checks (don't cash them) and record the source of each deposit on your bank statement. If the IRS finds a record of a check that you cashed instead of depositing, it may assume that check was income to you. If you have no record of that check, you may be required to pay taxes, penalties, and interest on the amount of the check.
- When you send in your return, send copies (not originals) of documentation for any transaction that may attract the IRS's attention. For example, if you made a large charitable deduction, voluntarily send in a copy of the receipt from the charity.
- If you do your own taxes, consider using a software program.
- If you have more than 24 transactions a month, use a computer program to track both income and expenses.
- Double-check your return: Is all the math correct? Have you included all schedules? Did you sign the return?

The IRS conducts three types of audits: (1) correspondence audits (the IRS sends you a letter with specific questions you must answer and you send back the required documentation); (2) office audits (you are asked to visit an IRS office); and (3) field audits (the IRS auditor visits you at home or at your office).

> **Hot Tip**
>
> You do not have to go to an office audit. You can hire someone else to represent you. Be sure to fill out the IRS's Form 2848 to give your substitute power of attorney to represent you. While tax pros are divided on whether you should go to the audit or stay away, they all agree that you need to hire someone to accompany you (or represent you) as you may not be able to understand the auditor's technical language.

If you are audited by the IRS, follow these steps:

- Do not panic!
- Do not offer more information than requested at any point during the audit.
- Never lose your cool no matter how upset you get.
- Hire a CPA, tax attorney, or enrolled agent to go with you to the audit.
- Organize your records as completely as you can. Staple canceled checks to receipts.
- Ask to postpone the audit if you are not prepared. You can postpone an audit for 30 days.

Remember: if you don't cooperate with the IRS, it has the power to drain your bank accounts, repossess your automobiles, place a lien on your real estate, and, in many states, force you to sell your home to pay your taxes.

Almost no one likes to pay taxes. Besides Social Security taxes and federal income taxes, you may pay state and local income taxes, sales taxes, property taxes, estate and inheritance taxes, and excise taxes (on airfares, telephone services, gasoline, cigarettes, and alcohol). Most middle and upper income families pay more in taxes than any other expense. You can save yourself a lot of grief if you have the discipline to become involved in the tax-filing programs described below.

Because the IRS would like to automate the filing of tax returns, you can benefit when you take advantage of the following options.

- *Direct deposit.* If you are owed a refund, fill out the section on the tax return that asks for your bank-routing and account numbers. Your refund check will arrive two or three weeks sooner and will be directly deposited to your checking or savings account.
- *TeleFile.* You may be eligible to file by using a Touch-Tone telephone (not a cordless or cellular phone). Your filing status must be single or married filing jointly, and you can not have celebrated your 65th birthday. In addition, you can only have

Hot Tip

Buy Fred Daily's book *Stand UP to the IRS* (Nolo Press) before you attend either an office or field audit. You'll also want to examine a copy of IRS Publication 556, Examination of Returns, Appeal Rights and Claims for Refunds. If you are not satisfied with the results of your audit, pick up a copy of *Settle Your Tax Debt* (Dearborn) by Sean P. Melvin, which explains in detail the IRS's little-publicized offer-in-compromise program that may allow you to settle for pennies on the dollar, depending on your circumstances.

received income from wages, salaries, or tips; income from scholarships or grants; or less than $400 in taxable interest income.
- *E-file.* If you have access to a computer with a modem, you or a tax professional can use tax preparation software to file your return online.

You cannot become financially fit if your income tax records are out of shape.

Financial Checkup Checklist

- Set up and use a good filing system to keep track of your tax records.

- Complete your W-4 properly. It's easy to overlook something simple.

- Start preparing your tax return as soon as you have received such all-important documentation as your W-2, 1099s, and a statement from your mortgage lender.

- Seek competent professional help when you encounter a problem.

- File your return on time.

19 Pay Uncle Sam Only What You Owe

Identify tax avoidance strategies you can use to reduce your tax liability.

> **I** was actually surprised that Kelly came to see me. He hated to pay anyone to do anything that he thought he could do, and Kelly thought that he could do just about anything. I like to review clients' tax returns to look for errors. If they have underpaid their taxes, it's better for me to catch the mistake before the IRS does. However, for everyone who has paid too little in taxes, there are five or six who have paid too much. Kelly was a member of the second group. In each of the last three years, he had missed tax-saving strategies that would have saved him more each year in taxes than my fees.

Each of us pays a substantial amount of our income in taxes. When we receive our first paycheck, we quickly learn that two different federal taxes are taken out of our wages: federal income taxes with rates ranging from 15 to 39.6 percent; and Social Security, including Medicare, which takes 7.65 percent of every dollar most of us earn. People in most states pay state and, in some cases, city income taxes.

Tax Reduction Strategies

It is important to know about tax-saving strategies so that you will be prepared to take advantage of them when you can. You must file Form 1040 to take advantage of most of these strategies.

Income from the following sources is not taxed by the federal government:

- Scholarships. You can exclude from taxation all money you receive from a scholarship or grant that is used to pay tuition and fees, books, and supplies. Scholarship money used to pay room and board, however, is subject to taxation.
- Gifts. Prizes you win, however, are taxed, including lottery winnings.
- Municipal bond interest. Interest income from most state and city bonds is exempt from federal income taxation.
- Interest received from Series EE federal government bonds used to pay college tuition.
- Employer-paid health and disability premiums.
- Federal income tax refunds.
- Child support payments.
- Proceeds from insurance policies.

> **Hot Tip**
>
> There isn't space enough to adequately discuss federal income taxes even if we devoted the entire book to the topic. If you need more information, call the IRS and order a free copy of Publication 17, *Your Federal Income Tax for Individuals.*

Reducing Gross Income

Calculating gross income is the starting point for completing a tax return. Total gross income is the amount of all taxable income that you receive during the year. Certain expenditures actually reduce your gross income.

Contributions to your employer's retirement plan. Are contributions to your employer's retirement plan withheld from your paycheck? Your contributions to a 401(k) or 403(b) plan reduce your gross

> **Hot Tip**
>
> You are missing out if you are not making the maximum contribution possible to your employer's retirement plan, especially when your employer matches your contributions.

income dollar for dollar. Normally, your employer subtracts these contributions from your gross income before your W-2 form is completed.

Jack and Jill are both employed by EZ Wash and earn $20,000 annually. Jack contributed $1,000 last year to the 401(k) retirement plan sponsored by EZ Wash. For every dollar Jack contributes to the 401(k) plan, EZ Wash contributes 50¢, or $500 last year. Last year Jack's 401(k) account received $1,500 in contributions. Jack's $1,000 contribution lowers his taxable income by $1,000. Jack also pays $150 less in federal income tax. Jill doesn't contribute to the EZ Wash 401(k) plan, so she pays $150 more in taxes than Jack does and has a zero balance in her retirement account.

	Jack's Taxable Income	Jill's Taxable Income
Salary	$20,000	$20,000
Less: 401(k) contribution	($ 1,000)	
Taxable income	$19,000	$20,000
401(k) contributions	$1,500	$0

Premium conversion plans. Does your employer offer a premium conversion plan that makes it possible for you to pay your health insurance premiums with before-tax dollars? Under a premium conversion plan, the amount that you pay in health insurance premiums reduces your gross income dollar for dollar. For example, EZ Wash offers a premium conversion plan; Jack participates, but Jill does not. Jack pays $100 a month for health insurance, but because he decided to participate in the premium conversion plan, Jack's annual gross income is reduced by the $1,200 he pays in premiums. Jack saves $180 in income taxes ($1200 × .15). Jill does not participate, so she doesn't receive any tax savings.

	Jack's Taxable Income	Jill's Taxable Income
Salary	$20,000	$20,000
Less: 401(k) contribution	($ 1,000)	
Health insurance premiums	($ 1,200)	
Taxable income	$17,800	$20,000

Medical care reimbursement accounts. Does your employer offer a medical care reimbursement account? You decide at the start of the year how much you expect to pay for medical, dental, prescription, and optical expenses for the year. One-twelfth of that amount is subtracted from your gross pay and deposited each month in a separate account. You will be reimbursed from this account for what you pay in medical bills up to the limit of your contribution to the account during the year. For example, suppose you contribute $50 a month starting in January. Your first medical bill for the year, which you pay in February, is $400. After you submit the bill, you will be reimbursed for $400 even through you have only contributed $100 to the medical reimbursement account so far this year. In fact, Jack contributed $50 a month to a medical reimbursement account.

	Jack's Taxable Income	Jill's Taxable Income
Salary	$20,000	$20,000
Less: 401(k) contribution	($ 1,000)	
Health insurance premiums	($ 1,200)	
Medical care	($ 600)	
Taxable income	$17,200	$20,000

As stated in a previous chapter, a drawback to medical reimbursement accounts is known as the "use it or lose it rule." If money is left in the account at the end of the year, you lose it. Last year Jack contributed $50 a month but only accumulated $540 in medical bills for the year. Jack lost $60. However, his $50 monthly contribution reduced his gross income for the year by $600, so he saved $90 in federal income taxes ($600 × .15). Jack is a little better off because the $90 in tax savings is more than the $60 he contributed to his medical reimbursement account but didn't use.

Dependent care reimbursement account. Does your employer offer a dependent care reimbursement account? It works about the same as the medical reimbursement account. You decide how much you want to contribute each month; the amount of that monthly contribution reduces your gross taxable income. You submit your dependent care expenses to the firm that handles your reimbursement account. If funds remain in the account at the end of the year, you lose those dollars. Jack contributes $110 a month to a dependent care reimbursement account.

	Jack's Taxable Income	Jill's Taxable Income
Salary	$20,000	$20,000
Less: 401(k) contribution	($ 1,000)	
Health insurance premiums	($ 1,200)	
Medical care	($ 600)	
Dependent care	($ 1,320)	
Taxable income	$15,880	$20,000

Business gains and losses. If you own a business, use the form known as Schedule C. Recordkeeping pays off here if you keep track of all your business expenses. Business expenses reduce the taxable income earned by the business dollar for dollar. If your business earns a profit, not only will you owe income taxes on your business's net income, but you will also owe Social Security taxes on that net income. Did you know that when your employer withholds Social Security taxes from your paycheck, the employer matches your Social Security contribution dollar for dollar? When you are both the owner and the employee, you will pay both the employee and employer share of Social Security taxes (technically known as self-employment taxes). So your first dollar of profit is subject to 15.3 percent Social Security taxes as well as 15 percent federal income taxes.

Last year Jack started selling Amway part-time. Because of his start-up expenses and related costs, he lost $400.

	Jack's Taxable Income	Jill's Taxable Income
Salary	$20,000	$20,000
Less: 401(k) contribution	($ 1,000)	
Health insurance premiums	($ 1,200)	
Medical care	($ 600)	
Dependent care	($ 1,320)	
Business loss	($ 400)	
Taxable income	$15,480	$20,000

Gains and losses on investments sold during the tax year. When you sell an investment at a loss you can use up to $3,000 of that loss to reduce gross income. Jack lost $5,000 when he sold the stock of XYZ company. He can use $3,000 of that loss in the year he made the sale (since he did not sell any investments at a profit). He must carry the remaining $2,000 loss forward to next year.

	Jack's Taxable Income	Jill's Taxable Income
Salary	$20,000	$20,000
Less: 401(k) contribution	($ 1,000)	
Health insurance premiums	($ 1,200)	
Medical care	($ 600)	
Dependent care	($ 1,320)	
Business loss	($ 400)	
Capital loss	($ 3,000)	
Taxable income	$12,480	$20,000

When you sell an investment at a profit, you will be taxed on the profit in the year the investment was sold. If Jack had sold his investment in ABC at a $9,000 profit, he could use the $5,000 loss from the sale of the XYZ investment to reduce the profit he made on the sale of his investment in ABC. His net gain would be $4,000 ($9,000 less $5,000).

Reducing Adjusted Gross Income

Adjusted gross income is income that remains after subtracting certain expenses from gross income. Let's examine these expenses.

The dollar amount of alimony payments that you pay to a former spouse.

Individual retirement account (IRA) contributions. These contributions are deductible up to $2,000 per person if an employer does not offer a qualified retirement plan. Even if an employer does offer such a plan, a person is still allowed to contribute and deduct up to $2,000 for 1999 if single and adjusted gross income (AGI) is less than $31,000 or if married and AGI is less than $51,000.

Figure 19.1 shows how the deductibility of contributions to an IRA phase out when an employee is covered by a qualified plan.

> **Hot Tip**
>
> The taxation of capital gains and losses is much more complex than presented here. Thanks to Congress, men and women you elect, the rules are now so complex that you almost always need professional advice whenever you generate a profit or loss by selling real estate, stocks, bonds, and mutual funds.

Self-employment deductions. Business owners can also reduce their gross income by 50 percent of the amount that they pay in self-employment (Social Security) taxes. For 1999, 45 percent of the premium paid for health insurance

Figure 19.1 IRA Deductibility Phaseout

Year	Single	Married Filing Jointly
1999	$31,000–41,000	$51,000–61,000
2000	32,000–42,000	52,000–62,000
2001	33,000–43,000	53,000–63,000
2002	34,000–44,000	54,000–64,000
2003	40,000–50,000	60,000–70,000
2004	45,000–55,000	65,000–75,000
2005	50,000–60,000	70,000–80,000
2006	50,000–60,000	75,000–85,000
2007	50,000–60,000	80,000–100,000

purchased by an owner also reduces the adjusted gross income for the self-employed. (The 45 percent grows to 100 percent in 2007.) Julie owns her business. She paid $5,000 in self-employment taxes last year; she is allowed to reduce her gross income by $2,500. Julie also paid $6,000 in health insurance premiums, so she is eligible for a $2,700 deduction in gross income.

Child support is neither deductible nor taxed.

Business owners can also make tax-deductible contributions to three different retirement accounts: simplified employee pensions (SEPs), Keogh plans, and SIMPLEs. If you are self-employed and are making enough money to contribute to a retirement account, ask your accountant or financial planner which of these three would be best for you. In many cases you may be required to make contributions on behalf of your employees.

Moving expense deductions. Before you move, order Form 3903 and Publication 521. To qualify for moving expenses, your new address must be a minimum of 50 miles farther from your job than was your old address. You must normally remain at the new address for 39 weeks during the first 12 months after you move.

Costs incurred moving your household goods can be used to reduce your taxable income, as can travel costs to your new location. These costs include transporting your possessions and the gas and lodging expenses incurred moving you and your family. The cost of meals is no longer an eligible moving expense.

If your employer reimburses you for the costs of moving, you can only deduct the amount of your expenses that exceed the amount that your employer reimburses you.

Interest on student loans. You can deduct interest paid during the first 60 months you make payments on student loans. The amount of interest that you can deduct is capped as follows:

1999	$1,500
2000	$2,000
2001	$2,500

You are only allowed to deduct interest on a student loan if no one else can claim you as a dependent. If you're married, you must file a joint return.

For example, Jan started repaying her student loans by making monthly payments on January 2, 1997. Because her interest deductions started in 1998, she can only deduct interest for the years 1998, 1999, 2000, and 2001. This interest deduction phases out for single taxpayers with adjusted gross incomes of $40,000 to $55,000 and for marrieds, filing jointly, with incomes ranging from $60,000 to $75,000.

Reducing Taxable Income

Taxable income is the figure used to compute your tax liability. In 1999 taxpayers could take an exemption deduction equal to $2,750 each for self, spouse, and every eligible dependent.

You should use the larger of either the standard deduction or the total of all of your itemized deductions. Itemizing one or more of the expenses listed below may result in an amount larger than the standard deduction. (If you itemize expenses, you have to complete Schedule A.) Expenses that can be itemized include the following:

- *Medical and dental expenses.* The amount of medical expenses that count as an itemized deduction is the amount that exceeds 7.5 percent of adjusted gross income. For example, Bill's out-of-pocket medical, dental, and optical insurance, which have not been covered or reimbursed by his medical insurance, come to $2,000. His adjusted gross income is $20,000; 7.5 percent of his AGI is $1,500. He has $500 of medical expenses that qualify as itemized expenses.
- *Nonfederal taxes you paid.* These include property taxes, and state and local income taxes.
- *Interest.* Mortgage interest paid as well as interest paid on a home equity loan.
- *Points.* All points paid to purchase a new home are deducted in the

> **Hot Tip**
>
> If you take a federal tax deduction for state income taxes paid, then you must claim any refund you receive from the state as income.

> **Hot Tip**
>
> Get in the habit of donating personal items you no longer use to charity. Make a detailed list of all items donated and estimate the current market value of each item. For example, President Clinton estimated that a pair of his used shorts was worth $1. Obtain a signed receipt from the charity. For any gift to a charity above $250, as noted in Chapter 18, you must have written documentation from the charity verifying the amount of the donation.

year they are paid. Points paid to refinance a home mortgage must be deducted over the life of the loan.
- *Gifts to charity.*
- *Casualty and theft losses.* You can deduct only the amount that exceeds 10 percent of your adjusted gross income plus $100.
- *Miscellaneous expenses.* Among a variety of miscellaneous deductible expenses are these:
  - Job-hunting expenses. Before you finish polishing up your résumé, call the IRS and order Form 2106. Job-hunting expenses count as itemized deductions if you are looking for a new job in your present occupation even if you don't get the job. You can use the following expenses as deductions so long as you have the documentation that proves you spent the money: the costs of preparing, printing, and mailing your résumé; fees paid to an employment agency; software purchased to find a job; and travel expenses associated with finding the job. You are allowed to deduct 32¢ a mile if driving your car while looking for a new job.
  - Expenses of a home office with several restrictions.
  - Work uniforms.
  - Investment and financial-planning advice.
  - Subscriptions to professional journals.
  - Tax advice.
  - Tax return preparation.
  - Business expenses for which your employer does not reimburse you, such as travel, education, car mileage, gifts, and publications.

> **Hot Tip**
>
> Buy a little notebook and record the mileage every time you travel to and from doing charity work (as well as parking and tolls). For example, if you teach Sunday school, you can deduct the mileage to and from church each week.

You will be allowed to deduct only the total amount of these expenses that are in excess of 2 percent of your adjusted gross income. For example, 2 percent of Mary's AGI is $200; her job-hunting expenses total $100 and work uniforms cost her $400. If she itemizes, she will be allowed to deduct $300.

Credits That Reduce Your Tax Liability

The previous discussions have focused on reducing your taxable income. In this section, I discuss income tax credits that you can use to reduce your income tax liability, dollar for dollar. Credits can save you more in taxes than the strategies previously discussed. For example, if you contribute $1,200 a year to a qualified retirement plan such as a 401(k), you have reduced your taxable income by $1,200 and can expect to save $180 in taxes. However, if you can take advantage of a $1,200 tax credit, you will reduce the taxes you owe by $1,200.

Earned income credit (EIC). Earned income credit is an important tax benefit for lower-income workers. If the credit is larger than your tax liability, you will receive the difference in cash. If you qualify, you can start receiving the credit now. The credit is considerably larger if you are supporting children, but you may be eligible for the credit whether you support a child or not.

Workers without children must satisfy the following requirements:

1. Married taxpayers must file a joint return.
2. You must be between the ages of 25 and 65 at the end of the year.
3. No one else can claim the taxpayer as a dependent.

EIC is available only to taxpayers who have earned income such as wages, salary, commissions, and tips as well as earnings from self-employment. Social Security, alimony, child support payments, and Aid to Families with Dependent Children are not considered earned income.

The dollar amount of the credit depends on the amount of your income and the number of your qualifying children. If you think that you qualify, request Form Schedule EIC and Publication 596, Earned Income Credit, from the IRS.

Credit for the elderly or the disabled. Call the IRS at 800-829-1040 and request:

- Publication 524, Credit for the Elderly or the Disabled;
- Publication 554, Tax Information for Older Americans; and
- Schedule 3 (if filing a 1040A) or Schedule R (if filing a 1040), Credit for the Elderly or the Disabled.

To qualify for credit for being elderly or disabled, you must be 65 by the end of the tax year or you must be permanently and totally disabled. Even if you qualify to be considered for the credit, you may not be eligible. Eligibility depends on the income limit for your filing class (single, married, or head of household). Since income limits change from year to year, call the IRS and order the materials listed above to see if your income is below this tax year's income limit.

Child tax credit. The credit is $500 for each dependent child under the age of 17 in 1999. The credit is phased out for singles whose adjusted gross incomes are above $75,000 and for married couples filing a joint return when their AGI rises above $110,000.

Child and dependent care credit. Maximum tax credit for one dependent is $720; maximum credit for two or more dependents is $1,440. Eligible expenses include paying for care for any dependent child or adult who is incapacitated when the taxpayer is going to school, looking for work, or working.

The credit is a function of the amount you pay in child and dependent care expenses and of your adjusted gross income, as shown in Figure 19.2.

Millie Martinez has an adjusted gross income of $35,000. She pays $1,800 a year for child care for her five-year-old and $10,000 for someone to take care of her dependent mother. She computes her credit as follows:

$$\$1,800 \times 20\% = \$360$$
$$\$2,400 \times 20\% = \underline{\$480}$$
$$\text{Total credit} \quad \$840$$

If you think you may be eligible, order Publication 503 and Form W-10 from the IRS.

Hope Scholarship credit (tuition credit). The credit equals 100 percent of the first $1,000 and 50 percent of the second $1,000 paid in tuition and related expenses

---

Figure 19.2 Child and Dependent Care Credit

Taxpayer's AGI	Percentage	Maximum Credit for One
0 to $10,000	30%	$720
$10,001 to $12,000	29	696
$12,001 to $14,000	28	672
$14,001 to $16,000	27	648
$16,001 to $18,000	26	624
$18,001 to $20,000	25	600
$20,001 to $22,000	24	576
$22,001 to $24,000	23	552
$24,001 to $26,000	22	528
$26,001 to $28,000	21	504
$28,001 and above	20	480

during a student's freshman and sophomore year in college. A parent can take this credit for each child.

Lifetime Learning credit. Taxpayers will be eligible for a credit of 20 percent of the first $5,000 of tuition (it increases to $10,000 in 2003) and related expenses at either the undergraduate or graduate level. Unlike the Hope Scholarship credit, this credit is limited to one per taxpayer.

You cannot take the Lifetime Learning credit for someone who is eligible for the Hope credit. Both phase out for single taxpayers whose adjusted gross incomes are between $40,000 and $50,000, and for married couples filing joint returns between $80,000 and $100,000.

Excess Social Security taxes. Did you pay excess Social Security taxes during the year? Not too likely unless you earned more than $72,600 (1999) and worked for two or more employers. Excess Social Security taxes withheld by more than one employer is a refundable credit on your tax return. If a single employer withheld too much, you must ask that employer for the refund.

Taxation of a Child's Income

For children 13 and younger, earned income is taxed at the child's rate. The first $700 of unearned income is not taxed; the second $700 is taxed at the child's rate; and unearned income above $1,400 is taxed at the parent's rate.

For children 14 and older, earned income is taxed at the child's rate as is unearned income.

Did you find one or more strategies that you were not aware of that can save you money? While this information was basically accurate at the time the book was published, many tax issues are far more complex than presented here. Before hiring a professional to answer your questions or prepare your return, ask for an estimate of the costs you can expect to pay. Many taxpayers pay too much in taxes because they refuse to seek help. You can successfully tackle most of the topics presented in this book by yourself. However, if you recently sold a house, made several investment transactions, own a business,

> **Hot Tip**
>
> While investing or depositing money in a child's name may save on income taxes, dollars so invested can reduce a child's financial aid when attending college. Also, funds in children's names are theirs to spend when they reach their majority.

or are taking care of a dependent parent, then a visit to a tax preparation professional may prove to be your best investment since buying this book.

Financial Checkup Checklist

- Try to complete your own return before hiring a professional. It's a good learning experience.

- Sign up for premium conversion, medical reimbursement, and/or a dependent care account.

- Think carefully before transferring assets to a child just to save on taxes. This can backfire.

20 Love What You Do

Focus on keeping your career on track and your résumé fresh.

> Linda wanted to know if a family currently living in one home could live almost as cheaply if she and the children moved out. She and her husband, Lance, had fought so long and hard about finances that the marriage was dead. However, their children—ages 6, 9, and 13—were very much alive. Linda had never graduated from college and had left the job market several months before the first child was born. Now she wanted separate quarters, seeking peace of mind. She wondered if she could make this work financially. She was not alone. I told her to create two budgets, one for her and the children and one for Lance, before our next visit.

This chapter looks at four questions:

1. How much income do you really bring home from your job?
2. How can you increase your income?
3. How do you create an electronic résumé and post it on the Web?
4. How do you conduct yourself in a job interview?

Job satisfaction is closely tied to happiness. If you hate your job, you need to explore your employment options, especially if you are inadequately paid. A good place to start when evaluating your present job is to find out what your real hourly take-home pay is.

What Is Your Actual Take-Home Pay?

If you think of your income in terms of your annual salary or your hourly wage, think again. The number in box one on your annual W-2 form may look like a lot of money, so why do you feel so poor much of the time? It is past time you found out.

How Much Do You Really Make an Hour?

Would you work for $1 an hour? How about $2? How about 25¢ an hour? You are about to discover how much you actually bring home for every hour you devote to your job. You may be shocked at what you discover. In the exercises that follow, you will be asked to calculate your actual hourly wage—that is, the dollar amount that you take home for every hour you spend involved in your work. You will be asked to make the following three adjustments to your income to calculate your actual hourly wage:

1. Subtract from your income any expenses that you incur because you have a job. An example of such an expense would be child care.
2. Add back in valuable benefits your employer pays for that you don't.
3. Divide your income by the actual number of hours you spend each week supporting your job, not just the hours your employer pays you to work. For example, the time you spend commuting is time the job requires but is not compensated by your employer.

Too often employees focus on their annual gross income or hourly wage. Few calculate what they have left to spend after subtracting all the expenses incurred to support their job. We often think of our job in terms of the number of hours our employer requires us to work, ignoring the many additional hours we spend to support our job. The following two exercises will help you compute your actual hourly wage.

Adjust Your Income According to Job-Related Expenses

To help you compute your actual hourly wage, meet Chris Popal, who earns $15 an hour and works 40 hours a week. Chris is single but has a two-year-old; he bought a car so he could get to and from work.

Read each description before you fill in the blanks in the Financial Costs and Benefits of a Job Worksheet. While your numbers are likely to be considerably different from Chris's, review each figure carefully. Consider using a pencil with a good eraser when filling in the blanks.

Hint: On the worksheet on the next page, include only expenses you incur (or benefits you receive) because you work. In Chris's column, he included car expenses because he did not need a car before he found his job. Now that Chris works 40 hours a week, he has less time to cook and shop, so his food costs have increased. He spends an additional $70 a month on food eaten at home because he buys more convenience foods; his costs of eating out have gone up by $50 a month. His annual clothing expenses have increased by $600 because his employer expects him to dress professionally.

Note: The numbers below are not Chris's budget but represent only the increases Chris incurred when he went to work. Before trying to fill in the last column—your figures—read the full explanation of each item following the worksheet.

To help you understand how to fill out this worksheet, let's discuss where Chris obtained most of his numbers:

1. In a marriage in which both partners are employed, food is more expensive than when one stays home. No one has time to prepare meals from scratch anymore. Such couples purchase mostly convenience foods, which increase food costs but are quick and easy to prepare. Chris now spends about $840 more a year on groceries.
2. As mentioned above, he spends about $50 more each month on fast food.
3. Chris has one child. If you have a young child, you know that quality child care is often hard to find as well as expensive. Child care expenses range from $80 to more than $200 a week. The expenses incurred for taking care of a baby are higher.
4. Chris spends $50 a month more on clothing now than he did when he wasn't working. Dry cleaning costs are included here, too.
5. Chris spends more on personal care because of the job, but you may not.
6. Chris does not make contributions to a church or other charitable organization. Do you?
7. Job costs include unreimbursed business expenses, such as education, subscriptions to journals related to your job, required clothing, gifts for fellow employees (who marry, have a baby or birthday, or suffer the death of a family member).
8. Do you ride public transportation or car-pool to work?
9. Chris found he needed a car once he got a job. You may not think it fair to charge all the costs of the car to Chris's job. But Chris rode the bus because he couldn't afford a car until he found his job. Some days he thinks he works just to support the car.
    a. Chris does not incur any bridge or toll road expenses traveling back and forth to work, but the parking spot at work costs $25 a month.

Financial Costs and Benefits of a Job Worksheet

Financial Data	Chris	You
A. Annual Income	$31,200	_____
B. Annual Expenditures		
1. Food at home	840	_____
2. Food out	600	_____
3. Child care	5,000	_____
4. Clothing	600	_____
5. Personal care	180	_____
6. Charitable contributions	0	_____
7. Job costs	0	_____
8. Public transportation	0	_____
9. Auto expenses		
a. parking fees	300	_____
b. gas	450	_____
c. insurance	1,400	_____
d. car repairs	600	_____
e. car payments	2,400	_____
10. Housekeeper	0	_____

(continued)

Financial Costs and Benefits of a Job Worksheet
(Continued)

    11. Federal income taxes   2,000   _____

    12. State income taxes   100   _____

    13. City income taxes   0   _____

    14. Social Security taxes   2,450   _____

    15. Payroll deductions (disability insurance)   840   _____

    16. Other job-related expenses:

         _____   _____   _____

         _____   _____   _____

C. Annual Benefits

    17. Vested retirement benefits   _____   _____

    18. Health and disability insurance   (3,000)   _____

    19. Life insurance   (200)   _____

    20. Child care   _____   _____

    21. Education expenses   (200)   _____

    22. Financial planning   _____   _____

    23. Other employer-paid benefits

         _____   _____   _____

    24. Total Expenses $14,360   _____

    25. Net contribution from job $16,840   _____

    b. Chris may have understated what he spends on gas.
    c. Insurance and car registration are $1,400 a year; insurance rates will be cut in half when Chris turns 25 or marries.
    d. Car repairs (including oil changes and tires) average about $600 a year.
    e. Chris makes payments of $200 a month on the auto loan.
10. Chris does not have a housekeeper. When both partners are employed, a housekeeper is not uncommon.
11. Federal income taxes Chris pays.
12. State income taxes Chris pays.
13. Chris is not required to pay a city income tax.
14. Chris pays Social Security taxes.
15. Many workers have disability premiums taken out of their pay.
16. Do you have job-related expenses that we failed to list here?
17. Include only contributions to a retirement plan made by your employer if those benefits are vested. If your employer now contributes to a retirement plan for you but you need to work several more years before you own those contributions, you receive no advantage from those benefits now. If you are partially vested in the contributions the employer makes to an account in your name, include the vested part.
18. Include only the amount of these benefits that the employer pays. You were not asked to include what you pay for health and disability insurance because you need such coverage.
19. You may be overstating a benefit received from your employer if the life insurance premium subtracted from your paycheck is higher than the premium you'd pay if you purchased a personal policy. Include what the employer charges you here anyway.
20. If your employer subsidizes the cost of child care for you, include it here.
21. What expenses did your employer incur to help you become a more valuable employee?
22. If your employer provides financial planning benefits, ask your benefits office how much the employer pays for those benefits for you.
23. What other benefits does your employer provide?

> **Hot Tip**
>
> **N**umbers recorded on lines 17 through 23 should be negative. Why? Because they are offsets to the expenses you incur to do your job. They actually benefit you, for you are better off because your employer purchases these services for you.

24. Add together all numbers on lines 1 through 23. Remember amounts on lines 17 through 23 are negative.
25. Subtract the amount on line 24 from the annual income on line A. This is the amount of income you have to spend after subtracting expenses you pay so that you can work.

Chris thought that earning $15 an hour would provide money for more leisure time activities. Chris was shocked to learn that nearly 50 percent of his income went for job-related expenses.

How many hours each week do you devote to supporting your job? Chris was paid for working 40 hours a week. However, he devoted much more than 40 hours to his job, including time spent dressing for and traveling to and from work. As you complete the Actual Hourly Wage Worksheet, estimate how many hours each year you spend on each category.

People who work through this exercise often become upset because their actual hourly wage is so low. I hope that your actual hourly wage is higher than Chris's. Some of my clients refuse to complete these worksheets, not wanting to find out what their actual hourly wage is. Many people become defensive when filling in the blanks. Some refuse to include any of the actual costs of owning and operating a car. Chris bought a car to travel to and from work, but some people get a job so they can pay for a car. Either way, the car consumes a significant amount of income. Many people tell themselves that they need the car when they could actually get by without it.

Many people who earn the lesser income in a two-earner family and must pay for child care are surprised to learn that their actual hourly wage is less than a dollar or sometimes even negative.

Before you buy an item, calculate the hours you had to work to purchase it. Once you have calculated your actual hourly wage (AHW), think in terms of the hours you must work to purchase any item. Since Chris's AHW is $6.67, he must work five hours to buy a shirt. To take a date to the movie, Chris must work more than two hours. When Chris learned that he was actually netting $6.67 an hour, he quickly became interested in what he could do to increase his actual hourly wage. Everyone needs to first evaluate his or her present job.

Can you say that basically you enjoy your job? Most of us have mornings when we roll out of bed dreading going to work. If you feel that way most of the time, what is it that you don't like? Is it the hours, the commute, your boss, fellow employees, the pay, or your job responsibilities? Do you find yourself watching the clock? If you have answered yes to any of these questions, you have something in common with a lot of people. When you dread your job, exchanging your time for money is extremely depressing. You realize that something must change, and the sooner the better.

Actual Hourly Wage Worksheet

Categories	Chris	You
1. Total hours worked in a year	2,000	_____
2. Hours preparing for work	125	_____
3. Hours traveling to and from work	125	_____
4. Hours working at home for free	0	_____
5. Job-support hours	50	_____
6. Lunch	200	_____
7. Job-related medical downtime	24	_____
8. Total work hours	2,524	_____
9. Actual income*	$16,840	_____
10. Actual hourly wage	$6.67	_____

*Net contribution from job on line 25 of previous worksheet (Financial Costs and Benefits of a Job).

How Chris calculated his numbers:

1. Fifty weeks times 40 hours a week equals total hours worked yearly.

2. Chris spends on average 30 minutes dressing for work.

3. Chris spends 30 minutes driving to and from work. Almost any employee in a large metro area will spend two to ten times as long commuting.

(continued)

Actual Hourly Wage Worksheet
(continued)

4. Chris does not bring work home. Do you?

5. Job support includes taking the car in for repairs, shopping for clothing worn at work, taking clothing to the cleaners, and so forth.

6. Chris has an hour for lunch. If he didn't work, he would still have to eat. However, he wouldn't spend an hour preparing and eating his lunch.

7. Illness from job-related stress and contagious sicknesses picked up at work caused Chris to miss work three days last year (way below average for an employee).

8. Chris initially believed the job consumed 40 hours each week when it actually consumed an average of 51 hours a week.

9. Get the figure for actual income from line 25 of Financial Costs and Benefits of a Job Worksheet.

10. Divide the amount on line 9 by the number on line 8. It turns out that Chris is earning $6.67 an hour for every hour the job demands. He is paid $15.00 an hour, but 44 percent of that income is spent supporting his job.

The happiest people seem to enjoy the work they do. A few days ago my wife told me about an interview that she had heard on the radio. A lady who ran an employment agency didn't care about her clients' credentials or work experience. She didn't want to hear about the kinds of jobs they didn't like. All she really wanted to know was what each applicant loved to do. If you could do anything (and be guaranteed that you could support yourself financially doing it), what would you choose? This is not an idle question. Right now people are earning a living doing things others only dream about. Someone once said, "If you can imagine it, you can achieve it; if you can achieve it, you can become it." You owe it to yourself to find a job on a career path that promises fulfillment.

Strategies to Increase Your Marketability and Income

You worked hard to complete your education. Perhaps you have earned a professional certification indicating your competency in your job or professional field. You work hard on the job and have gained a wide range of valuable experiences, yet when it comes to finding a job, nothing is more important than who you know. The best jobs are not found at your college's placement office, on the Internet, in the want ads, or at an employment agency. You discover them when someone you know tells you about them. Actually, this is logical when you think about it. Mr. Stein wants to hire someone to fill a vacancy in his firm. Yes, he may use a wide variety of resources to advertise his vacancy, but he also tells everyone about the kind of person he is seeking. If you know someone he tells, you are likely to have an inside shot at filling the vacancy.

You may find all of this upsetting because you spent years acquiring the knowledge stuff. However, who you know will open far more doors than what you know. Who you know gets you the interview; what you know gets you the job. Who you know actually has a name: networking.

Build Your Network

Right now you may be saying, "I don't know anyone who can help me find a job." You may be right, but you can change all of that if you will focus on networking.

Few activities are more enjoyable and rewarding than getting to know others who have similar professional interests. Anyone new to networking must learn how to do the following:

- Come in contact regularly with professionals whose career interests are similar to yours.
- Know how to interact with these professionals.
- Know what to do so that professionals will remember you.

Networking with professionals. Join a professional organization and attend local, regional, and national meetings. Such meetings provide many opportunities to meet others. Introduce yourself to the person sitting next to you at an education session, during lunch, or when everyone is standing around during a break. One of the best ways to get acquainted is to volunteer to become a member of one of the organization's committees. Every organization needs more volunteers.

Read the publications of professional organizations. When you read an article that interests you, write a letter to the author. Most authors receive fewer than five letters and phone calls after their articles appear. They will appreciate hearing from you. Your letter may be the beginning of an ongoing dialogue. Professional publications often carry employment ads (and for a modest fee may be willing to publish your position-wanted ad.) They are likely to carry announcements of professional conferences that you may want to attend. Most professional publications accept articles from members. Few entries on your résumé are more impressive than having published an article.

The higher you try to climb on your career ladder, the more important networking becomes. Once you learn to network effectively, you should never need to make cold calls to strangers about a job again. Your circle of influence should be large enough so that periodically you should be contacted about a vacancy. Remember, who you know gets you the interview; what you know gets you the job.

Keep up in your field. What do employers expect when they hire you? Most employers care more that you can think and communicate professionally than almost anything else. In almost all fields, employers expect excellent oral and written communication skills. If you hate to speak in public, take a course on public speaking or join Toastmasters. If your writing is not up to par, take a business or technical writing class. While communication skills have always been extremely important, communication skills, including computer skills, will be more important in the 21st century than ever before. Your communication skills enable you to network effectively.

Universities make the mistake of calling some degrees "terminal" degrees. Alumni of Texas Tech University are members of the "Ex-students" Association. Both *terminal* and *ex-students* are poorly chosen words. Today our career as students

> **Hot Tip**
>
> You can increase your networking opportunities and probably save yourself some money if you contact the professional organization you're interested in several months before its conference or convention is held and volunteer to help with the meeting. Attendees often pay a registration fee of $60 to $200 a day to attend. However, volunteers usually get to attend free. Volunteering gives you a networking edge over a regular attendee. Duties at the convention often include registering attendees, helping exhibitors set up booths, handing out brochures, and helping speakers with their presentation. Most volunteers are in constant contact with attendees and the officers of the professional organization. Meetings and conferences provide the best way to network.

never ends. If you are not periodically taking courses to keep up or get ahead in your job or profession, you should be. Most high schools offer adult education courses to distinguish them from the traditional classroom. Each college has a continuing education division. Professional organizations offer courses to their members. Employers provide in-house training. A growing number of commercial firms now provide classes on every topic imaginable. Increasingly, students who complete such courses never set foot on the campus of the organization offering the course.

Distance education is changing the way education is delivered. The computer and television make it possible to deliver education anywhere on earth. More progressive schools realize that they can no longer insist that the student come to them. They must deliver education to the learner. Where is your career headed? What courses should you enroll in next? Will your employer pay the costs of taking this course? No investment is more important than human capital.

Show off your work. Do you think that "show and tell" is only appropriate in first grade? Everyone wants his or her résumé to look good, but what can you pull out of your bag to show an interviewer that you actually have the right stuff? Have you written a report that was well received? Do you have a video showing you making an important presentation? How about a copy of an article you wrote that was published? Today, because the competition is so strong, a traditional résumé is just not enough. Be prepared to make a strong showing at the "show and tell" part of the job interview.

Creating a Résumé for the Web

Always Have Your Résumé Posted on the Internet

Create a winning electronic résumé. There is still a place for the traditional résumé, but it is going, going, and almost gone. While the Internet is impacting how we obtain and use information, the biggest opportunity of all may be employment. Increasingly, both employers and employees are using the Internet to find each other. By posting your résumé on the Net, you are opening the door to countless possibilities that you may never have considered. It is extremely important how you organize and present your information when writing an electronic résumé. When you are competing with people from around the globe, how you present what you have accomplished takes on a new meaning.

Hot Tip

Any professional organization worth anything will have a job bank on its Web page.

The Web changes the rules for creating and distributing your résumé. Because of the ease of posting your résumé at so many Web sites, plan to have your résumé posted and keep it updated continually. Employers are going to have to accept that their employees' résumés are always available to their competition. Your job is to create an electronic résumé that is distinctly different from one you mailed in the traditional way.

> **Hot Tip**
>
> After you post your résumé, always edit it. The format often changes; words get misplaced or even lost. Most Web sites make it easy to edit. You need to update your résumé periodically. Many sites will drop your résumé after 90 or 180 days if you have not made any changes.

The Difference between an Electronic and a Traditional Résumé

The following seven points distinguish an electronic résumé from a résumé on paper that is mailed to a potential employer.

1. Scanners have trouble reading most fonts, so use one of the common fonts to create your résumé.
2. The type size on the résumé should never be smaller than 10 points.
3. Anyone trying to fill a vacancy by surfing the Web will use key words to find qualified applicants. You can work hard to make sure that you include all key words as you write your résumé, or you can simply include a key word section in your résumé. Key words should be one-word, two-word, or three-word descriptions of the position you are seeking, your accomplishments, and your job responsibilities. The more key words you use the better.
4. Instead of the one-liner common on mail résumés, write a paragraph describing the opportunity you are seeking—that is, your objective.
5. Be sure to include a summary of your most significant work experiences. Because you don't know what vacancies are out there, a summary provides the employer a picture of who you are. Some résumé writers use the summary in place of the key word section.
6. You have a choice of two approaches when posting your résumé on the Web. You can simply post your résumé on several Web sites that are looked at by employ-

> **Hot Tip**
>
> A great book to help you post your résumé on the Web is *How to Get Your Dream Job Using the Web* by Shannon and Arthur Karl (Coriolis Group).

ers with vacancies you would like to fill. Expect to have to convert your résumé to both ASCII and html before you can post it on most sites.

Many Web sites have their own résumé format and often require you to fill in their blanks. Often you need to write paragraphs that answer the questions that are asked.

7. The following are some of the most widely used Web sites where people post their résumés:

About Work	www.aboutwork.com
America's Job Bank	www.ajb.dni.us
CareerMosaic	www.careermosaic.com
The Monster Board	www.monster.com/

List each Web site where you have posted your résumé (use pencil) on the following worksheet.

Some Web sites even tell you how many hits your résumé has received.

Résumé Web Site Posting Worksheet

Web site	Log-in/User name	Password	Date posted or updated
_____	_____	_____	_____
_____	_____	_____	_____
_____	_____	_____	_____
_____	_____	_____	_____
_____	_____	_____	_____
_____	_____	_____	_____
_____	_____	_____	_____

Preparing for and Handling the Interview

Interviews make most people nervous. You can eliminate most of that funny tummy feeling by being well prepared. Preparation includes the following:

- Learn all you can about the company.
- Dress for the interview.
- Bring questions to ask.
- Rehearse answers to commonly asked questions.

> **Hot Tip**
>
> **A**sk questions wisely. You may want to repeat some questions with everyone who interviews you. Others you may want to save for more-senior executives.

Research

Start your research about a firm on the Internet. Check Hoover's Online (www.hoovers.com/) with information on more than 4,000 companies. First review information on a company's Web page. Check with a search engine such as www.yahoo.com to learn what you can about a firm. Checking a search engine's sources will bring up current news articles about the company as well as financial information. If you really want this job, call company headquarters and ask to speak to someone in investor relations or shareholder services and ask the employee to send you a copy of the company's most recent annual report. Continue your research until you know the company's history, have uncovered the names of the key members of the management team, and know the issues (problems and opportunities) currently confronting the company.

If possible, try to interview one or more current or former employees before you go to your interview. Learn what they do (did) for the company, where they think the company is headed, and how satisfied they are (were) with their jobs. From your research, compile a list of questions about the firm. Put them on 3×5 cards to take to the interview. Include questions such as these:

- What would my primary job responsibilities be?
- What are my opportunities for promotion?
- What type of person are you looking for?
- Whom would I work with?
- Describe the greatest challenges this job offers.
- How often will I be expected to relocate?
- How long has the interviewer been with the firm?
- What has the interviewer gained from working for this company?

- Describe the strengths and weaknesses of the person I would report to (be careful with this question).

Always ask questions as if you are going to get the job. You want the interviewer to sense that you fit the position for which you are interviewing.

Rehearse

Practice your answers to the following questions commonly asked by interviewers:

- What are your greatest weaknesses? (Pause before answering.)
- What is your greatest (personal or professional) achievement?
- Why should this firm hire you?
- Where do you see yourself in five years?
- Why do you want to leave your present job?

The Interview Itself

Helpful hints:

- Come prepared to fill out paperwork before the interview.
- Bring along at least three copies of your résumé. (Also bring your Social Security card and driver's license—you may be offered the job on the spot.)
- Dress professionally; wear your best business suit. Pay attention to your entire wardrobe, including shoes. Keep to basic colors: black, gray and navy. Do not wear flashy colors or accessories.
- Make sure you know exactly where the interview will be held. Expect traffic and parking problems, so plan to arrive at least 15 to 30 min-

> **Hot Tip**
>
> Do not discuss salary until you are offered the job. If the interviewer brings it up before making an offer, tell him or her that you would prefer finding out if you really fit the opening before discussing salary. After you have been offered the job and a salary figure has been stated, repeat the offer and then pause several seconds before you respond. If you are offered a salary that you consider too low, counter by mentioning a higher figure. Some employers purposely offer less than they are willing to pay to see if the candidate will try to negotiate a higher salary. Such employers wonder if the candidate will not stand up for his or her best interests; will the candidate do his or her best when representing company concerns?

utes before your interview starts. You may be expected to complete forms before the interview starts.
- It is better to stand in the waiting room than to sit.
- When you name is called, hesitate a fraction of a second before stepping forward. Good posture and a warm smile are key here.
- Make sure you shake hands firmly (but do not squeeze).
- Make eye contact often.
- When offered a chair, move the chair slightly away from the interviewer. When sitting in the chair, do not cross your arms or legs (keep knees together). Keep your head upright. Sit so that you lean slightly toward the interviewer. Do not fidget or shift your weight.
- Use the interviewer's last name (never the first name unless asked to do so).
- Do not chew (gum or tobacco).
- Do not use slang (stay away from expressions like *you know, kids, guys,* etc.).
- Remember to ask your questions.

Earning a living can be an extremely satisfying experience. For many people their job defines who they are; it contributes more to their self-esteem than anything else. You are likely to be employed during most of your 60s and possibly into your 70s. You must find work that you like and that fairly compensates you. Do what you must to increase your real hourly wage. In this fast-moving information age, you should be currently enrolled in or be between courses so that you can keep your skills on the cutting edge. The Internet makes it easy for you to keep your résumé posted in several different locations. Rarely do people achieve financial fitness when they hate their job.

Financial Checkup Checklist

- Calculate your actual hourly wage.
- Join an appropriate professional organization.
- Enroll in a continuing education course.
- Post your electronic résumé on the Web.

21 Make Sure You Have a Plan for Your Estate

Make certain that your estate plan reflects your current thinking with particular attention paid to your dependents.

> Ethel did not want anybody to benefit by her death; yet she did not want to leave any of her money to charity. She certainly didn't want Uncle Sam to get his hands on her money. Ethel wanted to spend it all before she died, but she was terminally ill with cancer. With only a few more months to live, Ethel could spend very little of the money she had accumulated. During all of their married life, Doc often tried to get Ethel's money. Before she died, she did decide to leave every cent to him, hoping, but not believing, that he could manage it. In less than two years after her death, Doc and his new wife had spent it all.

The assets you own are considered your estate. Estate planning involves your deciding what should happen to those assets after your death. Estate planning is not just an activity that should interest elderly people. If you are young and single, your personal estate planning concerns are much less complex than your parents'. The fewer your assets, the less complex your estate planning needs to be. However, you need to be aware of the estate planning problems that confront persons of all ages. It is highly likely that loved ones, including senior members of your family and older friends and acquaintances, have not adequately planned how they want to dispose of their estates. Their failure to plan can create problems for you. Each of us shares some of the following concerns about our estates:

- After death, almost everyone wants his or her possessions to go to certain individuals and/or charities.
- People currently supporting one or more individuals want that financial support to continue after they are gone. Many people wish to continue managing their finances after their death for the benefit of their dependents.
- A parent of a minor child needs to nominate a guardian to raise the child in case of the parent or parents' premature death.
- Responsible individuals want all their debts repaid at their death. Most state laws provide that debts must be paid before distribution of assets, especially if the estate is probated.
- Wealthier individuals want to pay as little as possible in estate taxes and estate administrative fees. Almost everyone wants to save every tax dollar as well as attorney fees and court costs.
- Many individuals do not want their financial affairs to become public knowledge after their death.

Estate planning is also for the living. An accident could make it impossible for you to make rational decisions regarding your health care or how your finances should be handled. Planning for incapacity is an important part of estate planning. The odds are that younger persons will be disabled rather than meet an early death.

Estate Planning Tools

To help you learn how to deal with estate planning issues, you will find the following tools helpful:

Wills. A will identifies who will receive the assets in your estate. Your will names someone to serve as the guardian of your minor children. It also names the person (called an executor or personal representative) who manages your estate through the probate process (discussed on the following page).

Trusts. You can set up a trust to manage your financial affairs and investments during your life (or you can include a trust in your will). After your death, the assets in the trust will be managed as you specify in the trust document. You can desig-

> **Hot Tip**
>
> Using a trust may save a substantial amount of estate taxes at your death, but trusts do not save income taxes. Money earned inside the trust needs to be distributed annually or the trust will pay substantial income taxes at a much higher rate than individuals pay.

nate beneficiaries to receive income and/or assets from the trust. Trusts terminate when you decide that assets should be distributed. If you set up the trust during your lifetime, you can be the person who transfers assets to your trust, manages your trust, and receives income from your trust.

Contracts. Typically, most people are familiar with four different types of contracts:

1. A life insurance policy
2. An individual retirement account (IRA)
3. An employer's retirement plan
4. An annuity

You are required to designate a beneficiary who would receive the proceeds from each contract or account after your death. You may also specify contingent beneficiaries. A contingent beneficiary is a person or persons who would receive the proceeds from these contracts if the primary beneficiary you named dies before you do (and you fail to change the primary beneficiary).

Title. A title lists who owns property and how ownership is held. For example, if you hold title to property as a joint tenant with right of survivorship, at your death your share of the property will pass to the remaining joint tenant(s). Many married persons hold title to real estate (such as a home), bank accounts, and cars in joint tenancy. Any two or more individuals may hold title in joint tenancy in most states.

You can hold title several different ways: as a sole owner; as a joint tenant with right of survivorship; or as tenants in common, whereby each owner owns a distinct share or portion that does not pass at the death of one owner to the other owners but can be passed by will, trust, or intestacy laws.

Only certain assets, such as cars, houses, and bank accounts, have titles. Many people like to hold property in their own name and in the name of one or more persons as joint tenants with the right of survivorship so that it will automatically pass to the other titled individuals. For example, Evelyn and Angus bought a car together; they hold title as joint tenants. If one dies before the car is sold, the other becomes the sole owner of the car.

Myth: An item held in joint tenancy will not be subject to estate taxes because

> **Hot Tip**
>
> Property held in trust, property held as a joint tenancy, or property that transfers according to a beneficiary designation in a contract does not go through the probate process. An owner's will has no control over who receives property transferred by contract, trust, or title.

it avoids probate. This is not true. Avoiding probate has nothing to do with avoiding estate taxes. I don't discuss estate taxation in this text because if you leave a net estate of $650,000 or less in 1999 (the amount increases to $1 million as shown in the table below), you will not owe federal estate taxes. Nor will you owe taxes if you leave everything to your spouse.

Powers of attorney. These documents give someone the authority to act in your behalf if you are not able to do so yourself. Such documents are important if you become mentally or physically unable to make important financial and/or medical decisions.

Living wills. A living will gives someone the authority to turn off life support systems if a physician has declared you brain dead.

Letter of last instruction. This letter discusses your wishes for your funeral, indicates where you keep important documents, and often includes your personal concerns for your loved ones.

Probate. Probate is the process whereby a will is admitted to court or a deceased person is determined to have died without a will. The probate court appoints someone to handle the affairs of the deceased, to gather the deceased's assets, pay his or her debts, and distribute the remaining property according to the terms of the will or as the law dictates. Probate is usually handled in the local county court system.

Purpose of Estate Planning Tools

These tools are used for a variety of reasons. One reason is to reduce estate taxes. Actually, federal law offers anyone's estate in 1999 a unified credit that enables the first $650,000 of a person's estate to escape federal estate taxes. That amount increases as shown in the following chart.

Year	Amount of estate exempt from federal estate taxes
2000–1	$675,000
2002–3	700,000
2004	850,000
2005	950,000
2006	1,000,000

You may be surprised to learn that if you give anyone a gift larger than $10,000 in any one year, you will owe taxes on the amount in excess of the $10,000. If you fail to pay the tax during your lifetime, it will be assessed at your death. The unified credit can be used to reduce both gift taxes and estate taxes. For example, Bill gave his son Morris a $100,000 home a week before Morris married Myrtle. If Bill does not pay the gift tax on the $90,000 during his life, his estate will. In effect, the amount of his estate that is exempt from federal estate tax will be reduced by the $90,000.

Other purposes of the estate planning tools are to be as certain as possible that assets in a person's estate are distributed according to the wishes of the person who currently owns the assets; to make sure that a person's assets are used for his or her benefit if he or she is mentally or physically disabled. Estate planning also ensures that health care decisions can be made as needed, and that beneficiaries of the estate are taken care of adequately. This means that guardians are appointed to rear the children as well as manage money left to support them. Many people prefer that professionals, such as bank trust department officers, manage their estates.

While nearly everyone benefits from using the tools discussed above, none is more important than a will.

> **Hot Tip**
>
> If Bill is married, his wife can participate in the gift with each giving $10,000, so only $80,000 will be taxed. Had Bill made the gift after Morris's marriage, both he and his wife could have each given $10,000 tax-free to both the bride and groom, thus reducing the taxable gift to $60,000.

Wills

A will is a legal document that addresses the following issues:

- Who will receive your possessions after your death
- Who will serve as the guardian of your minor children
- Who will manage the money, and how they will manage the money your children inherit from you until they become adults

In addition, it directs that all of your debts be paid before your possessions are given to others; and it appoints an executor (male) or executrix (female) (or personal representative) to gather your assets, pay your bills, manage your affairs, and distribute what remains of your estate.

If you do not have a will, you may be tempted to write your own. Please think again! For example, do you know the correct number of witnesses required (0,1,2,3)? Should those signatures be notarized? Does your state accept handwritten wills or must they be typed? Handwritten wills often fail to comply with state law and are likely to be declared invalid by the probate judge. If you cross out part of a handwritten will, you may invalidate the entire will.

A will you draft yourself is unlikely to have certain key clauses that you may wish to include such as a simultaneous death clause. If someone named in your will dies 30, 60, or 90 days after you do, for legal purposes that person is assumed to have died before you did and will not receive any assets from your estate. Why is this important? A simultaneous death clause prevents your estate from being taxed twice: first at your death and second on the estate of the person who dies soon after you.

> **Hot Tip**
>
> If you are married, each spouse should have his or her own will. If one spouse dies, it's very difficult for the remaining spouse to change the terms of a joint will.

Do you know that you can stipulate that if someone named in your will contests the will, that person is to receive nothing from your estate? The person named in your will to manage the finances of your minor children can serve without bond. A bond guarantees to replace any of the children's inheritance that is stolen or lost as a result of poor management. Bonds will cost your estate money, so appoint a guardian of the children's money who is honest *and* competent. Stipulate in your will that this person may serve without having to buy a bond each year to ensure each child's inheritance.

Request that the executor be able to complete an informal probate, which is easier and less expensive than a formal probate. There are fewer forms to file and therefore fewer fees to pay. Ask that your will state that personal property can be distributed according to your handwritten list included with your will. Such a list, called a "listing agreement" in many states, can reduce or eliminate fights over who gets your baseball cards or Barbie dolls.

Include a trust, known as a testamentary trust, in your will. Much like an airbag that comes into existence on impact, the testamentary trust comes into existence after your death. Instead of directing assets to go directly to individuals, you may believe that your assets will be better managed if they are placed in a trust. For example, Louise has a $300,000 life insurance policy and two minor children. If her spouse is the beneficiary of her life insurance policy, she may feel that her spouse might not manage the proceeds in the best interest of the children. Instead of listing her spouse as the beneficiary of her life insurance policy, she lists the name of the trustee (or the trust itself) as the beneficiary. After her death, the proceeds of her insurance policy will be paid to the trust. Terms of the trust spell out how the money should be managed on behalf of her children. The trust document spells out exactly how the life insurance proceeds (and other assets from the deceased's estate that end up in the trust) are to be used to meet the financial needs of the remaining spouse and children. A spouse could be the trustee or, better yet, a cotrustee along with a competent friend or a bank's trust department.

There are some things a will cannot do. It cannot

- disinherit a spouse or minor children in most states;
- designate who receives property that has been transferred by trust, title, or contract;
- require someone to do something illegal to receive an inheritance; or
- handle any matters if you are incapacitated but not yet deceased.

> **Hot Tip**
>
> It could be in your best interest to show the will you drafted using the resources noted above to an attorney who specializes in estate planning. Also ask the attorney if there would be any advantages to videotaping your will. Frequently, people think their estate is small or simple; however, what they want or need is often more complex than they realize.

If you have an extremely simple, small estate or like to do everything yourself, you may want to obtain the book *The Will Kit* (Dearborn), by John Ventura. Quicken also offers Quicken Family Lawyer (800-223-6925). Both of these options are better than writing your own will or buying a blank will form at an office supply store.

Trusts

A trust is a contract between you (known as the donor or grantor) and the manager of the trust assets, known as the trustee. The trustee distributes income at least annually to the trust's income beneficiaries. When the trust is dissolved, all trust assets are distributed to the trust's beneficiaries or remaindermen according to the terms of the trust.

Trusts are either revocable or irrevocable. You gift assets to an irrevocable trust. Once the assets are transferred to the trust,

> **Hot Tip**
>
> You can place almost anything in a trust (as long as it is debt-free)! Because the Blankenships are still making mortgage payments, for example, they cannot place their home in a trust and have that home go directly to the named beneficiary.

you are not the owner of the asset and cannot at some future date remove the asset from the trust. People create irrevocable trusts when they wish to get an asset out of their taxable estate. Such an asset will not be included in their estate once it has been placed in an irrevocable trust. However, gifts made to the trust in excess of $10,000 ($20,000 for the married) are subject to gift taxes. If you set up a revocable trust, you have the authority to remove assets from the trust. Such trust assets will be included in your taxable estate at your death; however, after your death, the trust becomes irrevocable. It can also become irrevocable on your incapacity.

You can be the trustee and the beneficiary of your revocable trust. If you become mentally incompetent to manage the trust, wording in the trust document will result in another trustee replacing you as the trustee of your trust.

There are many different types of trusts. Testamentary trusts were discussed above. If your estate is approaching $1 million, you may need to visit with an attorney who specializes in trusts. Even if your estate is less than $500,000, you may benefit by setting up a living trust.

Living Trusts

Living trusts are the rage today. Although they are not for everyone, they do make sense under the following conditions:

- You own property in more than one state. A trust can keep your estate from having to go through probate in each state where you own property.
- You are contemplating a second marriage (especially if you plan to marry someone who has children and/or you have children by a first marriage). This strategy does not work as well in the eight community property states.
- You do not want your family to go through the hassle or costs of probate after your death.
- You are concerned about how your estate will be managed during your golden years when you may become incompetent to manage your financial affairs.

Hot Tip

Many attorneys prefer not to create living trusts. These trusts cost significantly more to set up and fund than does drafting a will ($1,000 to $2,000 versus $200 to $300). While most attorneys are happy to charge you for drafting a living trust, far fewer will make sure that your property is transferred to the trust. Before you pay the attorney's bill for the trust in full, make sure that title has been changed to all property that should be placed in the trust. Some assets which have beneficiaries, like life insurance policies, IRAs, and company pensions, must have the beneficiary designation changed, or after your death the dollars in these assets will not go into your trust.

- You are concerned about how finances will be managed for one or more family members after your death.

Living Wills and Durable Powers of Attorney

A living will expresses your wishes concerning life support systems should your doctor determine that you have no chance of survival. You can avoid being kept alive by artificial means if you complete a living will. State law governs the wording of living wills and the actual conditions under which living wills are valid. You need to make sure that you use a form approved by your state, but you don't need an attorney to draft a living will for you.

Filling out the blanks is just the beginning. You need to make copies of your living will. Put one copy with your will; give another to the executor or personal representative of your estate. Make sure your attorney has a copy. However, it is most important that both your doctor and your hospital have copies. Send them a copy stating that you will contact them if you revoke or change your living will. State law governs hospitals' and doctors' responsibility regarding compliance with the terms of living wills. You need to know that your wishes will be followed. A trusted friend or loved one who will insist that your wishes be carried out can be extremely valuable.

In a power of attorney you give someone else authority to act for you as your agent (or attorney-in-fact). However, unless a power of attorney is considered durable, it ceases to have any power once you are considered mentally incapable of managing your own affairs. If you do not wish anyone to have a power of attorney over your affairs until you are incapacitated, you will want a "springing" durable power of attorney. Such a power of attorney springs into existence once an appropriate person, such as a physician, has determined that you are not mentally capable of managing your affairs.

Choose carefully the person you select as your agent or attorney-in-fact. This person needs to be someone who knows you and your family well. You must be totally confident of this person's integrity and competence. Make sure you select at

> **Hot Tip**
>
> You may contact Choice in Dying, Inc., 1035 30th St., NW, Washington, DC 20007, (202-338-9790) to receive a free copy of a power of attorney and/or a living will that complies with your state's legal code. Your hospital may also have copies of blank documents that you can complete, and various organizations, such as the AARP, frequently offer them.

least two (three is better), so if one is unable to serve, another will be appointed in his or her place.

You may need two durable powers of attorney, one for financial affairs and one for health care—sometimes called a "health care proxy." The exact structure depends upon state law. To be sure the appropriate professionals will honor each, send or hand deliver to your doctor and banker a copy

Hot Tip

Each time you see your doctor, mention that you want him or her to honor your living will.

of your durable power of attorney; if you mail it, send it by certified letter. Ask them if they are willing to abide by the terms of your durable power of attorney and tell them you will inform them by certified letter if you revoke your durable power of attorney. Every time you visit with your financial advisers or medical professionals, reaffirm that your durable power of attorney expresses your current wishes. Make sure your attorney has a copy of both powers of attorney.

The medical profession is much more likely to comply with the terms of a durable power of attorney for health care. The person to whom you have given a durable power of attorney to handle your finances will have a more difficult time getting banks, brokerage houses, and insurance companies to comply with your terms. You must send copies to each institution that has one of your accounts. Try to get them to confirm in writing that they will honor your durable power of attorney. If any firm is reluctant, get your attorney involved.

If your parents are still living, do what you can to get them or others you care about to draft living wills and durable powers of attorney.

Using an Attorney

Before you see a lawyer to have a document drafted, fill in the blanks on the next worksheet with the following information.

- Name two or three individuals who could serve as the executor or personal representative of your will and/or trustee of your trust. Obtain each person's permission before including him or her in your will or trust.

Hot Tip

You benefit every time you update your living will or durable power of attorney because medical and financial professionals will regard the document as expressing your current thinking.

- Name two or three individuals (or couples) you want to serve as guardians for your minor children. Obtain each person's permission.
- Name two to three individuals you want to manage assets for your minor children. Obtain each person's permission.
- List individuals who are to receive your estate assets as well as a list of anyone who is to receive income from assets in your estate.
- Make a list showing how title is held to your home, automobiles, all bank and credit union accounts, securities (stocks, bonds, mutual funds) and certificates of deposit. Know the approximate value of each.
- Make a list showing who is the beneficiary of your life insurance policies, annuity contracts, IRAs, and other retirement plans. Know the approximate value of each.

> **Hot Tip**
>
> If you are no longer married to your children's mother or father and wish someone else (besides your ex) to serve as their guardian, write a separate letter to the probate judge (keep it with your will) explaining the reasons for this decision. The judge will consider your request. Without it, your former spouse is likely to be named as guardian no matter whom you appoint in your will.

Are you married? If you live in a community property state (Texas, Louisiana, California, Washington, Idaho, Arizona, Nevada, New Mexico), half of what you own belongs to your spouse. Technically, anything you owned before the marriage or received as an inheritance after the marriage belongs only to you. However, it is very easy for separate property to convert to community property. For example, before Cary marries, she puts $10,000 into a CD. At the time of the marriage the CD is Cary's separate property, but 50 percent of the interest that the CD earns after her marriage belongs to Cary's current spouse. The property will remain Cary's separate property if she gives the spouse 50 percent of the interest the CD earns each year. If she does not distribute the interest the CD earns each year, the money in the CD becomes community property in most community property states. This also holds true for profits from a business or the increase in value of other assets. Check with an attorney who specializes in estate planning if you live in a community property state and think some of your property is separate property or are uncertain exactly how the property would be viewed.

Consider reviewing and updating your legal documents every five years and when

- you acquire new real estate or valuable personal property;

Information Needed for Drafting a Document Worksheet

Personal Representative, Executor, or Executrix:

Name: _____ _____ _____

Address: _____ _____ _____

_____ _____ _____

Children's Guardian:

Name: _____ _____ _____

Address: _____ _____ _____

_____ _____ _____

Guardian of Children's Assets:

Name: _____ _____ _____

Address: _____ _____ _____

_____ _____ _____

Trustee:

Name: _____ _____ _____

Address: _____ _____ _____

_____ _____ _____

(continued)

Information Needed for Drafting a Document Worksheet
(continued)

Assets in Estate:	Value[1]	Title[2]	Beneficiary[3]	PP[4]

Bank Accounts:

_____ _____ _____ _____ _____

_____ _____ _____ _____ _____

_____ _____ _____ _____ _____

_____ _____ _____ _____ _____

Investments:

_____ _____ _____ _____ _____

_____ _____ _____ _____ _____

_____ _____ _____ _____ _____

_____ _____ _____ _____ _____

_____ _____ _____ _____ _____

_____ _____ _____ _____ _____

_____ _____ _____ _____ _____

_____ _____ _____ _____ _____

(continued)

Information Needed for Drafting a Document Worksheet
(continued)

Real Estate:

  Home   _____ _____ _____ _____

_____   _____ _____ _____ _____

_____   _____ _____ _____ _____

Retirement:

  Annuity   _____ _____ _____ _____

  Annuity   _____ _____ _____ _____

  IRA   _____ _____ _____ _____

  IRA   _____ _____ _____ _____

_____   _____ _____ _____ _____

_____   _____ _____ _____ _____

_____   _____ _____ _____ _____

[1]Value: Current market value of an asset.
[2]Title: Separate (one owner), community (husband and wife in the eight community property states), tenants in common (more than one owner), joint tenancy (more than one owner; at death proceeds go to remaining owner(s)), and tenancy by the entirety (husband and wife) in a few states.
[3]Beneficiary: The name of the person who receives one of your assets after your death.
[4]PP (how property is passed): How property is transferred from you to someone else—by *contract* (usually a life insurance policy, annuity, or retirement account); by *title* (document that determines ownership of a car, house, bank account); by *trust;* or by *will.*

- you move to a new state (your will, or parts of it, may not be legal after you change states);
- your spouse dies or you divorce;
- there is a death or divorce of someone named in your will;
- you marry or remarry;
- you receive a substantial inheritance;
- federal or state law changes;
- your health changes;
- there is a birth of a child; and
- you change your mind.

> **Hot Tip**
>
> **W**hen you have a new will or trust drafted, destroy all copies of previous wills and/or trusts.

How to Find an Estate Planning Attorney

Don't worry about finding an estate planning attorney. Here are some tips:

- Ask trusted friends if they use someone they like.
- Ask a trust officer at your bank for referrals to three attorneys.
- Ask other attorneys for references.
- Seek attorneys who are board certified in estate planning.
- Ask the local bar association for the names of attorneys serving on estate planning committees.
- Contact the following groups and ask for the names of estate planning attorneys in your area:

    National Network of Estate Planning Attorneys
    410 17th St., Suite 1260
    Denver, CO 80202
    800-638-8681

    American College of Trust and Estate Counsel
    3415 South Sepulveda Blvd., Suite 330
    Los Angeles, CA 90034-6060
    Fax 310-572-7280
    (Must request referrals by letter or fax.)

> **Hot Tip**
>
> **O**nce you receive a copy of a legal document, read it carefully. If you do not understand what is written, ask the attorney. *Do not pay the attorney's bill until you are satisfied that the document accurately reflects your wishes.* Leave a copy of your will and/or trust with your attorney, put one in your filing system, and give a copy to the person you named as personal representative or executor in your will, and the trustee of your trust.

Hot Tip

Interview at least two attorneys and explain exactly the services you want. You will be happier with quotes to complete the project than per hour rates (since neither you nor the attorney knows how many hours it will take to complete what you want accomplished). Find out if there is a charge for this initial meeting before you show up. Consider how much counseling, education, and follow-up is offered versus the mere drafting and generation of a document. You may want to ask the following:

- How much do you charge to draft a will, trust, or living will?
- Do you customize a document to fit my situation, or do you primarily use boilerplate documents?
- Should I include a trust in my will?
- Do you favor probating most estates?
- What year did you start specializing in estate planning?
- What can be done to reduce the cost of probating my estate?
- How much would you charge to probate my estate?
- How many wills and trusts did you draw up last year?
- Will you include a clause in my will that allows me to attach a handwritten list to my will identifying whom I want to receive my personal property?
- Will you be available to review my will or trust in the future and to make any needed changes?
- Will you be available for any estate planning problems that arise?

National Association of Estate Planning Councils
P. O. Box 46
Bryn Mawr, PA 19010
610-526-1389

- Check this Web site: www.lawyers.martindale.com/marhub

The documents discussed in this chapter can be a great aid in helping distribute the assets in your estate as well as providing proper care if you become disabled. While such documents can bring you great peace of mind, your family members and loved ones especially appreciate them. Make sure that they know you have drafted such documents and where you keep them. No one can be considered financially fit without a will, living will, and durable powers of attorney for health care and financial affairs. You may also benefit by having a trust drafted.

Financial Checkup Checklist

- Obtain permission of people I would like to name to represent me in these documents.

- Have my will and/or trust drafted or updated.

- Carefully read each legal document.

- Make a list describing whom I want to receive each of my personal belongings.

- Give a copy of my will to my executor or personal representative.

- Give a copy of my trust to my trustee

- Give a copy of my living will to my attorney, doctor, and hospital.

- Have a current durable power of attorney for health care.

- Give a copy of my durable power of attorney for health care to my attorney, doctor, and hospital.

- Have a current durable power of attorney for financial affairs.

- Give a copy of my durable power of attorney for financial affairs to my attorney and all appropriate financial institutions.

Financial Planning Calendar

After you have completed the exercises in *Financial Fitness for Life,* refer to the Financial Planning Calendar to keep yourself fit.

Month	Activities
January	Review the previous 12-month performance of each investment. Implement buy and sell decisions as appropriate. Calculate your net worth. Check to see if you are on track for achieving financial independence. Every three years obtain a copy of your Social Security benefit statement.
February	Prepare (or have a professional prepare) your income tax returns. File return if due a refund.
March	Review your auto and home insurance. Implement needed changes.
April	File tax return if you owe taxes.
May	Review your estate plan. Make changes if needed. Evaluate your donation strategies to include the worthiness of appropriate charities. Every five years review your life insurance coverage.
June	Review your lifetime goals, making sure you are adequately funding high priority goals.
July	Do nothing besides pay bills.
August	Review your career opportunities. Invest in your own human capital.
September	Review your spending plan with relevant members of your household. Make needed adjustments.
October	Review your debt obligations. Make sure you are on track for paying off expensive debt such as credit card balances.
November	Review your expected income tax liability for this year and next year. Make appropriate changes as necessary.
December	Review your employee benefit package. Make appropriate changes. Pay special attention to health and disability coverages plus the percentage of your salary contributed to a 401(k) plan.

Epilogue

Too many times clients do not implement the strategies they selected during our counseling session. If they carry out the strategy exactly as we discussed, they will achieve the financial goal they have selected. Too many readers buy books about personal finance, read the strategies, but then never implement them. Your success at becoming financially fit depends on your implementing strategies you have read about in this book. I hope you feel that you are doing a better job managing your finances after having read through the book. If you have worked through most of the worksheets in *Financial Fitness for Life,* I know that you are. You should feel a greater sense of control over your money; it should be doing a much better job for you. I also hope that you expect less of money now than when you started the book. The most important things in life are intangible; money at best can only indirectly help you work through issues of relationships, love, and memories. However, when money is not managed properly, stress generated by mismanagement often does destroy relationships and love, and creates unpleasant memories.

I hope you didn't read the book in one or two sittings. Reading too quickly about many financial topics that require your attention and action means too many issues were ignored. If you did, now is as good a time as any to turn to the table of contents. Which topic deserves your attention the most right now? Go back to that chapter; work through the exercises. Start to eliminate one of the financial stresses in your life today. Yes, you will need to change one or more behaviors. Change is threatening. We do not like change because change forces us to experience the unknown. Change is a gamble; we may be worse off because we have changed a behavior. However, all of us exhibit self-defeating behaviors. We write checks praying that a deposit will beat the check to the bank. We make purchases with a credit card hoping to lift our spirits. Some of us control the money in our households, forcing other family members to beg for or defend their use of money. We fail to buy the right kind and amount of insurance thinking (or hoping) that we will never need the coverage. We buy bonds when we really should be buying stocks because of fear that the stocks may lose value (when often it is the bonds that do). Fear plays too big a role in most people's financial affairs. Early in *Financial Fitness for Life,* I asked you to list your financial fears. If you still have one or more, it's time to reread the appropriate chapter. Knowledge will usually erase fear. You cannot become financially fit if you are afraid of the financial decisions you make.

Knowledge is power. Learn what *Financial Fitness for Life* can teach you about managing your money. No one is truly financially fit who cannot give generously of what he or she has received. For every dime that you put away for your retirement, give away a dime to someone in need. You have the power to make a difference in your life and in others. Use that power.

Index

A

A.M. Best, 161, 175–76
About Work Web site, 275
Accidental death insurance, 120, 126, 169–70
Accident insurance, 153
Accountants, 40, 41, 243–44
Actual cash value, 135
Advisers, professional, 37–42
   checklist, 42
   referrals, 41
Aggressive growth funds, 216. *See also* Mutual fund(s)
Alimony, 254
Alliance mutual funds, 212
American College of Trust and Estate Counsel, 293
American Express, 100, 134
American Institute of Certified Public Accountants, 41
American Institute of Philanthropy, 237
American Society of Appraisers, 137
America's Job Bank Web site, 275
Amica, 134
Annual benefit statement, 128
Annual percentage rate (APR), 78, 101, 105
Annual rate of return, 184
Annual renewable term insurance, 169
Annuities, 122, 227–35
   checklist, 235
   fixed or variable, 227–28, 232–33
   installment purchase of, 228–29
   lump sum purchase of, 228
   payout options of, 229–30
   pros and cons of, 230–32
   shopping for, 233
   worksheet, 234
Appraisals, of personal property, 137
Asset allocation, 224–25
Assets, 13
   cash, 14
   investment, 15, 21
   personal, 16
Attorney, estate planning and, 288–94
Auto(s)
   discounts on purchase of, with credit cards, 103
   expense of owning, 55
   insurance. *See* Auto insurance
   loan, 83
   market value of, 13
Auto insurance, 129–35
   collision insurance, 102–3, 130
   comprehensive insurance, 130–31
   as employee benefit, 120
   medical coverage, 131
   personal injury protection, 131
   rental car coverage, 132
   saving money on, 132–35
   towing/emergency road service, 132
   uninsured motorist coverage, 131–32
   uninsured motorist-property damage insurance, 132
Automatic transactions, 63
Average daily balance, 101–2

B

Baby Boomer Financial Wake-Up Call, The, 190
Bailout clause (annuity), 231, 233
Balanced funds, 216. *See also* Mutual fund(s)
Banking file, 31
Bankruptcy, 84, 87–88
Beating the Street, 198
Beneficiary, 174–75, 281
   of annuity, 229
   of IRA, 186
Billing, 38
Blue Book, 13
Bond(s), 7, 197–99, 205, 207–9
   government, 224, 250
   rating services, 207
   real after-tax rate of return for, 207–9

Bond funds, 216. *See also* Mutual fund(s)
Budget. *See* Money management
Building code, 139–40
Business
    expenses, 242
    gains and losses, 252–53
    risk, 207

C

Cafeteria plans, 121. *See also* Employee benefits
Cancer insurance, 153
Car(s)
    discounts on purchase of, with credit cards, 103
    expense of owning, 55
    insurance. *See* Auto insurance
    loan, 83
    market value of, 13
    rentals, credit cards and, 102–3
Career fulfillment, 262–78
    checklist, 278
    financial costs and benefits of a job worksheet, 265–66
    income, 263–64, 267–68
    interviews, 276–78
    networking, 271–73
    résumé, 273–75
    strategies, 271
CareerMosaic Web site, 275
Cash advance, on credit card, 102
Cash assets, 14, 16
Casualty and theft losses, 257
CDs, 7
Certified Financial Analyst (CFA), 40
Certified Financial Planner (CFP), 40
Certified Public Accountant (CPA), 40, 243–44
Charitable donations, 5, 236–40, 257
    checklist, 240
    contributions worksheet, 239
    donating time, 240
    personal items, 256
Charles Schwab (annuity purchase), 233
Chartered Life Underwriter (CLU), 40
Checking accounts, 97
Child care, as employee benefit, 121, 127
Child and dependent care credit, 259
Children
    debt and, 71
    guardians named for, 289
    protecting inheritance of, 284
Child support, 83
Child tax credit, 258

Choice in Dying, Inc., 287
Cliff vesting, 185
Clothing expenses, 54
COLA (cost-of-living adjustment), 185
Collection agency, 87–88
College education
    cost of, 164
    as employee benefit, 127
    Hope Scholarship credit, 259–60
    scholarships, 250
Collision insurance, 130
    car rentals and, 102
Commissions, 38, 41
    mutual funds and, 213, 215
Communication skills, 272
Comprehensive insurance, 130–31
Comprehensive major medical insurance, 145–46
Consumer Credit Counseling Service, 87
Consumer Reports, 218
Consumer Response Center (FTC), 88
Contingent beneficiaries, 281
Continuing education, as employee benefit, 127
Contracts, 281
Corporate bonds, 224
Correspondence audits, 246
Counseling
    divorce, 73
    shopping addiction and, 68
CPA, 40, 243–44
Credit
    building or improving, 96–98
    checklists, 90, 97
    report, 90–96
    rights, 88–90
Credit card management, 83, 99–112. *See also* Debt/debt elimination
    annual membership fee, 100
    annual percentage rate, 101, 105
    billing errors, 107–8
    card registry, 111
    cash advances, 102
    checklist, 112
    closing unused accounts, 95–96
    considerations, 109–10
    cutting up your cards, 69
    debit cards, 110–11
    defective product or service charged on card, 109–10
    denial of application, 108
    foreign travel and, 110
    fraud protection, 108
    grace period, 100–101
    insurance for lost or stolen, 103
    interest computations, 101–2
    introductory rate, 104–5
    minimum payments, 77
    900 numbers, 108
    perks offered, 102–4
    preapproved applications, 100
    transferring balances, 105–7
Credit life or disability, 169
Credit repair clinic, 96
Credit unions, 56
Currency exchange, 110

D

Debit cards, 110–11
Debt/debt elimination, 20, 65–98. *See also* Credit card management; Liabilities
    assessing problem worksheet, 67
    checklist, 75
    children and, 71
    counseling, 68
    credit cards, 69, 71–72, 77
    debt elimination calendar, 79–82, 86
    divorce and, 72–73
    family business, 73–74
    financial records, failing to keep, 70
    loan ledger worksheet, 78–79
    needs vs. wants, 74–75
    self-esteem and consumerism, 70
    shopping addiction, 66, 68–69
    -to-income ratio, 104
Debt Counselors of America, 87
Debtors Anonymous, 87
Decreasing term insurance, 169
Deductibles, insurance, 136, 141, 149
Deductions, 243
Deferred annuities, 228. *See also* Annuities
Deficiency judgment, 83–84
Defined benefit retirement plan, 120, 122, 180
    cost-of-living adjustment, 185
Defined contribution retirement plan, 120, 122, 180
Dent, Harry, 209
Dental expenses, taxes and, 256
Dependent care
    flexible spending accounts and, 124
    reimbursement account, 252
Depression, and shopping, 66, 68
Direct deposit, 247
Disabled, tax credit for, 258
Disability income policy, 155
Disability insurance, 126, 154–61
    analysis of disability needs worksheet, 155

buying a policy, 158, 160
comparing your policy worksheet, 159–60
credit cards and, 104
definition of disability, 157
disability income policy, 155
elimination period, 157
as employee benefit, 120
inflation and, 157
length of coverage, 157
noncancelable, 158
rehabilitation benefits, 158
residual benefits rider, 156
self-employed and, 160–61
Social Security, 116, 154
waiver of premium, 158
women and, 160
workers' compensation, 154
Discover Card, 101
Diversification, mutual funds and, 216–17
Dividend reinvestment, mutual funds and, 213
Divorce, 72–73
Doctor(s)
second opinions and, 151
specialist referrals, 147
Documents, filing. *See* Filing system
Dollar cost averaging, 211, 223
Dominguez, Joe, 64
Dow Jones Industrial Average, 22
Downing, Neil, 186
Dread disease insurance, 153
Dreyfus S&P 500, 123

E

EAFE index, 221
Earned income credit, 258
Earthquake insurance, 140, 143
Education. *See also* College education
benefits, 127
ongoing, 272–73
E-file, 248
Elderly, tax credit for, 258
Emergency accounts, 56, 97
Emergency road service insurance, 132
Employee benefits, 119–28
annual benefit statement, 128
checklist, 128
educational benefits, 127
flexible spending accounts, 124–25
insurance, 125–26
125 plans, 123–24
mutual funds, 123
quality-of-life benefits, 127–28

retirement plans, 122
vacation and sick pay, 126
worksheet, 120–21
Employer(s)
benefit specialist, 152
credit checks and, 93
Employment. *See* Career fulfillment; Job
Equifax, 91, 94
Estate planning, 279–95
attorneys and, 288–89, 293–94
checklist, 295
contracts, 281
executor, 284
file folder, 31
gifting, 282–83
information needed for drafting a document worksheet, 290–92
IRA payments and, 186
letter of last instruction, 282
living trusts, 286–87
living wills, 282, 287–88
powers of attorney, 282, 287–88
probate, 282
title, 281–82
trusts, 280–81, 285–86
unified credit, 282
wills, 280, 283–85
Expenses
mutual funds, 218
unexpected, 71–72
Experian, 91, 94

F

Fair Credit Billing Act, 89
Fair Credit Reporting Act, 89
Fair Debt Collection Practices Act, 89–90
Family business, 73–74
Family-friendly employee benefits, 127–28
Federal Trade Commission, 88
Fee-based payments, 41
Fee for Service, 173
Fee-offset payments, 41
Fee only compensation, 41
Fidelity (annuity purchase), 233
Fidelity Magellan Fund, 217
Fidelity Spartan, 123
Field audits, 246
Filing system, 29–35
annual discards, 34–35
finding and filing documents, 34
labels for folders, 31–33
setting up, 30–31
supplies, 30
Financial advisers, 40–42, 190

Financial beliefs/behavior, 2–8
fitness quiz and answers, 3–4, 5–8
Financial calculator, 82
Financial independence, 19, 178–96, 216
investment portfolio, 186–87
monthly investments, 181, 183–84
pension indexing, 185–86
pension plans for self-employed, 187, 189
retirement calculator worksheet, 191–94
retirement crisis, 179–81
vesting, 185
Financial planning. *See also* Money management
as employee benefit, 121
calendar, 296
file folder, 32
Financial records, failing to keep, 70
Fire extinguishers, 141, 143
Fixed annuities, 228. *See also* Annuities
Flexible spending accounts, 124–25
Flextime, 121, 127
Flight insurance, 103–4, 169
Flood insurance, 140–41, 143
Food expenses, 53–54
Forbes magazine, 218
401(k), 122, 184
403(b), 184
Franklin mutual funds, 212
Fraud, credit cards and, 108
Frequent flier miles, 103

G

Garnishee of wages, 83, 85
Geico, 134
Gifts, taxation of, 250
Global/international funds, 216. *See also* Mutual fund(s)
Goals, 23–29, 46
investments and, 208
personal goals worksheet, 26–27
Goddard, John, 25
Government bonds, 224, 250
Grace period, 100–101
Graded vesting, 185
Group insurance policies, 125–26
Growth funds, 216. *See also* Mutual fund(s)
Growth and income funds, 216. *See also* Mutual fund(s)
Growth investment, 224
Guarantees, 136
Guardians, for minor children, 289

H

Hardy, Dorcas, 115
Health care proxy, 288
Health insurance, 144–53
    compare policies worksheet, 148
    as employee benefit, 120, 124
    fee for service, 145–46
    finding a policy, 147–49
    flexible spending accounts and, 124
    group policies, 125–26
    liabilities and, 138
    managed care, 146–47
    Medicare/Medicaid, 152–53
    paying doctor or hospital bill, 151–53
    policies to avoid, 153
    rates, 151
    reducing cost of, 149–51
    stop-loss limit, 163, 164
Hobbies, 194–95
Homeowners policy, 137–40
Hoover's Online, 202, 276
Hope Scholarship credit, 259–60
Hospital insurance, 145. *See also* Health insurance
Household file folder, 32
Housing expense, 54
How to Get Your Dream Job Using the Web, 274

I

Immediate annuities, 228. *See also* Annuities
Income, 263–64, 267–68
    actual hourly wage worksheet, 269–70
    garnishee of wages, 83, 85
    health insurance premium conversion option and, 149–50
    investments and, 5, 19
    proof of, and IRS, 242
    reducing adjusted gross, 253
    reducing gross, 250–51
    reducing taxable, 256–57
    rental, 243
    spending plan and, 56, 59–60
    take-home pay, 263
Index funds, 222–24, 223
Inflation
    annuities and, 231
    disability insurance and, 157
    retirement and, 180–81
    Social Security and, 156
Institute of Certified Financial Planners, 41

Insurance
    auto, 102–3, 129–35
    beneficiary, 174–75
    disability, 154–61
    face amount, 176
    flight, 103–4
    health, 144–53
    inadequate, 72
    liability, 137–40
    life, 120, 126. *See also* Life insurance
    long-term care, 121
    lost or stolen credit cards, 103
    property, 135–40
Insurance companies, credit checks and, 93
Insurance News Network, 134
InsuranceQuote, 173
Insweb, 134
Interactive life insurance needs calculator, 167
Interest
    annual percentage rate, 101, 105
    annuities and, 231
    credit card, 101–2, 104–5, 107, 109
    taxable income and, 256
Interest rate risk, 207
International Association for Financial Planning, 41
International funds, 216. *See also* Mutual fund(s)
International securities, 224
Internal Revenue Service. *See* IRS
Internet, résumés posted on, 273–75
INVESCO S&P 500, 123
Investment(s), 15, 16. *See also* Bond(s); Stock(s)
    buying, 20, 21
    file folder, 32
    gains and losses, taxation of, 253
    income and, 5–6, 19
    investment risk, 198–99
    objectives, mutual funds and, 216
IRA, 185–86
    deductibility phaseout, 254
    estate taxes and, 186
    self-employed and, 187
    taxes and, 254
IRS, 83. *See also* Tax(es)
    accuracy of records for, 242–43
    audits, 246
    dependent care and, 124
    late fees and, 244
    tax preparation, 243–44
    W-4 form, 242
Irrevocable trust, 285–86
Itemized deductions, 243

J

Job. *See also* Career fulfillment
    certification, 127
    file folder, 32
    financial costs and benefits of worksheet, 265
    interviews, 276–78
Joint-and-survivor (annuity) option, 229–30
Joint tenant with right of survivorship, 281–82

K

Karl, Shannon and Arthur, 274
Kelley Blue Book, 13
Keogh plan, 187
Kiplinger's Personal Finance Magazine, 104, 218

L

Landlords, credit checks and, 92
Law and ordinance clause, 140
Legal services, as employee benefit, 120
Leisure time, 7
Liabilities, 13, 16, 18
Liability insurance, 130–31, 135, 142
Life insurance, 162–77
    A.M. Best rating, 175–76
    agent, 176–77
    annual premium, 176
    beneficiary, 174–75
    cancellation warning, 167
    checklist, 177
    credit cards and, 104
    as employee benefit, 120, 126
    interactive life insurance needs calculator, 167
    needs analysis worksheet, 165–66, 168
    shopping for, 173–74, 175
    term, 169–73
    universal life, 170, 171
    whole life (permanent insurance), 170, 171–72
LifeRates of America, 173
Lifetime Learning credit, 260
Life with a period certain (annuity) option, 229
Living trusts, 286–87
Living wills, 282, 287
Loan(s)
    debt elimination calendar, 79–82

Index 303

ledger worksheet, 78–79
student, 83
Locus of control, 68
Long-term liabilities, 16
Lynch, Peter, 198, 217

M

Maintenance fee, annuity, 231–32
Managed care, 146–47
Married couples, health insurance and, 150
MasterCard, 95, 102
MasterQuote, 173
Maximize Your IRA, 186
Medicaid, 153
Medical bills, 79, 83
Medical care reimbursement accounts, 124–25, 150, 251–52
Medical coverage in an auto policy, 131
Medical expenses
 insurance, 145. *See also* Health insurance
 taxes and, 256
Medical file folder, 32–33
Medical insurance. *See* Health insurance
Medicare, 114, 117, 152–53, 179
Millionaire Next Door, 70
Mission statement worksheet, 10
Money.com, 190
Money management, 43–64. *See also* Financial planning
 cash flow for 12 months worksheet, 44–45
 checklists, 52, 64
 financial planning calendar, 296
 periodic review of spending, 63–64
 retirement budget worksheet, 181–84
 sacred cows, 53
 spending diary evaluation worksheet, 47–48
 spending plan, creating, 55–63
 tracking spending, 46–55
 where my money went worksheet, 50
Money magazine, 104, 218
Monster Board Web site, 275
Moody's, 207
Morningstar, annuities and, 234
Morningstar Mutual Funds, 219
Mortality charge (annuity), 231
Mortgage, 83
 insurance, 169
 interest, 256

points, 256–57
Moving expenses, 255
Municipal bond interest, 250
Mutual fund(s), 123, 210–26
 annuities and, 228, 232
 asset allocation, 224–25
 checklist, 225
 commissions, 213, 215
 defined, 210–11
 dollar cost averaging, 211–13, 215
 evaluation tools, 225
 families, 212
 index funds, 222–23
 investment objectives and, 216
 managers of, 211, 217–18, 219, 222
 net asset value, 219
 newspaper table of prices, 221
 performance ratings, 218–19
 purchases worksheet, 226
 rate of return, 217
 risk rating, 217
 selecting, 215–19, 220–22
 tracking performance of, 219
 worksheet, 226

N

National Association of Enrolled Agents, 243
National Association of Estate Planning Councils, 294
National Association of Personal Financial Advisors, 41
National Association of Securities Dealers, 40, 41
National Charities Information Bureau, Inc., 237
National Flood Insurance, 141
National Insurance Consumer, 143
National Network of Estate Planning Attorneys, 293
Needs vs. wants, 74–75
Net asset value, 219
Networking, 271–73
Net worth, 12–22
 assets and liabilities defined, 13
 date on statement, 13–14
 financial data columns, 14–16, 18
 increasing, 20
 sample statements, 15, 21
 statement, 17
No-load funds, 213. *See also* Mutual fund(s)
North American Securities Administrators Association, 42

O

Office audits, 246
125 plans, 123–24
1001 Ways to Cut Your Expenses, 61
One Up on Wall Street, 198, 208–9
Oppenheimer mutual funds, 212
Organization, 23–41
 advisers, professional, 37–42
 checklist, 29, 37
 file system, 29–37
 goals, 23–29
 personal data worksheet, 36
 personal goals worksheet, 26–27
Overdraft protection, 97

P

Pension indexing, 185–86
Pension plans, 180. *See also* Retirement plans/planning
Performance ratings, on mutual funds, 218
Permanent life insurance, 170
Personal assets, 16, 18
Personal data, 35–36
Personal Earnings and Benefit Statement, 115
Personal file folder, 33
Personal injury protection, 131
Personal property insurance, 135
Philanthropic Advisory Service, 237
Philanthropy. *See* Charitable donations
Physicians. *See* Doctor(s)
PIN numbers, 111
Points, 256–57
Pond, Jonathan, 61
Portfolio diversification, mutual funds and, 211
Powers of attorney, 282, 287–88
Premium conversion option, 124, 149, 251
Prime rate, 105
Private insurance, 146. *See also* Health insurance
Prizes, taxation of, 250
Profit-sharing plan(s), 122
Property insurance coverage, 135–37
 earthquake insurance, 140
 flood insurance, 140–41
 homeowners policies, 137–40
 saving money on, 141–43
Property lien, 84, 85
Provident Life, 158
Publications, professional, 271–72
Putnam mutual funds, 212

Index

Q–R

Quality-of-life benefits, 127–28
Quotesmith, 174
Rate of return, 217
Real property, 135
Receipts, 143
Referrals, 39–40
Registered Investment Advisor (RIA), 40
Rehabilitation benefits, 158. *See also* Disability insurance
Remodeling, and property insurance, 140
Rental car coverage, 132
Rental income, 243
Renter insurance policies, 135, 141–43
Replacement cost, 135
Request for Earnings and Benefit Estimate Statement, 113, 115
Restaurant expenses, 54
Résumé, 273–75
Retirement benefits, Social Security, 116
Retirement calculator worksheet, 191–94
Retirement plans/planning
    annuities, 227–28
    budget worksheet, 182
    calculators, 190, 191–94
    as employee benefit, 122
    investment portfolio, 186–87
    monthly investments, 181, 183–84
    needs analysis worksheet, 188
    pension indexing, 185–86
    retirement crisis, 179–81
    self-employed and, 187–89
    software, 190
    vesting, 185
Revocable trust, 285–86
Risk rating, 217
Risk score, 93
Roaring 2000s, The, 209
Robin, Vicki, 64
Rockefeller, John, 240
Roth IRA, 186
Russell 2000 index, 221

S

Sacred cows, 53, 55
Safe deposit box, 34–35
Savings accounts, 56, 72
Savings Are Vital to Everyone's Retirement (SAVER) Act, 179
Savings Incentive Match Plan for Employees (SIMPLE), 187
Schedule C, 252
Scholarships, 250
Schwab S&P 500, 123
Scudder S&P 500, 123
Sector funds, 216, 224. *See also* Mutual fund(s)
Secured creditors, 78, 83–84, 87
Securities and Exchange Commission, 40, 41
Select Quote, 174
Self-employed
    disability insurance and, 155, 160–61
    pension plans, 187–89
    taxes and, 245, 254
Shirley, Kay R., 190
Shopping addiction, 65–66, 68–69
    self-esteem and, 70
Short-term disability insurance, 126
Short-term liabilities, 16
Sick pay, 126
Simplification, 8–9
Simplified Employee Pension (SEP), 187
Simultaneous death clause, 284
Single-life (annuity) option, 229
Skill enhancement, as employee benefit, 127
Small capital class, 224
Social Security, 113–18, 179, 260
    disability benefits, 116, 154, 156
    earnings record, 115
    estimated benefits, 115–16
    medical reimbursement account and, 124–25
    Medicare, 117
    Personal Earnings and Benefit Statement, 115
    reduced benefits for employed retirees, 117–18
    Request for Earnings and Benefit Estimate Statement, 113, 115
    retirement benefits, 116
    survivor benefits, 116–17
    taxation and, 118
    Web site, 115
Society of Financial Service Professionals, 41
Software, for tax preparation, 244
Spending, tracking. *See* Money management
Spouses, health insurance and, 150
Standard and Poor's 500 (S&P 500) index, 123, 221–22
Standard and Poor's rating service, 207
Stanley, Thomas J., 70
Stock(s), 198, 199–206, 209
    accurate records of transactions, 205, 206
    buying, 199–204
    goals and, 205
    purchase plan, 120, 122–23
    selling, 204–5
    when not to buy, 205
Strong Index 500, 123
Student loans, 83, 85, 86
    taxation and, 255–56
Surgical insurance, 145. *See also* Health insurance
Surrender charge, annuity, 231
Survivor benefits, Social Security, 116–17

T

T. Rowe Price (annuity purchase), 233
T. Rowe Price Asset Builder, 223
T. Rowe Price Equity Index, 123
Tax(es), 241–48. *See also* IRS
    accuracy of records, 242
    audits, 246
    avoiding overpayment of, 249–61
    checklists, 248, 261
    child's income and, 260–61
    dependent care and, 124
    file folder, 33
    health insurance premium conversion option and, 124, 149–50
    income tax credits, 257–60
    marginal tax bracket, at retirement, 183
    medical reimbursement account and, 150
    payment extensions, 245
    preparation of, 243–44
    property, 140
    reduction strategies, 250–60
    self-employment and, 245
    Social Security and, 118
    underwithholding, 244
    W–4 forms, 242
Tax Counseling for the Elderly, 243
TaxCut software, 244
Tax Simplification Act, 179
TeleFile, 247–48
Templeton mutual funds, 212
Tenants in common, 281
Term life insurance, 169–73
    whole life vs., 172
TermQuote, 158
Testamentary trust, 284
Theft losses, 257
Title, 281–82, 289
Towing/emergency road service insurance, 132

Transportation expenses, 55
Transunion, 91, 94
Trusts, 280–81, 285–86
Truth-in-Lending Act, 90
TurboTax, 244
Two-cycle average daily balance, 102

U

Umbrella liability policy, 142
Uninsured motorist coverage, 131–32
Uninsured motorist-property damage insurance, 132
United Way, 240
Universal life insurance, 170, 171
Unsecured creditors, 78–79, 85–86
UNUM, 158
USAA, 134
    annuity purchase, 233

S&P 500 Index, 123
Utilities, 83

V

Vacation pay, 126
Value, 224
Value Line Mutual Fund Survey, 219
Vanguard
    annuity purchase, 233
    500 Portfolio, 123, 225
Van Kampen mutual funds, 212
Variable annuities, 228. *See also* Annuities
Vehicles file folder, 33
Ventura, John, 285
Vesting, 185
Visa card, 95, 102
Volunteer Income Tax Assistance, 243

W–Y

Waddell & Reed mutual funds, 212
Wages, garnishee of, 83, 85
Waiver of premium, 158, 170
Wardrobe expenses, 54
Warranties, 136, 143
Web sites, résumés and, 273–75
Welfare system, 179
Whole life insurance, 170, 171–72
Wholesale Insurance Network, 158, 174
Will Kit, The, 285
Wills, 35, 280, 283–85, 293
Wilshire 5000 index, 123, 221
Withdrawal charge, annuity, 231, 233
Women, disability insurance and, 160
Workers' compensation, 154
Your Money or Your Life, 64